IDEAS AND THINK TANKS IN CONTEMPORARY BRITAIN

Volume I

Ideas and Think Tanks in Contemporary Britain

Volume I

edited by

MICHAEL DAVID KANDIAH

and

ANTHONY SELDON

FRANK CASS

LONDON • PORTLAND, OR

First published in 1996 in Great Britain by
FRANK CASS & CO. LTD.
Newbury House, 900 Eastern Avenue, London IG2 7HH, England

and in the United States of America by
FRANK CASS
c/o ISBS, Inc.
5804 N.E. Hassalo Street
Portland, Oregon 97213-3644

Transferred to Digital Printing 2004

British Library Cataloguing in Publication Data
A catalogue record for this book is available from the British Library

ISBN 0 7146 4743 8 (hardback)
0 7146 4301 7 (paperback)

Library of Congress Cataloging-in-Publication Data

A catalog record for this book is available from the Library of Congress

This group of studies first appeared in a Special Issue:
'Ideas and Think Tanks in Contemporary Britain, Part I'
of *Contemporary British History*, Vol.10, No.1, Spring 1996,
published by Frank Cass and Company Limited.

Contents

Introduction   **Michael David Kandiah and Anthony Seldon**   1

Political Ideas since 1945, Or How Long was the Twentieth Century?   **Rodney Barker**   2

The Beveridge Strait-jacket: Policy Formation and the Problem of Poverty in Old Age   **Helen Fawcett**   20

The Nature and Impact of Think Tanks in Contemporary Britain   **Andrew Denham and Mark Garnett**   43

The Social Market Foundation   **Lewis Baston**   62

'Blueprint for a Revolution'? The Politics of the Adam Smith Institute   **Richard Heffernan**   73

The Institute of Economic Affairs: Undermining the Post-war Consensus   **Christopher Muller**   88

WITNESS SEMINAR
The Number 10 Policy Unit   (editor) **Michael David Kandiah**   111

INTERVIEWS
The Influence of Collectivist Ideas
(**Anthony Seldon** interviews **Bernard Crick**)   126

The Influence of Liberal Ideas in Post-War Britain
(**Anthony Seldon** interviews **Lord Dahrendorf**)   137

The Influence of Sociology in Post-War Britain
(**Anthony Seldon** interviews **Anthony Giddens**)   144

The Influences on Economic Policy
(**Anthony Seldon** interviews **Andrew Graham**)   152

The Influence of Ideas on the Modern Conservative Party
(**Anthony Seldon** interviews **John Ramsden**)   168

The Influence of Ideas on Economic Policy (I)
(**Anthony Seldon** interviews **Lord Roll of Ipsden, KCMG, CB**)   186

The Influence of Classical Liberalism and Monetarist Economics
(**Christopher Muller** interviews **Arthur Seldon**)   199

Introduction

MICHAEL DAVID KANDIAH and ANTHONY SELDON

This is the first of two volumes on 'Ideas and Think Tanks in Contemporary British History'. We have concentrated on the influences on politics and policy-making and offer the following: a transcript of a round-table interview on think tanks, taken from Radio Four's *Analysis* programme; interviews with participants, academics and former government insiders; articles on a number of think tanks, ranging from the Fabians to the Adam Smith Institute; and a Witness Seminar on the Number Ten Policy Unit. These are preceded by articles on the place and significance of ideas in the shaping of British policy-making.

In subsequent issues scholars working on different areas of contemporary British history will be given the opportunity to publish the results of their ongoing research. The review section in this issue gives a flavour of the work which will be featured. The best articles from *Contemporary British History*'s predecessor journal, *Contemporary Record,* will be published in a series of books, while some of the Witness Seminars will be published as pamphlets. Eventually, some material will be stored 'on-line' for access on the internet. In this way, we hope that the role of contemporary history in Britain will come to be ever more appreciated.

Michael David Kandiah and Anthony Seldon, Institute of Contemporary British History.

Political Ideas since 1945, Or How Long was the Twentieth Century?

RODNEY BARKER

1945 is given too much importance as a turning point in the history of political thinking. Most of the changes which occurred at and after the end of the Second World War were intensifications of existing conceptions and aspirations, rather than new departures. By the 1990s, in contrast, a new intellectual century, however uncertain its features, had begun. Socialism and conservatism were dead, and in their place was a division between left and right, with elements of liberalism on each side of the divide. At the same time society has been replaced by societies, and both gender and religion have emerged as major themes. And yet, paradoxically, much of what was new drew on the recessive themes of the past.

Scholars are familiar with historical centuries which take subtle liberties with the arbitrary chronology of one hundred years, no more, and no less. There are short and long eighteenth centuries, and various candidates for the most useful delineation of the nineteenth which extend it on either side of both 1800 and 1900. But until recently the twentieth century has been left alone, or left alone save for meticulous argumentation over whether 31 December 2000, or 31 December 2001 was the date on which we ought to be celebrating the millennium. That may be in part because there have been so many cataclysmic events since 1900 that there are more than enough identifying characteristics of the last 95 years to remove the need for any more subtle delineation. The twentieth century imposes itself so violently on our consciousness that definition seems superfluous. But it can still be worth asking what the defining events are, what they define, and what kind of narrative it is that leads us to see things in one way rather than another. As the chronological century comes near to its end, Eric Hobsbawm has taken the bull by the horns, or the clock by the hands, and identified a 'short twentieth century' running from 1914 to 1991.[1] The first date is chosen because it marks the assassination in Sarajevo of the Archduke Franz Ferdinand and the outbreak of the First World War, the second because 'the world that went to pieces at the end of the 1980s was the world shaped by the impact of the Russian Revolution of 1917'.[2]

That does not bring discussion to an end. On the contrary, it provokes a

Rodney Barker Department of Government, London School of Economics and Political Science.

continuing discussion of how we should arrange our histories, and to what purpose. If the twentieth century is indeed the 'Bolshevik century', then 1917 might seem a more appropriate starting date than 1914, and 1989 than 1991. The periodisation which we choose arises from the way we characterise history in the first place – not just what we consider significant, but what we seek significance about. The account we give is an aspect of what story it is we want to tell. So it is worth not only questioning the periodisation with which we are most familiar when talking of the twentieth century, but asking what sort of stories historians and others have wanted to tell and how this has been related to their choice of significant dates. Is it to be a story of the extending influence of warfare? Or of the spread of democracy? Or of governmental control? Or the conflict between eastern managerial communism and western liberal capitalism? Each narrative leads to different questions, and different chronologies. Whether the narrative begins with assassination in Sarajevo, with the Bolshevik Revolution of 1917 or, as Quentin Bell has suggested, with conversations about sex amongst Bloomsbury intellectuals in 1908, depends on what sort of century you want to describe.[3]

The Turning Point of 1945?

Centuries are not the only way in which history is chopped up. Both world wars, as Hobsbawm's chosen starting date illustrates, have widely been used to mark off events into pre- and post- eras. Whenever the twentieth century is taken to have begun, if we are dealing with shorter historical periods, with milestones rather than with boundary signs, then 1945 has often seemed the obvious place to start. There is a widespread convention in historical narratives of beginning accounts which focus on the later part of the century with the end of the Second World War. Wars are the great instigators of change, and the Second great war of the century changed the domestic landscape just as irrevocably as it did that of Europe and the rest of the world . With the end of the war in 1945, America and Russia were irrefutably world powers, Nazism and Fascism had been destroyed, and democracy and socialism were advancing with the election of the first majority Labour government and the final introduction of one person one vote.[4] Evacuation and the disruptive domestic migrations of war had confronted different classes with each other as never before, and a 'People's War' had called into question both social and political deference. Government had massively extended its power, and whether or not voters had been inspired by visions of socialism, they had been provided with an illustration of the possible benefits of collectivism.[5]

Nor is this judgement one only of subsequent historians. The end of the war seemed an event of huge significance for contemporary political writers whatever their allegiance or aspirations. Those who feared what they saw as a possible future were as clear on this as those who welcomed what they saw as a new dawn. F.A. Hayek, warning of the dangers of collectivist economic planning and a 'road to serfdom' in 1944, assumed none the less that it was a time for new departures, and that whatever else might divide him from the 'socialists of all parties' to whom he dedicated his tract, he shared with them an assumption that the end of the war marked a time for decisions to be made and Rubicons to be crossed. 'If we are to build a better world we must have the courage to make a new start.'[6] *Let Us Face the Future* was the title of the Labour Party's election manifesto, and it caught the tone well. Unemployment, poverty, ill health and lack of education would at last be overcome, and all the old hopes for peace, progress, justice and security finally realised. John Strachey, writing in 1944, was not modest about quoting Lincoln Steffens on the Soviet Union – 'I have seen the future, and it works' – in recommending as a post-war future for Britain, 'a supremely high ideal of how men and women shall some day live on this earth.'[7] Everything, it was hoped or feared, had changed, or was about to.

Reconstruction or Reform?

But if 1945 can be seen as a starting point, it can be seen also as an intensification of or development within a political world whose domestic problems, aspirations, institutions and solutions were rooted in the years before the Second World War, perhaps even in the years before the First, and whose international context of strategic and ideological threats was set by the existence of the Soviet Union. Far from being brought to a close in 1945, this agenda was shortly to be intensified in the cold war. What is as striking as the prevalence of new dawns and new starts in the language of political writing around 1945, are the backward-looking images of threat and promise which were associated with them. Both the dangers to be avoided and the prizes to be grasped were conceived within understandings derived from the past. Hayek might talk in the language of the time of new starts, and Labour supporters sing enthusiastically if uncritically the words of Blake's *Jerusalem*, but what was clear was the extent to which perceived threats and perceived goals were traditional ones, and the degree to which problems were familiar and solutions well tried, or at least well talked about. The 'fear' which Aneurin Bevan wanted to banish when he set out his version of socialism in 1952 was fear of familiar deprivations: poverty, unemployment, poor housing, ill health.[8] The 'serfdom' which Hayek wanted to avoid was not some new and barely imagined horror, but a distillation of the totalitarianism of the 1930s and 1940s. Even the most imaginative of post-war speculations about the dangers ahead, George Orwell's *1984*, was an extrapolation of every abuse of power the author had known, from boarding schools to Stalinism.[9]

The solutions were equally familiar. For social democrats, a rigorous extension of conventional socialism, public control under the stewardship of the state to create a society where social and economic injustice in the form familiar during the previous half century was brought to an end. For economic liberals – of all parties, as Hayek might have said[10] – a return to the lost rigours of the market. For conservatives, a recognition of the imperilled verities of traditional society. Being conservative more than being either liberal or socialist, meant doing familiar if neglected things, not creating new worlds. The conservative disposition wrote Michael Oakeshott in 1956, was 'appropriate to a man who is acutely aware of having something to lose which he has learned to care for'.[11] But people of all parties hoped, feared, speculated and planned not in terms of an imagined future but with reference to an experienced past.[12] 1945 might provide new opportunities, but they were opportunities to do what should have been done in 1935 or 1925. The election of a Labour government and the wartime extension of state powers may have threatened conservative conceptions of society or economic liberal theories of markets, but the threats were not new, merely intensified.

The years of reform which followed under the Attlee Government of 1945–51 were a culmination, not a new departure. The new ideas were all full square in the tradition of the old. Nor was this location at the end rather than at the beginning of a political tradition a characteristic only of the party of reform. Socialism might soon be furiously scouring its traditions for its true essence, but conservatism was defensive of property and imagined social orders and liberalism was insisting on the economic and social rights which would have been recognised a hundred years before. Quintin Hogg, writing in 1947 located conservatism firmly within a period of 'revolutionary change' which over the previous forty years had made a mockery of the optimistic phrase 'century of the common man'.[13] As striking as any rhetorical suggestions that people were living in new times, was the hope, or fear, that they could return to, or avoid, or set right, the social, economic, and political arrangements with which they had been familiar before the catastrophe of war.

The debates were conducted, too, within an implicit rationalist, modernist, and collectivist framework which set them firmly in the succession of both Fabian Socialism, Liberal Imperialism, and Tory reform, a blend Samuel Beer identified in 1964 as embracing all parties,[14] and which constituted one more link with a style of politics running back at least to the closing years of the nineteenth century. A.V. Dicey had in 1905 described a new politics of collectivism,[15] and though the governmental responsibilities extended after 1945 went far beyond what he had feared and warned against, they nonetheless fell still within that broad collectivist tradition. Government in the form of an intelligent, democratic, sovereign state would pursue the common good by the application of science and through the expression of the common will channelled and harmonised by representative parliamentary politics. The years after 1945 witnessed not so much a change of course, as a fruition or culmination of old arguments, a manoeuvring and negotiation within familiar perimeters.

The End of the Twentieth Century?

If we are looking for fault lines over the last hundred years, the most spectacular events are not necessarily the most important, nor the most devastating interruptions of and assaults on ordinary life, the most powerful in altering patterns of thought or culture. Traumas can make people more firmly set in their ways just as often as they can jolt them out of them. Whatever accelerations or intensifications of political life and thought 1945 may have been the occasion for, it does not provide us with a major transition. If we are looking for the frontiers of the twentieth century, however long or short we expect it to be, we must look elsewhere than the end of the war and the election of the Attlee government, and though 1914, or 1917 may provide a starting point, 1945 provides neither an end nor a beginning.

In political thought the transformations have become evident relatively recently. Whilst the language of the 1940s may stand in line with that of the past, the language of the 1990s clearly does not. Looking back at 1945, something has changed very substantially, and we need to ask what, when, and how. If the 1940s and 1950s remained resolutely part of the twentieth century rather than something new, then now we are looking back on a century that has ended, and from a vantage point which must be described in terms quite different from those appropriate for the 1940s and 1950s. The way in which political thinking is carried on now bears only superficial resemblances to the manner in which it was conducted in the 1940s. Arguments are different, but so are the key words and the things about which the arguments are conducted. Socialism, capitalism, class, cold war, equality, rationalism, modernisation, society have been replaced or eclipsed by nationalism, religion, pluralism, autonomy, citizenship, post-modernism, and gender. Whether we accept Hobsbawm's date of 1991, or settle for 1979, 1989, or 1973, somewhere between 1945 and 1995 a transition has occurred.

Political Argument after the End of the Short Twentieth Century

The extent of the change is most evident in retrospect, and it is easier to see how different things have become, than to identify precisely when or in what manner the change took place. There are two obvious candidates for the role of catalyst: the emergence of the New Right at home from the end of the 1970s, and the collapse of managerial communist despotism in Eastern Europe from 1989 onwards. The flourishing of New Right arguments and assumptions called into question broad assumptions about the appropriateness or competence of public bodies under governmental supervision, and made familiar and powerful the belief that individual choices in some form of market were more meaningful and effective than collective, political choices. The disappearance of managerial communism removed from the New Right at the very moment of its triumphs, the demonology with which it had buttressed its arguments, and the ideological polarisation which had shaped thinking on both right and left. But in investigating the causes, something more may be discovered not only about the origins of the change, but also about its nature. Hobsbawm's date of 1991 may not be the most appropriate, but whenever the most illuminating date is thought to be, we can nonetheless talk of a short twentieth century, and place ourselves beyond it. The date of its demise, and the identity of its assassins, depend upon each other.

The Disappearance of Socialism and Conservatism, and the Emergence of New Rights and Lefts

The most striking change is the virtually complete disappearance of socialism and conservatism. There remain of course political parties of whom these titles are descriptively used, either by the parties themselves or by their opponents.[16] But in the political writings of those who can be broadly termed 'left' or 'right' the words socialism and conservatism and the aspirations and aversions which they expressed, no longer play a role of any importance. Arguments from the New Right may continue to be described by some of their proponents as conservative, but they represent a complete departure from conservatism. Arguments on the left, by contrast, although they draw on elements of socialism, go to some lengths to find new terms, usually either 'left' or 'radical' to describe themselves. The contemporary left uses both the word radical and the word left, but not the word socialism. Were we, in other words, to undertake an account of contemporary political thought without possessing either the words or the concepts of socialism and conservatism, it would not occur to us to invent them. The old, rough and ready terms 'left' and 'right', on the other hand, still retain their usefulness.

Conservatism has been variously described as a liking for familiar customs, institutions and values; as a belief that it is wise to be deferential in the face of social or other arrangements which, by surviving, have proved themselves; as a belief in the unequal distribution of ability and hence of responsibility.[17] Philip Norton has recently boiled it down to 'scepticism as to the power of man's reason' and 'a concern for, and in essence an adherence to, society as it presently exists.'[18] What has been termed the 'New Right' has sometimes been presented as a continuation of familiar conservative or liberal doctrines. But none of these values is to be found on the right wing of political thought in the last decade of the century.[19] The New Right in fact represents a direct rejection of and attack on at least some of them.

New Right thinking represents a break with conservatism in two respects. First, although an advocacy of private property and economic markets has for over a century been a component of conservative thinking, the markets were not liberal markets in either function or outcome. Markets were seen as maintaining, and flourishing within, the hierarchical structures of a society stratified on grounds of merit and ability. It was stratified also on grounds of responsibility. Not only *noblesse*, but worldly success and eminence in all its forms, placed upon those who enjoyed it and upon the government which was their rightful sphere of operation, the responsibility both of social and cultural leadership, and also of paternal care for the rest of their fellow subjects. Second, conservatism was, unlike liberalism, not a combative, radical or aggressive doctrine. It neither attacked established institutions nor set out to transform the way in which economic or any other kinds of social activity were carried on. The New Right by contrast has concentrated paternal responsibilities upon the family, but treats them when found within society at large as presumptuous, debilitating, and subversive of individual enterprise. There remain of course those who describe themselves as conservative, and advance a case for a welfare state,[20] but the principal thrust of argument is for an assertive economic liberalism which departs from conservatism both in its commitment to innovation, and in its increasing separation of economics from social or cultural traditions.

The break with liberalism is equally marked. Liberalism had economic and political strands, the one advocating markets and property and individual economic choices, the other advocating the political and social autonomy of the individual. The first, in an intensified form, composed one element of the New Right: the second was almost entirely absent from it. Thus Roger Scruton, a writer who arrived at a New Right position from a conservative direction could state that individual rights had no place in what he still called conservatism. The 'business of politics is to maintain the civil order, and to prevent the "dust and powder of individuality" that was once described as its ruin.'[21]

Socialism disappeared just as had conservatism. The distinguishing feature of socialism had been the combination of a moral commitment to equality with an expectation that the means of achieving equality was through state action applied to a population whose needs were assumed to be broadly uniform, and whose wants were assumed to be coterminous with their needs.[22] By the 1990s, although appeals could be found to rediscover such a classic socialism – together with a classic Marxism,[23] the predominant tone of writing on the left argued for autonomy rather than for equality, and argued for a reform which would recognise varieties of culture rather than stratifications of class in a manner which made little if any use of even the word 'socialism'. A collection of essays edited in 1994 by David Miliband which drew on both the academic and the parliamentary strands of what has come to be termed the 'left' and which saw itself as naturally advisory too, though neither subordinate to or limited by, the Labour Party, covered a broad sweep of both theory and policy with hardly any use of the 's' word.[24]

At the same time as a radical or left, rather than socialist, political position has been developed, a form of 'market socialism' has been advocated which sees the actions, either in co-operation or alone, of individuals as the most effective way to express and achieve the varieties of individual purpose, giving to the state a facilitating but not an achieving role.[25] Market socialism of this kind incorporates some of the criticisms of writers such as Hayek, in particular the objection to collective provision that only individuals can properly decide what it is that they want. Popular power, it was argued, was not the same as state power, the aspirations of ordinary people were immediate and mundane, rather than visionary, and one people could harbour a myriad identities and aspirations.

The Replacement of 'Society' with 'Societies'

It had been an assumption of the short twentieth century that people inhabited a common society, and that though they might be ranked or even divided by class or by region, there were needs which were common to all, or which were a feature of phases of life through which all passed: childhood, work, old age. This had been an assumption of the Beveridge Report in 1942, but it was neither new then, nor discarded subsequently. In such a society is made perfect sense for government to make general provision for common needs, and to govern on the assumption that there was a broad identity of interest between people considered collectively, and individual citizens. That assumption was neither so strong nor so prevalent by the end of the century. It had been subject to well-publicised attack by Margaret Thatcher when as Prime Minister she had declared that she had no perception of society, only of families and individuals. But it was not only politicians of the New Right who denied that social life could be understood as homogeneous. Feminists, nationalists, members of religious and ethnic minorities, gay activists, could all be found arguing that social life was conducted in a myriad of groups and associations, and that whilst no one was an island, nor did we all inhabit a single uniform continent.[26] Post-modernist theory gave sustenance to the political argument that there was not one society, but many.[27]

For those on the radical left of the 1990s, the implication of this was that a new form of subsidiarity, far more extensive and downwardly devolving than the national subsidiarity proposed by John Major as a check on European federalist ambitions, should be introduced at levels of politics below the state, central, national level.[28] Associative democracy, as Paul Hirst called it, was an attempt to give political expression to a new multifarious social life.[29] The 'new political forces' were 'too diverse, to concerned with different issues, to be placed on a single spectrum', and whilst some overall form of political association was necessary, people would 'need a political community that will enable them to be different, and not one that exhorts them to be the same'.[30]

A society could be stratified into classes. But the fading of the concept of a homogeneous society was accompanied by a decline in the stress on traditional class. As the electoral importance of class and the historical link between the working class, socialism, and the Labour Party was eroded, so the place of class in strategic political thinking began to crumble. A society segmented by class is still one where all its parts are described with reference to a single system. A plural society is not.

The Replacement of Secular Anglicanism with Religion in Public Life

Although Britain was a religious country in the twentieth century, its public life was not religious, at least not in England. But by the 1990s ordinary Anglicans were discussing employment, housing, poverty, education and the condition of the urban poor in relation to conceptions of Christian citizenship, whilst those who beliefs placed them alongside, but not at the centre, of traditional religious practice in Britain, such as Catholics and Baptists, or well away from the centre, such as Muslims, were making vigorous contributions, based on statements of religious faith, to public debate over abortion and censorship. The arguments of those who have opposed the greater availability of abortion, let alone the prospect of abortion at the discretion of the woman, have invoked religious grounds for insisting on the sanctity of life.

Whilst political liberals were arguing for constitutional reform and a working conception of citizenship to provide a regulated space within which politics could be conducted, and a set of rules which would be neutral as to particular parties or policies, there was at the same time a growth in the use of religious foundations for political argument, involving the claim that policies could not be all treated equally within the constitution, but that the pursuit of godly ideals took precedence over, indeed could in certain circumstances monopolise or replace, conceptions of constitutional neutrality.

There is a paradox here. The short twentieth century may not have been a time of religious faith, but it was none the less one where politics were organised and motivated along lines of fideistic allegiance to a degree not found in this country since the seventeenth and eighteenth centuries. A confluence of values was clustered around competing secular powers: class affiliations, ideological predispositions, and states could be grouped in loose association. The end of the cold war and the collapse or abdication of managerial communism in Eastern Europe brought this to an end. But rather than bringing fideistic political argument to an end, this created more space for other, less secular forms of transcendental appeal.

The Replacement of Policies with Constitutions, and of Class with Citizenship

When men and women could be assumed to share broadly similar needs and aspirations, politics could devote its attention to arguments over policy. It could be assumed, with whatever qualifications, that there was some policy or set of policies which would best serve the interests of all. When that assumption of homogeneity is replaced with pluralism, attention is moved to the consideration of forms of association and negotiation which will provide the fairest means of bargaining and discussion, and which will avoid settling too much power in any one place. Policies are replaced by procedures, and radicals begin to discuss constitutional reform.

The constitutional debate was enhanced by the growing presence within British politics of the European Union.[31] The existence of appeals from the British courts to the European Court of Human Rights, the transferability of professional qualifications across European national frontiers, the enfranchisement of non-nationals within nations other than their own for European elections, all raised the question of citizenship in a form which cut across the conception of the sovereign state, and raised questions of multiple identity.[32]

Even within the United Kingdom, the decreasing presence of class, and the growing presence of other, less homogeneously structured categories of identity – gender, religion, nationality, ethnicity – raised problems for those who wished to argue for people to be seen as citizens as well as subjects. A means had to be found, as David Miller argued, to discover or create a conception of citizenship which was sufficiently 'thick' to justify and sustain social services and public goods, but sufficiently 'thin' to encompass a great variety of persons.[33]

The New, or Different, Internationalism of Political Thought

Both liberalism and socialism had been avowedly international in their derivation of ideas, setting their arguments in the context of an at least European debate. The very words liberty and equality proclaimed a lineage linking British thinking with the revolutionary doctrines of Europe. Conservatism on the other hand had been almost as insular as it presented itself as being.[34] But whilst conservatism could be described without reference to argument outside Britain, the New Right could not. Austrian economics and Chicago and Virginia political theory were as much a foundation for the New Right as were any strictly indigenous doctrines.

Once conservatism, which necessarily eschewed the potential internationalism of theory for the rooted pragmatism of tradition, was replaced by a different kind of right wing thinking, a different range of justificatory reference became appropriate. To recommend that we carry on much as before does not involve an appeal to theory in the way that proposals for radical change do, and as the New Right was combative and innovative, rather than conservative, so too it drew on theory rather than indigenous practice for both its justification and its rhetoric.

When, and Why, was the Twentieth Century

There are moments, of which the collapse of state communist managerial despotism in Eastern Europe after 1989 was one, when people are acutely aware of change. But at the same time, since the causes of large scale transformations in the way in which people think are not normally either single, or simple, or contemporaneous, there are also moments when people become aware that things have changed already, at some time in the recent past. There is no particular date or event to which they can point, but it is clear that things are now done differently and that a comparison with even a few years ago will show great differences.[35]

The changes in the way politics is thought, written and argued about have not come about at an instant, or from a single cause. But there are a few events of overwhelming consequence which clearly were major causes of the change: the new east European revolutions of 1989; the rise – and perhaps decline – of New Right government after 1979; the end of the cold war.

But the change in political thought is not best understood as the result or expression of some one underlying cause. The coherence or unity is to be found not in the circumstances of the change, but in the confluence of various events which themselves constitute the change. These events, though often reciprocally affecting each other, have also independent histories, and are united in the observation of the historian who makes them components, not aspects, of a 'single' historical phenomenon.

One explanation which has been put forward of the immediate causes of the transformation of political thought is similar to that put forward for the advance of socialism at the beginning of the short twentieth century. Just as the credit was given then to the hard work and manoeuvrings of the Fabian Society, so now it is given to the Institute of Economic Affairs.[36] From a different stance, an explanation in terms of the resolute action of committed groups is dismissed as mistaking effect for cause. If the advance of economic liberalism in its New Right version is a conditioned response to the changing needs of capitalism, then it is an effect of changes in economy or society.[37] But there are two responses to such an argument. The first is to say that all causes can also be represented as effects, and there are *no* independent pristine causes. The second is to respond that since the dominant political ideas of the 1950s and 1960s were *also* described in terms of their service to capitalism, capitalism has become a cause so flexible that, by explaining everything, of itself it explains very little.

An approach which combines some of the insights of both these approaches, but which also acknowledges the autonomous role of political argument draws attention to the importance of developments within institutions – states, political parties, international organisations – without making ideas dependent upon them.[38]

Nothing New Under the Sun: Recessive Themes in Political Thought

Major changes in the way people think about politics, whether they are called revolutions, or paradigmatic shifts, or radical transitions, are never so neat and clean when viewed in detail. The end of socialism or conservatism is never final: there are continuities and similarities which at numerous points link the present to the past. To say that socialism has come to an end is not to say that no one writes socialist articles or books any more, but that the predominant arguments are no longer best summarised by such a title. But nor should the fact that there is never such a thing as a clean break lead us to deny that significant changes occur. Nor should we omit to ask what kinds of continuities there are. It is frequently the case that the continuities are with elements of past thinking which were not previously of major importance, that the new present is built in part not out of the major themes of the past, but out of its minor or neglected ones. New arguments are shaped in part out of themes which were previously, like latent genes, recessive or of secondary importance. Those who argue that change is manufactured from existing materials are therefore right, but so are those who present change as a series of innovations. Such an account does not preclude the existence of genuine invention, ideas that have never before been thought. Nor does it preclude the working assumption that such invention is likely to be rare. Post-modernist theory is usefully seen as taking up again some of the concerns and conceptions of early twentieth century (pre-Bolshevik) pluralism. But it is also usefully seen as an innovation.

Looked at from the 1990s the years back to 1945 look rather different from the way they looked before 1989. One reason for this is that we are interested in different things, and so find different elements of the past significant. Another is that themes which, like recessive genes, were present but relatively mute, can from a different chronological vantage point be seen to have carried ways of talking about politics which provided some of the language of later years. This means that though we will not give a *truer* account of the short twentieth century, we will come to give a *different* one, or an account of a *different century*. This does not mean that we should provide new accounts of history which concentrate on the ideas that 'won' in the end. Rather, that from the perspective of the 1990s, after the end of the short twentieth century, other themes are of interest. Earlier accounts are not less true, nor less important, but simply less appropriate for what at the moment happen to be the principal interests of historians.

Looked at in this way, the history of the years between 1945 and 1989 can be painted with different emphases. The lingering interest in workers' control, the anarcho-communism of the New Left, the stress on neighbourhood and participation, all can seem less peripheral in the light of the concern, in the 1990s, for community, subsidiarity, and the multiplicity of identities.[39] The earlier writings of Laski and Cole, which had been eclipsed – though not obliterated – by their latter, more collectivists socialisms, have been recovered with new interest.[40] The 'revisionism' of the 1950s and 1960s, of which Anthony Crosland was the principal exponent, can be seen not only as an attempt to 'rediscover' the essential principles of socialism, but as a stress on freedom, variety, and co-operative and individual autonomy. Crosland's discussion of what people did with the spaces in which they lived made possible, or was a precursor to, a departure from a 'leftism' of collective provision to a belief in individual control.[41] The New Left of the 1960s and 1970s, in its concern with quality of life and non-economic aspirations, its attack on centralism and oligarchy in government and politics, is attempt to discover indigenous roots for universal aspirations, cannot so readily be dismissed as a romantic diversion from the vantage point of the last decade of the chronological century.

In the 1940s two prominent members of the Church of England were continuing to relate their religion to their politics, though in very different ways. But the placing of religion within the body of their social doctrine by both Tawney and Eliot was conducted in circumstances which did not encourage links between the two spheres. Established religion in the Church of England was the faith of the state and the establishment, and whatever individuals amongst either laity or clergy might write or say, Anglicanism in this form placed an insulating barrier between religion and politics. At the same time the conventions of religious toleration within the United Kingdom discouraged the use of fideistic arguments to recommend secular policies to those who did not share the religious persuasions of the person arguing the case. Yet viewed from the 1990s, these efforts at fideistic politics seem less peripheral than they did at the time.

National identity, like religious allegiance, had been a virtually dormant theme in political argument during the whole of the short twentieth century. Orwell had discussed it in a way which de-politicised it, and dismissed more specifically political nationalisms in Scotland, Wales, or Ireland.[42] The writings of men such as Saunders Lewis or Hugh McDiarmid remained marginalised until the collapse of cold war, class, and socialist/conservative political argument left space for other forms of identification and allegiance. If nationalist political argument had been dormant, the most unfamiliar aspect of political thought after the end of the short twentieth century had been virtually underground. The argument for political reform and constitutional reform, though it lingered throughout the years after the great debates of the pre-1914 era, emerged in the 1980s as an issue of such novelty that it seemed more appropriate to identify it by reference to events in Czheckoslovakia than to traditions of political thought in Britain.[43]

Hayek provides a further instance of the way in which ideas emerge into the political mainstream. Although *The Road to Serfdom* received widespread attention from socialists, conservatives and liberals, even gaining praise of a qualified kind from George Orwell,[44] Hayek's political arguments remained for many years at one remove from the mainstream, and were criticised for being an incoherent connection of economic liberalism with social and cultural conservatism.[45] Yet with the ascendancy of the New Right Hayek's work became the most powerful and sophisticated argument for the new doctrines, and their principal exposition. One major strand within political thought between 1945 and the present does not fit this model of recessive themes, and that is feminism. Whilst non-feminists have been slow to take up the contributions which feminism has made to political thought in particular and to social theory generally, feminism cannot be described as recessive in the way that religious political thought, or pluralism, or nationalism can be. From the end of the 1960s a broad and increasingly variegated body of writing which was marked off by its insistence on the importance of gender in analysing political power, or the distribution of advantage, or the character of ideology, or law, or political institutions began to make major re-thinkings necessary across the whole spectrum of political enquiry. But it was a body of work which was in parallel with the prevailing orthodoxies of socialism, conservatism and liberalism. Now that socialism and conservatism have disappeared, and political argument is based increasingly on an assumption that there will be wide differences within society which politics must express, gender is located as a major line of division.

The Importance of Enemies

One of the most important thing that has happened with the end of the short twentieth century is that there has been a disappearance of enemies. The identification of the values and practices which one opposes, and which may even be actively threatening, is one of the prior conditions and sustaining nourishments of political argument.

Socialism was expounded as an opposition to capitalism, conservatism and liberalism as a defence against socialism. Even Anthony Crosland, who spent many pages setting out what a socialist society might be like, none the less could organise his later work around an account of *The Conservative Enemy*.[46] Hayek spent more time warning of the dangers of 'serfdom' than discussing the virtues of catallaxy.

Hobsbawm, amongst many others, makes the point: 'we have all been marked [by the impact of the Russian Revolution of 1917] inasmuch as we got used to thinking of the modern industrial economy in terms of binary opposites, "capitalism" and "socialism" as alternatives mutually excluding one another'.[47]

The disappearance of the managerial communism of Eastern Europe removed, almost at a stroke, both Marxism and end-of-ideology conservatism from play. Those who had presented politics as a defence against the excesses of democracy, romantic principle, and socialism were left like hell fire preachers who had just witnessed the re-development of the underworld as a *crèche* and community centre, whilst Marxism, despite valiant efforts, almost in an instant came to seem as relevant to contemporary discussion as the disputes between the Celtic and Roman churches or a debate over the existence of phlogiston.[48]

A Long Twenty First Century?

We have come out on the other side of the short twentieth century, without being sure what exactly it is we have left, and without any fully precise idea of where we have arrived. Nor do we quite know how we got here: certainly it was not because anyone intended to break through the walls which marked out the territory of the twentieth century. Whatever the New Right thought it was doing, it did not think it was doing this, any more than its opponents imagined that the alternative to the New Right was something it would have contributed to and yet would also find deeply uncongenial. For the moment, even the identity of our enemies is uncertain, and whilst there are plenty of tentative and less than tentative predictions, the most imaginative political thought remains optimistic rather than confident, and eclectic rather than didactic. Interesting times, as the old curse has it, can be dangerous. They can also be disconcertingly difficult to interpret for those who are not prepared to wait for the judgement of history.

Most of the predictions and conclusions that are possible are little more therefore than qualifications, or suggestions about what is *unlikely* to happen. Because the conception of an enemy or an other is important in defining political ideas, the disappearance of socialism and conservatism makes some kinds of political argument unlikely. At the same time the variety of political identities and hence of political aspirations, suggests that the greatest need for the immediate future is not to find appropriate social or economic policies, but to discover a form of political association which will enable a politics without grand causes but with strong sectional allegiances to be carried on in a way which co-ordinates but does not subordinate difference. Such constitutional speculation, if it occurs, will not have a great deal on which to draw when it looks for help to the short twentieth century.

NOTES

1. Eric Hobsbawm, *The Age of Extremes: The Short Twentieth Century 1914–1991* (London: Michael Joseph, 1994).
2. Ibid., p.4.
3. Quentin Bell, *Virginia Woolf: A Biography. Volume One. Virginia Stephen 1882–1912* (London: The Hogarth Press, 1973), pp.124–5.
4. Though only if the person was over 21.
5. See the recent book by Fielding, Thompson and Tiratsoo for an argument that the aspirations of ordinary voters were far more mundane. Steven Fielding, Peter Thompson and Nick Tiratsoo, *England Arise! The Labour Party and Popular Politics in the 1940s* (Manchester: Manchester University Press, 1995).
6. F.A. Hayek, *The Road to Serfdom* (London: Routledge, 1944), p.177.
7. John Strachey, *Why You Should be a Socialist* (London: Gollancz, 1944), pp.77 and 90.
8. Aneurin Bevan, *In Place of Fear* (London: Heinemann, 1952).

9. George Orwell, *1984* (London: Secker and Warburg, 1949). There has been considerable controversy over what it was that Orwell was describing in *1984*, but his own denial that it was a satire on socialism is unequivocal. A useful account is to be found in Bernard Crick, *George Orwell: A Life* (London: Secker & Warburg, 1980), pp.396–9.
10. Hayek had dedicated *The Road to Serfdom* to 'The Socialists of All Parties'. See op. cit., p.iv.
11. Michael Oakeshott, *Rationalism in Politics and Other Essays* (1967 edn.) (London: Methuen, 1962), p.169.
12. *Ibid.* It would of course have been Oakeshott's own response that that is all that people ever do, or ever can do. But what they make of their inherited raw materials, even when doing no more than 'pursuing intimations', can vary so widely as to still enable us to distinguish between periods of continuity and periods of discontinuity.
13. Quintin Hogg, *The Case for Conservatism* (West Drayton: Penguin, 1947), pp.7–8.
14. S.H. Beer, *Modern British Politics* (London: Faber, 1965, 1969).
15. A.V. Dicey, *Lectures on the Relation between Law and Public Opinion in England during the Nineteenth Century* (London: Macmillan, 1905).
16. Political parties are, moreover, important as institutional centres around which ideas form, cluster, and change, the grit around which the pearl of political thought forms in the oyster shell of the body politic. This symbiotic relationship, the 'Constantine relationship' is discussed in Rodney Barker, 'A Future for Liberalism or a Liberal Future?', in James Meadowcroft (ed.), *The Liberal Political Tradition: Contemporary Reappraisals* (Aldershot: Edward Elgar, 1995).
17. A number of attempts have been made to catch the 'essence' of conservatism, an enterprise which W.H. Greenleaf has dismissed as misconceived from the start. For some of these, and some of the criticisms, see: W.H. Greenleaf, *The British Political Tradition, volume two: The Ideological Heritage* (London: Methuen, 1983).
18. Philip Norton, 'Conservatism', in Michael Foley (ed.), *Ideas that Shape Politics* (Manchester: Manchester University Press, 1994), p.40.
19. A fact observed more in sadness than in triumph by Neville Johnson when he wrote that 'there may no longer be any substantial social or moral foundation for a body of practice and thought that can realistically be designated "conservative"'. Neville Johnson, 'What Will You Conserve', *Times Literary Supplement*, 9 Oct. 1992, p.10, quoted in David Miliband (ed.), *Reinventing the Left* (Cambridge: Polity, 1994), p.4.
20. David Willetts, *Modern Conservatism* (London: Penguin, 1992).
21. Roger Scruton, *The Meaning of Conservatism* (Harmondsworth: Penguin, 1980), p.34.
22. Though the 'essence' of socialism has been contended over at least as much as has that of conservatism. Anthony Crosland's attempt to discover a 'true' socialism by looking back amongst the ancestral texts was one only of many. C.A.R. Crosland, *The Future of Socialism* (London: Jonathan Cape, 1956).
23. Ralph Miliband, *Socialism for a Sceptical Age* (Oxford: Polity, 1994); Leo Panitch (ed.), *Why Not Capitalism: The Socialist Register 1995* (London: The Merlin Press, 1995).
24. David Miliband (ed.), *Reinventing the Left* (Cambridge: Polity, 1994), but see also Chantal Mouffe (ed.), *Dimensions of Radical Democracy: Pluralism, Citizenship, Community* (London: Verso, 1992).
25. Avner De-Shalit, 'David Miller's Model of Market Socialism and the Recent Reforms in Kibbutzim', *Political Studies*, Vol.40, No.1 (1992), pp.116-23.
26. Geof Andrews (ed.), *Citizenship* (London: Lawrence & Wishart, 1991).
27. Geof Mulgan, *Politics in An Antipolitical Age* (Cambridge: Polity, 1994).
28. There is a parallel here with disputes in political theory between liberal foundationalists and communitarians.
29. Paul Hirst, *Associative Democracy: New Forms of Economic and Social Governance* (Cambridge: Polity, 1994).
30. *Ibid.*, pp.9 and 14.
31. Cynics might suggest that the presence of the European Union within British politics was considerably greater than the presence within the politics of the European Union of Britain.
32. Elizabeth Meehan, *Citizenship and the European Community* (London: Sage, 1993).
33. David Miller, *Market, State, and Community: Theoretical Foundations of Market Socialism*

(Oxford: Clarendon, 1990).

34. The self-presentation of conservatism was in general of a body of doctrine averse to theory, but there were always those who ignored this demeanour. Both Mallock and Eliot, in their very different ways, consciously and openly drew on continental European thinkers. On conservative anti-intellectual diffidence, see Rodney Barker, *Politics, Peoples and Government: Themes in British Political Thought Since the Nineteenth Century* (Basingstoke: Macmillan, 1994).

35. It might of course be argued that since the short twentieth century was the Bolshevik century, its conclusion allows us to carry on where we left off. The agenda of the 1990s, in other words, picks up the loose threads of the 1910s, and we can all get on with pursuing the implications of New Liberalism. After the short twentieth century, comes the Hobhousian decade.

36. Richard Cockett, *Thinking the Unthinkable; Think Tanks and the Economic Counter-Revolution, 1931–1983* (London: HarperCollins, 1994).

37. Radhika Desai, 'Second Hand Dealers in Ideas: Think Tanks and Thatcherite Hegemony', *New Left Review* 203: Jan./Feb. (1994).

38. The 'Constantine syndrome', for a discussion of which see Barker, 'A Future for Liberalism or a Liberal Future?', op.cit.

39. J.A. Hobson had argued in 1920 that the development of collectivism would lead to the relative unimportance of collective provision, and the proliferation of private, individual, or small scale enterprises. J.A. Hobson, *The Crisis of Liberalism: New Issues of Democracy* (first published 1909; reprinted Brighton: Harvester, 1974), pp.172–3. Stephen Brooke has detected the seeds of disruption for socialist collectivism in its very successes after 1945 when he comments that 'It is an inevitable paradox, perhaps, that the triumph of the "public" nation, with the election of a socialist government dedicated to collectivism and state welfare, coincided with, or encouraged the ascendancy of a "private" nation of frustrated materialist desires.' Stephen Brooke, *Reform and Reconstruction: Britain After the War, 1945–51* (Manchester: Manchester University Press, 1995), p.24.

40. Paul Hirst (ed.), *The Pluralist Theory of the State: Selected Writings of G. D. H. Cole, J. N. Figgis, and H. J. Laski* (London: Routledge, 1989).

41. Crosland, *The Future of Socialism*, op. cit.

42. George Orwell, 'Notes on Nationalism' (1945), George Orwell, *The Collected Essays, Journalism and Letters of George Orwell*, edited by Sonia Orwell and Ian Angus, 4 vols. (1970 Penguin edn.) (London: Secker & Warburg, 1968), Vol.3.

43. The absence of constitutional discussion from the political thought of the short twentieth century contributed to an account, during that time, of nineteenth century politics which reflected this neglect of issues not prominent after 1917. This, appropriately, is now being addressed by historians. For example, by Patrick Joyce, *Democratic Subjects: The Self and the Social in Nineteenth Century England* (Cambridge: Cambridge University Pre, 1994); James Meadowcroft, 'State, "Statelessness", and The British Political Tradition', *Contemporary Politics*, 1:2 Summer (1995), pp.37–56.

44. Orwell reviewing *The Road to Serfdom* declared that collectivism 'leads to concentration camps, leader worship and war'. The trouble was that capitalism led to 'dole queues, the scramble for markets and war'. Orwell, *Collected Essays*, op. cit., p.144.

45. An account of Hayek's influence which treats it as just such a move from wilderness to temple is contained in Richard Cockett, op. cit.

46. C.A.R, Crosland, *The Conservative Enemy: A Programme of Radical Reform for the 1960s*, (London: Jonathan Cape , 1962).

47. Eric Hobsbawm, *The Age of Extremes*, op. cit., p.4.

48. Etienne Balibar and Immanuel Wallerstein, *Race, Nation, Class: Ambiguous Identities* (New York & London: Verso, 1991) and Ephraim Nimni, *Marxism and Nationalism: Theoretical Origins of a Political Crisis* (Pluto: London, 1991) provide good examples of discussions which set out either to examine the consequences for Marxism of the political revolutions of the 1990s, or to see what of value can still be extracted from a Marxist approach to politics.

The Beveridge Strait-jacket:
Policy Formation and the Problem of
Poverty in Old Age

HELEN FAWCETT

In the late 1950s, the Labour Party devised a radical plan to reform the British welfare state. The policy document, *National Superannuation: Labour's Policy for Security in Old Age*, aimed to move away from the flat-rate universalism of the Beveridge model of income maintenance and to institute an earnings-related system of contributions and benefits. In comparative perspective, the development was of great significance since many European countries were developing comparable schemes in the 1950s. However, the Labour Party failed to implement any structural reforms until 1975 when it launched the State Earnings Related Pension Scheme which was substantially less radical than the original proposals. This article argues that the feedback effects generated by the Beveridge model itself were a powerful barrier to long-term change. By creating short-term pressures for increases in the basic retirement pension, and causing, through the very inadequacy of that pension, the growth of a powerful private sector policy 'lock-in' effects developed, and it became progressively more difficult to reform the system..

> 'Everyone knows I am cooking this marvellous vote winner.
> I hope to God it is'.
> R.H.S. Crossman[1]

Towards the end of the 1950s policy-makers in both the Labour and Conservative Parties were forced to admit that the dream, embodied in the Beveridge Report, of a welfare state which protected society from the conditions of poverty and deprivation experienced in the 1930s, had failed to become a reality. The Beveridge model of social security, was based on a contractual relationship between individual citizens and the state based on the principle of insurance. Beveridge proposed a system in which benefits were earned by contributions made during working life which guaranteed a basic minimum pension entitlement. However, it had become apparent that flat-rate contributions were incapable of securing enough revenue to maintain the state pension at an acceptable level. The level of contribution

Helen Fawcett, Department of Social Policy, University of York.

had to be determined by what the poorest wage-earners could reasonably be expected to pay, making it impossible to increase the pension without increasing the Exchequer contribution. Thus, by the 1950s, the model of social welfare which was supposed to liberate society from want was being described as a 'strait-jacket'.

It was against this background that the Labour Party set up the Study Group on Security and Old Age, under the chairmanship of Richard Crossman. During the 1950s the Labour Party conducted a number of enquiries into party policy but the Study Group was remarkable for two reasons. First of all, it employed the expertise of three leading academics based at the London School of Economics, Professor Richard Titmuss and his students Brian Abel-Smith and Peter Townsend, who set the agenda for the Groups' discussions. Secondly, its report is rare amongst opposition party policy papers in being a fully worked out blueprint rather than a statement of general principles and desirable objectives. The 1957 document, 'National Superannuation: Labour's Policy for Security in Old Age' represented a major break-through. It advocated moving to a system of earnings-related contributions and benefits which would solve the problems associated with financing the basic state pension, increase the standard of living for those already in retirement, and secure the financial security of future generations of the elderly.

Yet despite the skill and effort which was dedicated to the construction of the new policy, and the enthusiasm which greeted its publication, National Superannuation was never translated into legislation in its original form and it took nearly 20 years before the Labour party could launch an earnings-related pension scheme. Since a number of European countries adopted state superannuation systems in the 1950s and early 1960s and have maintained them ever since, it is implausible to think that the work of the Study Group was fundamentally flawed.

This paper argues that the Study Group's proposals were hindered by the structural obstacles which confronted policy-makers and contends that the flat-rate universalism of the Beveridge model itself produced some intractable problems which were difficult to overcome. In particular, policy-makers were faced with the requirement to (a) reconcile the short-term interests of those already in retirement, with the long-term need to establish a pension scheme which would be suitable for future cohorts of pensioners and, (b), a private sector which had expanded to bridge the gap in provision caused by the absence of adequate state support for the elderly.

Previous analyses have tended to under-rate these structural obstacles. A number of authors, puzzling over the reasons why Crossman's vision of National Superannuation was never translated into reality, have dwelt on a number of inter-mediate political and economic variables. These are, of course, of considerable importance. For instance, when Labour came to power in 1964 it did not prioritise this large and complicated piece of legislation and Crossman was not placed in charge of the DHSS until 1968. In October 1974, the Labour government had a very slim majority, and emphasis was placed on winning the co-operation of the Conservative opposition in order to steer the State Earnings Related Pension Scheme through parliament. In addition, the ideological predispositions of the leadership and the political will to prioritise superannuation were subject to fluctuations throughout this period.

All of these factors are valid in providing a historical account of the slow and laborious progress of Crossman's vote winner. However, such discussions often neglect the basic context of policy-making which is fundamental to all that follows. As Heclo argues, it is impossible to understand the development of superannuation without taking into account the perceived failings of the Beveridge report which underpinned the policy-making environment.[2] This insight can be developed further, however the Beveridge model was to prove extremely durable and resistant to change because the longer it took to reform the system, the more compelling the need to resolve the problem of existing pensioners and the more difficult it was to overcome the problems created by a thriving private sector. In this sense, the feedback effects emanating from the Beveridge model gathered momentum and made it progressively more difficult to construct a new model of social security which would halt them.

The case of National Superannuation highlights the need to consider policy inheritance and feedback when evaluating policy development and implementation. The ease with which it is possible to move from one structure to another is evidently crucial to the possibility of change. Any discussion of the history of this particular initiative is incomplete without acknowledging that it became increasingly difficult to implement National Superannuation precisely because the universal flat-rate pension remained in place. Although the policy response may have remained appropriate, the facility with which it could be effected declined during the 1960s and 1970s as the private sector grew.

By focusing on the quality of advice and the structural political and economic factors which inhibit purposive government action, it is possible to disguise or neglect the role of policy inheritance and policy feedback. It is the argument of this paper that the Beveridge model of social security created a powerful and rigid structure for social welfare. Once it was in place, it proved extremely hard to either abandon, ameliorate or reform. The most propitious time to implement any change was arguably in the 1950s when there may have been enough flexibility to ease the path of new legislation. Thereafter, the feedback effects generated by the Beveridge model gathered momentum. There was a dual pressure to improve the position of those already in retirement and living on an inadequate flat-rate pension, whilst attempting to launch a new system which would supersede the Beveridge model and provide a higher standard of living and a better means of financing retirement pensions.

In addition, the poor quality of state provision encouraged the growth of the private sector which expanded to fill the vacuum in provision. This was compatible with Beveridge's original vision of a basic minimum for all, set at subsistence levels, and supplemented by private provision for those able to afford it. As the private sector grew in size and scale it became a powerful interest group and the sheer numbers of people covered meant that it had to be accommodated within any attempt at reform. Even as early as the 1960s, over half the workforce were covered by occupational pension schemes, and the longer it took for the state to provide an alternative, the more employers were convinced to provide occupational pension schemes[3] and the more employees opted for this type of provision. Consequently, any attempt to launch an alternative would be forced to take account of the importance of market provision. Therefore, radical reform would most feasible prior to the growth of the private sector.

The slow progress of National Superannuation emphasises the degree to which structural factors can inhibit policy options and thereby limit the role of those involved in policy development. It also highlights the importance of historical contingency, and how difficulties in implementation will increase if action is not taken at the most opportune time.

The Beveridge Report from the Cradle to the Grave

Late in 1942 Beveridge produced his plan for Social Security, *Social Insurance and Allied Services*.[4] His aim was to establish a comprehensive social insurance scheme to cover the main contingencies of unemployment, sickness and old age. Benefits would be flat-rate and financed by flat-rate contributions. They would be set at a subsistence level, so as to be just sufficient to meet basic needs without recourse to means-tested benefit, but no more than subsistence so as to encourage individuals to provide for themselves on a voluntary basis. Social insurance benefits supplemented by private insurance or savings were to be the major source of income during interruptions of earnings or retirement, with social assistance being reduced to a safety net to deal with emergencies and those with special needs.

In 1944 a White Paper on Social Insurance was issued to which all parties in the coalition were committed, and a Ministry of National Insurance was established. However, the new provisions for social security enacted in the next few years fell short of those proposed by Beveridge.

Although a major achievement, they harboured the difficulties which were to emerge more plainly as early as the 1950s.

The National Insurance Act of 1946 was the first piece of social policy legislation brought forward after the war. The Act departed from the Beveridge proposals in a number of ways. In particular, full-rate old age pensions would be introduced immediately, whereas Beveridge had envisaged a 20-year-phasing in period to spread the increased expenditure. The level of benefits would be fixed substantially above the level recommended by Beveridge which had been based on 1938 prices. Although this reflected the increase in the cost of living index since 1938, the index had been distorted by several years of rationing and food subsidies and probably under-estimated the actual increase in living expenses.

The safety net of means-tested National Assistance was also introduced. The level of National Assistance was below that of National Insurance, although when rent was taken into account, could be higher. It was thought that only one in five pensioners would require assistance and that most non-pensioners, who it was assumed would be short-term cases, would not need to apply. Thus it was widely believed that the stigma and means-testing which characterised the social security system of the 1930s had been abolished and a universal system based on rights and entitlements had been introduced. The Beveridge plan survived as the basis for British social security for the next 35 years. The report inspired great public enthusiasm and the Labour Party adopted the principles of the scheme without a full evaluation of the scheme and its implications.[5]

In 1955 the Labour Party argued that social security must be developed a stage further. It promised that a Ministry of Social Welfare would be created to combine the work of the Ministry of Pensions and National Insurance and that of the National Assistance Board.[6] It was hoped that a new ministry might be able to remove the 'taint of public assistance'. In the space of four years the mood had changed from one of self-congratulation to one of concern with the image of National Assistance. In part this reflected Labour party's new role as a party in opposition rather than that of the outgoing government defending its record; but it also reflected the beginning of the disenchantment with which members of the Labour Party viewed the social security system created under the Attlee government.

The flat-rate national insurance system introduced in 1946 was under considerable stress throughout the 1950s. On the one hand the current and projected costs of social security benefits – especially pensions – and their distribution between employee, employer and the Exchequer were issues of controversy. On the other hand, despite their apparent costliness, insurance benefits had visibly failed to achieve the goal of removing the retired, the sick, the unemployed and the widowed from poverty. Unless they had income from other sources, or very low rents, people drawing these benefits were almost certainly living on an income below national assistance benefit scales. National Insurance benefits were judged inadequate, particularly within the Labour Party, for three reasons: the flat-rate benefits were low relative to the definition of poverty embodied in national assistance; they were almost continually eroded by inflation but only periodically revised; and they bore no precise relationship either to the individual standards of living experienced by people during working life or to any measure of the national average standard of living. The system of financing the scheme left little room for removing these defects. Unless costs were shifted towards the Exchequer, substantial improvements in benefits could only be financed by greatly increasing the burden of the regressive flat-rate contributions on lower paid workers.

The position of the elderly was obviously central to the discussion of national insurance and assistance not only because they were the largest group of beneficiaries but also because they were permanently obliged to live on a very low income. Although the 1960s is often regarded as the decade when poverty was 'rediscovered',[7] the question of poverty in old age was, in fact, a central concern in domestic social policy in the 1950s. Indeed, it was shared throughout post-war Europe where a number of countries began to redesign their pension schemes. The inadequacies of National Insurance were underlined by the fact that some, but by no means all, employees received occupational benefits which were additional to their entitlement under the state scheme. The core issue, as perceived by the Labour Party, was summarised by a speaker at the 1957 conference: 'the system we have at the present time is creating wider inequalities in old age than exist in working life. We are developing two classes in our society; a class dependent on the national pension and more and more National Assistance, and another class gaining from private superannuated schemes.'[8]

In May 1957 the Labour Party published *National Superannuation: Labour's Policy for Security in Old Age*. It marked a complete break with the Beveridge flat-rate system and served as the corner-stone of Labour's social security policy from 1957 until it formed a government in 1964. In the aftermath of the election defeat of 1959 the principle of an earnings-related state pension which it proposed was extended to other national insurance benefits for the unemployed, sick and disabled. If it had been implemented it would have represented a complete re-writing of the Beveridge system.

In comparative perspective the scheme was as advanced as any of those under discussion in the social democratic parties of Europe, and demonstrated that at this historical juncture the Labour Party had a policy which, if implemented, would place Britain among those European countries with the most advanced welfare states.

The development of *National Superannuation: Labour's Policy for Security in Old Age* provides strong support for Heclo's contention that change in social policy has been strongly influenced by the intervention of individuals in the policy process.[9]

> Typically, social policies have been most directly influenced by middlemen at the interfaces of various groups. These have been men with transcendable groups commitments, in but not always of their host body. While not the most powerful participants, these agents of change have usually had access to information, ideas and positions outside the normal run of organisational actors. Their formal party allegiances have differed greatly but all have used their various positions to bring pensions, unemployment insurance or superannuation questions onto political agendas.

The re-orientation of Labour Party policy owed a great deal to the influence of outside academic experts. Richard Titmuss, Brian Abel-Smith and Peter Townsend played a key role in designing the new strategy.

The idea for earnings-related contributions and benefits first appeared in 1953 in a Fabian Society Pamphlet, 'The Reform of Social Security'[10] and two years later the ideas which formed the basis of National Superannuation were published in 'New Pensions for Old'.[11] These pamphlets were discussed in Labour Party circles and came to the attention of Peter Shore, the Head of the Research Department. He passed the pamphlets on to Richard Crossman who had been asked to reply to the Social Services debate at the 1955 Annual Conference.[12] Between 1952 and 1955 the financing of the Beveridge scheme had been the subject of national debate. The Labour Party had rejected the findings of the Phillips Committee[13] which had recommended that the retirement age should be increased to reduce costs. The Labour Party's Social Security Committee had been examining the crisis of the Beveridge system but had failed to make any recommendations because of the trade union movement's staunch commitment to the contributory principle. This commitment was based on the assumption that if workers made identifiable contributions, it would be difficult for the government at a later stage to reduce benefits. In replying to the debate on National Assistance and National Insurance benefits, Crossman stressed the urgent need for the Labour Party to form a pensions policy which would offer a solution to the crisis in social security. *The Study Group on Security and Old Age*[14] (a sub-committee of the Home Policy Committee of the National Executive) was asked to investigate the area. However, it was clear from the composition of the committee that debate would centre on the ways and means of moving to a system of earnings-related contributions and benefits. The final version of the superannuation report was produced in April 1957[15] and was accepted by Conference later that year.

The Study Group's Strategy

The Study Group was concerned to defuse all the resistance to their new proposals which might be rooted in from the party's commitment to the Beveridge report. Whilst they understood that some important factions such as the trade union movement had a well-founded case for maintaining their allegiance to the report, they also understood that the party membership's self-image as the authors and defenders of the welfare state was a strong emotional tie, and that to appear to be directly attacking the adoption of the Beveridge report as a mistake would be counterproductive.

The main task of the Study Group was to attack the central notion of flat-rate contributions as a basis from which to determine the financing of the scheme. To this end they employed arguments based on changed circumstances and unforeseen difficulties. The Study Group argued that the national insurance pension had failed because Beveridge had been concerned with the problems of mass unemployment and a dead-level of poverty in the 1930s. These circumstances had made a compelling case for uniform flat-rate benefits and a uniform pension. But the conditions of the 1950s were very different because mass unemployment had been eliminated and the economy was experiencing a period of growth. With a shortage of labour it was clearly desirable that people should postpone retirement as long as possible and hence the retirement rule (which prevented the payment of the pension before retirement rather than the payment of the pension when a certain age is reached) did not appear to be so desirable. Likewise the earnings rule discouraged pensioners from taking up some form of employment after retirement.[16]

Most importantly, they argued, contributions based on the uniform flat-rate principle were out of place in the conditions of the 1950s. This form of contribution was having a restrictive effect on the level of benefits because the size of the employee's contribution necessarily was determined by what the low paid could reasonably be expected to pay.[17] Contribution levels could not be raised without penalising the low paid and consequently benefits could not be increased.

Financing Benefits from General Taxation

Possible responses to the crisis of the Beveridge system under discussion since the beginning of the 1950s had directed the attention of politicians to two possible alternative solutions: graded contributions or benefits which would be financed from general taxation. The latter option had found favour with the left wing of the party. Clearly, the study group needed to question the feasibility of the general taxation option in order to win support for their scheme The study group chose to argue that subsistence benefits might be more difficult to achieve under a tax financed system of benefits than they were under the existing system.

Within the Labour Party tax resistance was believed to be prevalent among all social groups and thus, the Study Group argued, there would be a very real limit to the amount of revenue which could be raised by general taxation. If this was the case, the party would face the unpalatable choice of whether to increase the level of taxation or whether to make economies in other area of the manifesto programme so that there would be sufficient resources available for providing subsistence pensions. In their view, the electorate's gratitude for being relieved of the burden of contributions would not last long in the public memory and would be of no help in mitigating tax resistance. The Study Group shrewdly avoided mentioning the arguments about which approach would conform more closely with the general socialist aims of the party; in particular which would be more re-distributive, which would be a more effective measure as the agent of social justice, or which would better serve the long term goals of creating a socialist society. There was certainly no attempt to counter the obvious argument that superannuation would perpetuate the wage differentials which existed among the work-force after retirement.[18]

Accommodating the Trade Unions: The Case for the Insurance Principle

The Study Group's main concern was with the response of the trade union movement. Despite their negotiations with the TUC, they were naturally aware that only a few years before, the possibility of a change in policy had been effectively vetoed because maintenance of the insurance principle was still Congress policy.[19] It was obviously necessary to anticipate the possibility of further trade union resistance. By paying tribute to the justifications for support of the insurance principle they undermined the arguments in support of funding pensions from direct taxation but more importantly gave themselves the tactic with which to win support for their proposals, namely to create a logical and inextricable link between support for the insurance principle and support for superannuation. The one could not be maintained without acceptance of the other.

The Study Group began by accepting the TUC's legitimate fears that, without the insurance principle, the state might be able to slash benefits in order to weather some future economic storm: 'As long as benefits are earned by payment of contributions and financed out an insurance fund, they are felt to be something which the worker receives as of right and which no politician can take away from him.'[20] The authors sought to create an indissoluble bond between support for the principle of national insurance and superannuation, hence taking advantage of the emotional and political support for the principles of Beveridge and portraying the new scheme as the only way of preserving the essence of the old.

They argued that it was the form of contribution rather than the contributory principle itself which was causing the problem. Contributions could not be increased because of the burden that would be placed on the lower paid worker. However, if pensions were increased by the Exchequer, the deficit in the National Insurance fund would do the same. Hence there was no way of providing adequate pensions under the current system. By clinging to the insurance principle but refusing to change the system of contributions the actuarial basis of the scheme would become a 'hollow shell'.[21]

Occupational Pensions

The second line of attack was based on the conditions of inequality in old age; namely the vast difference in the financial circumstances of those who were dependent on the state pension and those who were able to supplement it with an occupational pension. The Study Group wanted to make it clear that the only way in which the state could provide benefits comparable to those of the occupational schemes was by adopting superannuation.

They attacked the private sector on the grounds of inadequate transferability of pension rights, that is to say, the absence of a mechanism whereby the contributions paid whilst in one job could be transferred, or in some other way preserved, if the worker changed his job. It was usually the case that the employee was forced to forfeit the contributions and had to start paying into a pension fund from scratch on starting a new job.

Nevertheless, the Study Group emphasised that the advantages of an occupational scheme outweighed this disadvantage because they were able to offer pensions which were superior to those offered by the state. However, these benefits were only available to a privileged minority. Two-thirds of the work-force had little chance of ever being included in such schemes. Access to superannuation was confined to the higher grades of professional and white collar workers and to a minority of industrial workers who were employed by large firms.

The benefits offered by occupational schemes were substantial: the middle ranges of civil servants and other white collar workers could expect to receive half or even as much as two-thirds pay on retirement. This was a marked contrast to the conditions on which pensions were available to blue-collar workers.[22] Nevertheless, even the occupational provision available in the industrial sector was far superior to the quality of pension offered by the state.

The Study Group made it clear that the taxpayer was subsidising privileges for this minority. The Phillips Committee estimated that the tax concessions to superannuation schemes were costing the Exchequer £100 million in 1954.[23] This had to be compared with the sum which was contributed to National Insurance pensions, a mere £3 million. The tax concessions to occupational schemes were encouraging the growth of superannuation schemes which were benefiting a mere third of the population while the government was spending much less on the national scheme designed for the whole population.

In concluding their case for change the Study Group argued that the Beveridge scheme had become an anachronism and that it was now time to: 'rise above this concept of fair shares in poverty. Wage-related pensions satisfied the conditions of the second half of the twentieth century just as flat-rate pensions suited the first.'[24]

The Principles of National Superannuation

Under the terms of the Labour Party's new scheme, employees would pay earnings-related contributions of 3 percent of their wages, employers would pay 5 percent and the Exchequer would contribute two per cent. In return, the average worker who contributed to the scheme throughout working life (approximately forty years) could expect to receive a pension which represented half his final salary – 'half-pay on retirement'. The party also undertook to ensure the pension was protected against inflation once it was in payment.

The most important political advantage of the scheme was its solution to the low level of benefits which were being paid to existing pensioners. The group gave a definite commitment that this basic element of the pension would be raised by 50 percent when Labour came to office.[25] The funds accumulated from the contributions of workers inside and outside the state scheme would be enough to allow this dramatic increase in the basic level of pension and would quell any discontent over the inability to pay existing pensioners earning-related benefits under the new scheme. Moreover the Labour Party under took to protect the £3 pension against inflation.

The state scheme would differ from the occupational schemes operating in the commercial sector because it would be a mechanism for the reduction of inequality. There would be a ceiling beyond which contributions would not be payable and consequently benefits would not be available. But more importantly, at the other end of the scale, there would be a floor below which no pension would be permitted to fall. Hence it was quite conceivable that a low-paid worker would receive a higher income on retirement than that which s/he had earned during their working lives. This was the main re-distributive element in the report.[26]

A further advantage of the national scheme was the manner in which it solved the problem of transferability discussed earlier. The existence of a state scheme would provide the private sector with strong competition because one of the conditions for the approval of an occupational scheme would be the addition of transferability rights if they did not exist already. This would mean that the worker's contribution to the occupational scheme could be saved and moved to the scheme which was run by the next employer if s/he chose to change jobs. The implementation of the new plan would mean that there would be increased mobility of labour in the workforce; and in particular, freedom of movement would be restored to middle-aged workers who were often reluctant to change jobs for fear of losing their pension entitlement.

Another difference between the occupational sector and the new proposals was the way in which the level of benefit would be assessed. It was the practice in the private sector to base the retirement pension upon the salary earned during the last three or four years of working life. This was clearly to the advantage of professional and white collar workers who were at the peak of their earning power at this time. However, it was to the disadvantage of manual workers whose earning power tended to decline as they approached retirement. The Labour Party undertook to provide 'dynamic' pensions. The group proposed an index which would relate lifetime earnings to the precise fraction such earnings either rose above or fell below national earnings. This system would not only preserve the real value of contributions throughout life but would also give each worker a credit for the increase in the national standard of living. In an attempt to preserve the pensioner's standard of living after retirement, the earnings-related supplement would be re-valued to take account of inflation, although the Labour leadership chose to be more equivocal on this point than they had been on the inflation-proofing for the £3 basic pension.[27]

The Retirement Condition and the Earnings Rule

The Study Group did not trim its views in anticipation of union hostility. They made it quite clear that there was no reason to maintain the retirement condition if the new scheme was adopted. National Superannuation would be perfectly efficient if the pension was paid at a statutory age with no retirement rule or earnings condition attached. The plan would provide half pay at 65 rather than half pay on retirement. The group was willing to concede that if there was a likelihood of a return to mass unemployment it would be advisable to retain the retirement condition but were quite unequivocal in their own preferences: 'We see much to be said for the gradual easing of the earnings rule and the eventual abolition of the retirement condition. But this is an issue where the final decision must be left to the next Labour Government in consultation with the TUC.'[28] This was a wise strategic move because the maintenance of the retirement condition would not compromise the scheme. If trade union opposition seemed intense it would be possible to concede the point.

Contracting Out – The Relationship Between the State and the Private Sector

An important feature of the proposals was the extremely exacting terms on which private occupational pension schemes would be allowed to contract out of the state scheme. First of all, their contributions and benefits would have to compare favourably with those offered by the state. Secondly, occupational pensions would have to be completely transferable from one place of employment to another. Thirdly, individuals would be allowed to contract into the state scheme if they so wished and it would be illegal for membership of an occupational scheme to be a condition of employment. The occupational sector would have found it difficult to adapt to these stringent conditions as Hannah observes:

> Occupational pensions by now already covered a third or more of the work-force, and many employers were considering introducing, upgrading or expanding schemes. This did, then, probably represent the last practical moment at which a state earnings-related pension scheme could have wiped out the bulk of demand for private provision in Britain. When the Labour scheme was announced, the shares of insurance companies fell sharply. Shareholders were right to be worried: this scheme could kill the bulk of their expanding business in pensions.[29]

However, the Study Group avoided the possibility of making a second key structural change in the pensions package. The most important sense in which we can see the influence of policy feedback was the decision to retain the national insurance pension. The option of excluding those already in receipt of state pensions and older workers who were over the age of fifty and would not have time to contribute to a new scheme was rejected on the grounds of social justice. The Study Group argued it was impossible to create any fair mechanism by which to determine who would be in the old scheme and who in the new.

There was also the question of the rights which workers had already established by contributing to the basic state pension scheme during their working life. Their contributions entitled them to a flat-rate pension as a legal right. This was something of a rationalisation since few people would be concerned about legal rights if they were being offered substantially improved benefits. However, in setting out the terms and conditions of the new scheme, Labour's planners did not feel able to confront the problem of the inequalities which would arise between the different age cohorts of pensioners once the scheme came into operation. This demonstrates how the established interests created under Beveridge were powerful enough to go almost unchallenged in the design of a new scheme: the Beveridge pension was to be incorporated, not abolished.

National Saving

The outline of the general principles of the report ended with a discussion of the possibilities which superannuation afforded for national saving. The credit which would accumulate in the national fund would in fact provide a system of national savings which could be used to carry through a large scale programme of capital investment to the general good of the national economy. This aspect of the scheme had inspired a great deal of interest among the 'Revisionists', who saw it as a means of countering further demands for nationalisation with a proposal which was equally radical.

The presentation of National Superannuation had a broad appeal. For the Labour Party member, the effective 'back-door' nationalisation of the insurance companies was attractive. Nationalisation had been in the party's programme during the 1950s but had not been seriously placed in the general strategy of the party. The growth of the insurance companies and their importance as investors was a growing concern. However, nationalisation was electorally unpopular and the cause of great dissension between the party's factions. If the insurance companies were taken into public ownership directly, the Conservative opposition would be able to make great political capital about the issue. But superannuation would lead to the withering away of the private sector because it could not compete with the benefits and conditions on offer in the state scheme. The proposals were attractive to both right and left because they provided the means to curtail the growth of the private sector without nationalisation and provided an important source of capital for a future chancellor.

But for the electorate in general, there was little attraction in a superannuation scheme which would not have any tangible results until it matured over some considerable period of time. Throughout the 1950s, a major issue in party conflict on the domestic front had been the scandal of the growing levels of poverty in old age. In 1951 the Exchequer contribution had been reduced, quickly followed by the revelation that millions of pensioners were dependent upon means-tested National Assistance benefits. The quinquennial review of the Beveridge Report in 1954, the Phillips Committee, had revealed the inadequacy of pension levels and their decline in real terms since the 1940s, but had proposed that pensions should not be payable until the age of 70. Hence the real issue was which party would find a way of increasing the basic pension for existing pensioners not which party could develop the best actuarially sound plan for future decades. National Superannuation was a way of achieving the massive increase of 50 per cent. This had the dual advantage of distracting attention from the difficult problem of finding an equitable solution to the problem of the transition and the fact that the scheme would enforce strict actuarial principles on the benefits available to the middle-aged worker. Such a decision could be justified by the high level of the basic pension.

The Study Group had devised a plan which constituted a politically acceptable way of re-writing the Beveridge Report. It would solve the immediate problem of poverty in old age which was of fundamental concern to the party, the trade union movement and the electorate while finding a way of moving from the principles of the Beveridge report to superannuation and the concept of graded contributions and benefits. However, we can see how the legacy of past policy shaped the construction of the scheme. There was a consistency of support for a universal uniform pension which the Study Group preferred to incorporate, thus creating a two-tier system of pension provision rather than a completely earnings-related system. Moreover, the contractual relationship between the state and the individual in the form of a contributory system had also established strong roots which it was easier to maintain. As Heclo argues the technique of social insurance has tended to become considered the 'natural' policy response for problems of income maintenance.[30] Beveridge created both traditions and difficulties, and the two together became the motor behind policy change.

The Implementation of State Superannuation: Policy Feedback and 'Lock-in'

The slow progress from blueprint to legislation provides compelling evidence of the role of policy feedback effects. This concept refers to the ways in which previous political choices affect the current political agenda and the options open to political parties. As Schattschneider wrote, 'new policies create a new politics'.[31] Discussion of policy feedback focuses on two components of political change. First of all, it is argued public policies give rise to structures and resources which either encourage or inhibit the formation of interest groups. This is the inverse of the classic pluralist position in which interest group activity is seen as shaping public policy. Policy feedback highlights the way in which policies themselves contrive to spawn interest groups and generate incentives which either facilitate or retard their expansion. Secondly, existing policies influence the perceptions and agendas of key political actors. In short 'political learning' encapsulates the way in which politicians adapt their behaviour in the light of experience. This concept is open to some criticism as Pierson writes:

> Learning processes seem likely to be more important when policy-making remains insulated from broader conflicts. Policy learning is also likely to play different roles at different stages in the policy making process. Learning effects will be most apparent in the identification of particular policy alternatives, since this is when detailed knowledge is most crucial. It is less clear that policy learning is central to the formation of government agendas or the final choice between alternative policies.[32]

While the relevance of political learning is apparent in the development of National Superannuation, the impact of other feedback effects are central to what happened in the aftermath of the Study Group's report.

National superannuation never became legislation: indeed in comparison to the earnings-related systems in place elsewhere in Europe, Britain became something of a welfare state laggard. It was not until the launch of the State Earnings Related Pension Scheme in 1974[33] that a full state superannuation scheme was inaugurated, by which time similar schemes had been available in Sweden and Germany from the late 1950s and early 1960s. Moreover, the legislation departed from some of the principles of the 1957 proposals, and was a testimony to the feedback effects which acted as a constraint on policy-makers who were influenced by two key considerations. First of all, there was the priority of meeting the needs of existing pensioners within any scheme of earnings-related provision: and secondly, there was the necessity to adapt to the expansion of earnings-related provision in the private sector.

Existing Pensioners

The legacy of Beveridge is at its most apparent when we examine the way in which policy was shaped by the problem of existing pensioners. The political imperative to raise the basic state pension was a constant factor in the deliberations and a continuing dilemma which explains many of the twists and turns of policy-making. For instance, in 1964, when Labour took power, the government's first initiative was not to launch National Superannuation, but to increase the basic state pension.[34] This was an important factor contributing to the delay in preparing the legislation. Although, the government was blown off-course by the problems of implementing the Income Guarantee, the remedial action taken in respect of the basic pension, outside the context of the new scheme, bred a sense of complacency. The delay also created practical difficulties in that it is preferable to begin work on ambitious new proposals of such magnitude at an early stage in the life of a government.

The problem of existing pensioners re-emerged during the 1970s. On this occasion, it led to a complete reorientation of party policy, and for a time, it appeared as if superannuation might be jettisoned altogether in favour of a substantial flat-rate pension. The abandonment of the Crossman proposals by the Heath government re-opened the debate on the best way of alleviating poverty in old age.[35] From the period 1970–74, powerful sections of the labour movement preferred to re-affirm the Beveridge system and improve the basic state pension. This would have the advantage of establishing a basic minimum standard of provision available to all, and would particularly operate in the interests of the poorer members of society. Many believed that superannuation was now an irrelevance compared with the immediate priority of improving the living standards of those already in retirement.[36]

Both the number of people covered and the social composition of those dependent on the state scheme created a community of interest and re-enforced support for the Beveridge system. Blue-collar workers in the industrial sector of the economy, whose earning power declined as they grew older, were still less likely to be covered by occupational provision. Thus, there was a social division of welfare in this respect, leaving traditional working class employees far more likely to rely on the basic state pension.

In 1971, the trade union movement, led by Jack Jones the general secretary of the Transport and General Workers Union, began to campaign for a substantial increase in the basic pension, indexed so it would be protected against inflation.[37] The Labour leadership was seeking a *rapprochement* with the trade union movement, following the friction caused during the 1964–70 government by their incomes policy and attempt to reform industrial relations 'In Place of Strife'. It was now hoped to repair party-union relationships and to involve the trade unions in a process of political exchange: in return for wage restraint, the Labour Party undertook to guarantee the implementation of certain policies when it returned to office. The party ratified a substantial increase in the basic state pension and this became one of the first measures to be implemented by the Labour government of 1974. By 1973, the pledge to increase the basic pension to £10/£16 a week for a single person and a couple respectively was part of the Social Contract.[38] Very little consideration was given to how this would effect plans for superannuation, and thereafter, the party's proposals had to be constructed around the assumption of a large basic state pension. Thus the State Earnings Related Pension Scheme would be built as a second tier of earnings-related provision on top of the basic state pension. Although superannuation was not abandoned altogether it became less prominent on Labour's agenda.

Policy Lock-in

The progress of National Superannuation from the 1950s illustrates a further critical aspect of policy feedback: namely, the impact previous policy choices have for society as a whole, beyond the realm of elite decision-making and interest group politics. The development of the private sector demonstrates how the ordinary public as well as policy-makers can become 'locked-in' to a particular course of action which greatly inhibits any attempt to pursue alternative policies. Government decision-making in this area of public sector activity has major implications for individual citizens. The absence of adequate state provision creates a strong incentive to seek private sector coverage. However, given the contributory nature of financing occupational pensions, exiting from a pension scheme is only feasible if pension rights are fully preserved. Moreover, the complexity of pension schemes implies that individuals need significant levels of information to make appropriate choices. Thirdly, de-stabilising private sector coverage, by either demanding that the quality of pension schemes should be improved, increasing regulation, or setting up a state scheme in competition is likely to provoke opposition from the pension providers and to incur resistance from those who have now become clients of the private sector. As Pierson writes:

> Policies may create incentives that encourage the emergence of elaborate social and economic networks, greatly increasing the cost of adopting once-possible alternatives and inhibiting exit from a current policy path. Individuals make important commitments in response to certain types of government action. These commitments, in turn, may vastly increase the disruption caused by new politics, effectively locking in previous decisions.[39]

The growth of the private sector during the 1960s demonstrates the importance of lock-in effects and shows the way in which the accelerating momentum behind the growth of the private sector rendered previously viable strategies increasingly problematic.

The key turning point in the development of the private sector took place under the Conservative government of 1959–64. Conservative policy was determined by policy inheritance and the need to respond to the increasing deficit in the National Insurance Fund. Indeed, the result of their strategy was to re-affirm Beveridge's vision of a dual system comprising of flat-rate universal provision supplemented by more generous market provision for those who could afford it. During this period government policy was geared to supporting the expansion of the private sector and in this respect was congruent with Beveridge's original intentions.

The financial pressure on state pension arrangements was increased in 1958 when the number of people eligible for the state pension increased dramatically as 400,000 older workers with only ten years of contributions became eligible for the state pension. Even before this date the Conservatives had started to investigate earnings-related benefits and contributions.[40] However, there was an important qualitative difference between the Labour and Conservative approaches: the Conservatives' interest in earnings-relation stemmed exclusively from the desire to reduce the deficit in the National Insurance Fund without increasing the Exchequer contribution. Their response to the Labour Party scheme was hostile, opposing it both as a means of improving the living standards of the elderly and as an attack on the private insurance industry. The Conservative party chairman, Oliver Poole, described National Superannuation as 'half pie in the sky rather than half pay on retirement' and the Prime Minister himself attacked the proposals as an attempt to nationalise the insurance industry by stealth.[41]

The graduated pension scheme proposed by the Conservative government was not comparable to the Labour party's 1957 proposals, because although it instituted graduated contributions it only provided the most minimal earnings-related benefits in return. The lower paid were to remain reliant on the basic pension and the higher paid were also ineligible for the scheme. Under the Conservative legislation, earnings-related contributions were levied on those earning between £9 and £15 per week at a time when the average wage was about £13 a week. The graduated pension only added a small additional sum to the basic pension and was not protected against inflation. In addition, the Conservative scheme incorporated very lenient contracting out conditions which allowed employees to leave the state scheme and contribute to private sector schemes which guaranteed comparable benefits. In fact, most earnings related contributions flowing into the graduated scheme were not used to finance earnings-related pensions at all but instead were used to shore up the deficit in the National Insurance Fund. Consequently, when the scheme came into operation in April 1961, many of those eligible to join chose to contract out. As Hannah comments:

> As the insurance world recognised, Boyd-Carpenter's plan was 'a political gimmick not a pension scheme'. Nonetheless, as it left them a relatively clear field, the main pension interests understandably supported it .... The Conservative strategy had been to achieve as little for the state scheme as politically possible; and if the primary measure of success is the consonance of objectives and achievements, their graduated pension scheme must rank as the most successful piece of pension legislation ever. The plan achieved little in the way of Earnings-Related State Pension, and did so at considerable cost.[42]

The feedback effects of this departure can be seen in the adaptation of Labour Party policy. It would be incorrect to regard the private pension interest groups as invulnerable. The private sector was open to criticism for its inability to provide good quality coverage for the lower paid and to compete with the benefits the state would be able to provide under superannuation. In fact, as Hannah and other commentators record, the occupational sector was often keen to foster a partnership with government.[43] However, as the private sector became more powerful – particularly in terms of the number of people it served – so politicians grew increasingly reluctant to challenge it. So it was, the proposals to regulate the private sector set out in National Superannuation were effectively abandoned, and the Labour Party conceded a dual system, consisting of a mixture of state and market provision without any significant attempt to implement their original proposals. Although the Study Group continued to refine its proposals during the opposition years of 1959–64, seeking to extend the principle of earnings relation throughout the social security system, the problem of contracting out was only discussed on one occasion and did not form an extensive part of the discussion. Thus the Labour Party came to power in 1964 without any well-worked out vision of the relationship between state and market provision beyond that which had been elaborated in 1957.

The Crossman White Paper of 1969 made two significant departures from the 1957 proposals.[44] First of all, it was a fully earnings-related system without a first tier of flat-rate provision. Secondly, it relaxed its position *vis-à-vis* its relationship with the private sector. National superannuation had deliberately made the conditions under which private schemes would be allowed to contract out extremely onerous. The 1969 proposals advanced a system of 'partial contracting out' in which employers and employees would pay a reduced national insurance contribution and the latter would receive a reduced state pension. However, instead of providing comparable benefits, occupational schemes were only required to guarantee a pension of a fixed cash value. Moreover, occupational schemes would not be forced to inflation-proof their pension or to re-value them in line with increases in living standards. Instead, the state undertook to offer additional protection to those who contracted out. If the level of the occupational pension was less than that available from the state scheme, the government undertook to fund the difference. Thus the cost of pension increases would be met by the state, while the occupational schemes would be responsible for paying a fixed amount irrespective of increases in inflation or the level of earnings. The state would also take responsibility for widows' pensions. The ceiling placed on contributions was seen as a way of giving the private sector a free hand to cover higher paid employees who would be ineligible for the state scheme.

Former members of the Study Group, such as Richard Titmuss and Tony Lynes, criticised the new proposals for failing to improve the quality of pensions offered by the private sector.[45] Indeed some regarded it as objectionable that the state should effectively subsidise occupational pensions However, these concessions were made in recognition of the size of the private sector and the number of people it covered. Indeed, the public sector unions were extremely hostile because they feared the scheme would threaten their occupational pensions.

The theme of partnership was taken up again in the State Earnings Related Pension Scheme. Once again, the state offered the private sector a form of subsidised competition. Occupational schemes were not obliged to provide any inflation-proofing, and the state undertook to underwrite the indexation. Occupational schemes were obliged to provide a guaranteed minimum pension at the point of retirement without guaranteeing any indexation to cover increases in inflation. The state assumed responsibility for inflation-proofing. These terms were highly congenial and by 1979 there were 11.6 million members of occupational schemes.

Conclusion

This discussion has explored the way in which policy inheritance has influenced the development of income maintenance policy for the elderly. Although Heclo's contention that the influence of key actors – 'middlemen' – has had a decisive effect on major policy innovation is persuasive in the case of the Study Group on Security and Old Age, it is equally important to assess the role of individuals in the context of the political and structural constraints inhibiting policy development. This particular case confirms the innovatory capacity of the Study Group on Security and Old Age. However, it also show the importance of the historical circumstances in which their task was conducted. The crisis of the Beveridge system created conditions of flux and openness which allowed the idea for state superannuation to enter the political debate. However, the capability to launch this initiative progressively grew less as the dynamic of the Beveridge model took hold. The imperatives of improving the condition of those already in retirement and improving the financial viability of state pensions was the foundation of all policy-making. Moreover, as the private sector expanded in response to the inadequacies of the state system, significant social change occurred. the private sector may have become a powerful interest group, but the efforts the Labour party made to protect those covered by occupational schemes indicates the importance of policy 'lock-in'. Government action was strongly influenced by the sheer numbers of employees covered by the private sector.

The feedback effects emanating from the Beveridge model of social security acted as a protective shield around the basic liberal-collectivist framework of social welfare it had established. An examination of this case reminds us of the dangers of adopting an individualistic approach to the development and implementation of new initiatives. As time went by, the space for policy advisers to 'think the unthinkable' grew less, and the possibility of pursuing alternative courses of action became increasingly impractical.

NOTES

1. J. Morgan (ed.), *The Backbench Diaries of Richard Crossman* (London: Hamish Hamilton and Jonathan Cape, 1981), p.581.
2. H. Heclo, *Modern Social Politics in Britain and Sweden* (New Haven, CT.: Yale University Press, 1974).
3. L. Hannah, *Inventing Retirement. The development of Occupational Pensions in Britain* (Cambridge: Cambridge University Press, 1986), Table A.1, Statistical Appendix.
4. *Social Insurance and Allied Services*, Cmnd 6404 (London: HMSO, 1942).
5. Jose Harris, 'Social Planning in War-Time: Some Aspects of the Beveridge; Report, in J. M. Winter (ed.), *War and Economic Development* (Cambridge: Cambridge University Press, 1975), and 'Political Ideas and the Debate on State Welfare, 1940–45', in Harold L. Smith (ed.), *War and Social Change. British Society in the Second World War* (Manchester: Manchester University Press, 1986).
6. Labour Party 1955 General Election Manifesto, *Forward with Labour*.
7. See Rodney Lowe and Paul Nicholson (eds.), 'The Child Poverty Action Group and the Rediscovery of Poverty in the 1960s', *Contemporary Record*, Vol.3, No.3.
8. Report of the 56th Annual Conference of the Labour Party, 1957, p.107.
9. Heclo, *Modern Social Politics in Britain and Sweden*, op. cit., pp.308–9
10. B. Abel-Smith, *The Reform of Social Security* (London: Fabian Society, 1953).
11. B. Abel-Smith and P. Townsend, *New Pensions for Old* (London: Fabian Society, 1955).
12. R.H.S. Crossman, *The Politics of Pensions*, Eleanor Rathbone Memorial Lecture (Liverpool: Liverpool University Press, 1972).
13. *The Report of the Committee on the Economic and Financial Problems of the Provision for Old Age*, Cmnd.9333 (London, HMSO, Dec. 1954).

14. The membership of the Study Group on Security and Old Age was as follows: NEC members – R.H.S. Crossman, G.I. Brinham, H. Gaitskell, J. Griffiths, R.J. Gunter, M. Herbison, E. Summerskill, H. Wilson; Co-opted members – B. Abel Smith, D. Jay, H. Marquand, Professor R.M. Titmuss.

15. Labour Party Archives, Manchester (henceforward LPA): Re.152/April 1957 (revised): Draft Policy Statement on National Superannuation, 'Labour's Policy for Security in Old Age'.

16. Ibid., p.4.

17. Ibid., p.4.

18. Ibid., p.5.

19. LPA: R.508/April 1955 Policy and Publicity sub-committee: p.2. 'very little help can be expected from the TUC they are obviously not in a mood to consider changes in the present position. They are completely wedded to the contributory system, and it will take lengthy discussions to modify their views'.

20. LPA: Re 152 /April 1957(revised), p.6.

21. Ibid., p.7.

22 In 1955 the National Insurance pension represented 18.4 percent of the average earnings of a male manual worker. *Social Security Statistics 1982* (London, HMSO, 1982), p.251.

23. Cmnd. 9333, op. cit.

24. *National Superannuation*, Re. 152, op. cit., p.14.

25. Benefits would be raised to £3 which represented 25 per cent of average national earnings. *National Superannuation: Labour's Policy for Security in Old Age* (London: Labour Party, 1957), p.37.

26. Hannah, *Modern Social Politics in Britain and Sweden*, op. cit., p.55.

27. *National Superannuation*, op. cit., pp.27–8.

28. LPA: Re 152/April 1957, p.25.

29. Hannah, *Modern Social Politics in Britain and Sweden*, op. cit., p.56.

30. Heclo, *Modern Social Politics in Britain and Sweden*, op. cit. pp.315–16.

31. E.E. Schattschneider, *Politics, Pressures and the Tariff* (New York: Prentice Hall, 1935), p.288.

32. Paul Pierson, *Dismantling the Welfare State? Reagan, Thatcher and the Politics of Retrenchment* (New York: Cambridge University Press, 1994), pp.41–2.

33. Better Pensions: Proposals for a New Pensions Scheme Fully Protected Against Inflation, Cmnd 5713.,1974.

34. *Hansard*, House of Commons Debates, vol. 707, col. 1031-2, Nov. 1964.

35. National Superannuation and Social Insurance: Proposals for Earnings Related Social Security, Cmnd 3883, 1969.

36. c.f. Bill Simpson, *A New Approach to Retirement Pensions,* Labour Party Research Series, Rd. 583 and Judith Hart, *Draft Paper on Pensions,* Labour Party Research Series, Rd.580, 1973.

37. Cf. Labour Party Conference Annual Report, 1971, p.190.

38. 'Economic Policy and the Cost of Living', TUC/Labour Party Liaison Committee Joint Statement, February, 1973.

39. Pierson, op. cit. pp.42–3.

40. Heclo, *Modern Social Politics in Britain and Sweden,* op. cit., p.264.

41. Ibid., p266.

42. Hannah, *Inventing Retirement* op. cit., p.58.

43. Ibid., p.59.

44. Cmnd. 3883 op. cit.

45. See Tony Lynes, *Labour's Pension Plan,* Fabian Tract 396, (London: Fabian Society, 1969) and 'Superannuation For All: A Broader View', *New Society,* Feb. 1969, pp.315–17.

The Nature and Impact of Think Tanks in Contemporary Britain

ANDREW DENHAM and MARK GARNETT

This contribution surveys the impact of and literature on think tanks in Britain since 1945. The subject has been comparatively neglected until the publication in 1994 of Richard Cockett's *Thinking the Unthinkable*, a book which this survey critically examines. Denham and Garnett first examine what a think tank might and might not be, before going on to show that they are not a new phenomenon as is widely believed. Several nineteenth-century antecedents are adduced to show the long history of these intermediate bodies between informed public opinion and political and governmental institutions. The heart of the survey is a sceptical analysis about the extent that 'New Right' think tanks actually did lead to changes in government policy from Keynesian social democracy to a greater emphasis on the free market since the 1970s.

Introduction

Despite the growing interest in 'think tanks' on both sides of the Atlantic since 1990, the American academic literature is still much more substantial than the British and dominates international discourse on the subject.[1] The British literature has increased in recent years, but published work in the 1990s consists of a solitary book, a few journal articles and occasional references in studies of the impact and aftermath of Thatcherism.[2] In short, the British literature on 'think tanks' is strikingly modest, given the high profile enjoyed by groups such as the Institute of Economic Affairs (IEA), the Adam Smith Institute (ASI) and the Centre for Policy Studies (CPS) since the 1970s. Great claims have been made for the political influence of these bodies (collectively dubbed 'think tanks of the New Right'[3]), both by themselves and by the media, especially the quality press.[4] Yet while media perceptions of their credibility and influence are important (see below), academic analyses of the role and impact of 'think tanks' in British politics are urgently required.[5]

Here we re-examine three important questions in the light of recent developments in the study and practical experience of 'think tanks' in Britain. The first section discusses the problem of defining these groups in the context of British politics. The second explores the history of 'think

Andrew Denham, Department of Politics, University of Nottingham, and Mark Garnett, Department of Politics, University of Bristol.

tanks' in Britain and rejects the widely-held view that their appearance on this side of the Atlantic is only a recent phenomenon. The final section identifies the objectives of 'think tanks' and evaluates the extent to which the claims advanced on behalf of New Right groups are justified. It also explores the 'think tank' record since the fall of Margaret Thatcher.

The Problem of Definition

The term 'think tank' is notoriously difficult to define. Borrowed from Second World War military jargon for a secure room where plans and strategies could be discussed, the term was first used during the 1950s to denote the contract research organisations (such as the RAND Corporation) that were set up by the United States military after the war. By the 1960s, 'think tank' had entered the popular lexicon, but the term is used to refer to many kinds of research groups.[6] As the American political scientist David Ricci points out, no-one in the United States 'has yet decided exactly what think tanks are'.[7] The confusion about the functions performed by 'think tanks' extends beyond academic commentators, and is 'sometimes shared by the managers, trustees and researchers at these institutions'.[8] Hames and Feasey have suggested that a broad definition of the term would be 'a non-profit public policy research institution with substantial organisational autonomy', but concede that this 'hardly reveals much about the nature and character of these entities'.[9] In the US, the sheer number and diversity of private research groups hampers accurate definition. American scholars have attempted to resolve this difficulty by identifying and distinguishing between three categories of 'think tank': 'universities without students', 'contract research organisations', and 'advocacy tanks'.[10]

The first category describes large institutions with considerable staff, mostly academic researchers, working mainly on book-length projects. These institutes differ from universities in two ways. First, staff are not required to teach students in the same way that (most) full-time academics are. Secondly, the subject areas investigated have a stronger policy focus than the research and analysis carried out in universities which is typically 'more academic, theoretical and less palatable for general consumption'.[11] Groups in this category have long-term horizons focused on changing the 'climate' of elite opinion and draw most of their core funding from a variety of corporations, foundations and private individuals, diversifying their sources of financial support in order to reduce the risk of client backlash over particular research results.[12] The number of American research institutes in this category is small and members vary in respect of the range of policy issues they deal with; American research institutes that appear to fit this model include the Brookings Institution and the American Enterprise

Institute. An insider has described the work atmosphere at the former as 'like a university when the students are away and the professors are trying frantically to catch up on research'.[13]

The second category – 'contract research organisations' – serve *2nd cat.* government agencies and private sponsors on a contractual basis by executing research solicited in a number of fields. Groups in this category are likely to be subject to influence in their choice of topics and the conclusions they reach, because if their findings are too much at odds with a client's interests, future research contracts may be awarded to their competitors. The emphasis of these groups, then, is on excellence defined by contract success rather than by the 'peer group recognition offered within research communities such as academic disciplines'.[14] There are many 'think tanks' in Washington – such as the Mitre Corporation – that work on one contract after another. More famous American 'think tanks' in this category include the RAND Corporation (in defence-related fields) and the Urban Institute (covering domestic policy issues).

'Advocacy tanks' are the last (and latest) group of 'think tanks'. These *3rd cat.* groups have a strong policy partisanship (often derived from an equally determined ideological position) and campaign aggressively on current policy issues. American examples of 'advocacy tanks' include the Heritage Foundation and the Institute for Policy Studies. Heritage, in particular, is quick to admit that its purpose is advocacy, rather than academic research; staff at Heritage are told by their employers that the Foundation is not an academic body, but one committed to certain beliefs.[15] The format chosen for the research output of 'advocacy tanks' is, typically, short pamphlets and papers rather than book-length studies. This approach indicates a further obstacle to a satisfactory definition; just as 'think tanks' in the 'universities without students' category are quasi-academic bodies, 'advocacy tanks' are difficult to distinguish from pressure groups in that both are essentially interested in political lobbying.[16]

According to Jeremy Richardson, 'A pressure group may be regarded as any group which articulates demands that the political authorities in the political system or sub-system should make an authoritative allocation'.[17] Richardson adds a caveat which excludes bodies seeking to take over government, but this has no effect on 'think tanks'. Similar fund-raising activities enhance the temptation to draw parallels; the British IEA, for example, now sells items such as 'Great Economist' mugs, Adam Smith money clips and IEA teddy bears. Meanwhile, pressure groups are becoming increasingly dependent on professional research in order to lend authority to their claims. Are we to conclude, therefore, that 'think tanks' are merely a pretentious sub-set of pressure-groups? To date, this question has been strangely overlooked in work on pressure-groups, but an important difference between the two is that 'think tanks' tend to operate across a broad range of policy areas, whereas pressure groups tend to focus on issues that relate to one in particular. As the number and variety of bodies claiming the status of 'think tanks' increases, however, even this distinction comes under strain.

Even if the American model has some validity for organisational purposes, it should be used with caution. Models of this sort do not always allow a perfect fit and grey areas persist.[18] While the three categories outlined above are analytically clear and distinct, the reality is more complicated. In fact, the aims and activities of individual 'think tanks' are diverse. The American Enterprise Institute, for example, has undertaken studies that would fit into all three categories.[19] Scholars in the United States have discovered that 'think tanks' do not have a generic form in the same sense as families, armies, churches or industrial corporations. Instead, the term 'think tank' refers to institutions 'whose aims may vary across time and whose researchers may associate with one another only temporarily and for personal convenience'.[20]

Moreover, as Dickson has shown, a further source of confusion is that 'most groups that *are* think tanks don't like the term', yet 'pretentious little research groups' often invoke it to look and sound important.[21] Genuine 'think tanks', according to Dickson, consider the term limiting, confusing, even demeaning; it sounds too passive, and connotes non-accomplishment (a place where thinking is an end in itself, irrespective of the utility of the thinking). As Rivlin recalls, staff at Brookings used to disdain the 'faintly pejorative' appellation 'think tank' – even if they now use it as freely as everyone else.[22] At the other end of the spectrum, meanwhile, it has been argued that the term 'think tank' carries an unmistakable prestige which is sometimes undeserved.[23] Margaret Thatcher, for instance, thought that the Centre for Policy Studies 'could not properly be called a "think tank" for it had none of the corporate grandeur of the prestigious American foundations which that term evokes'.[24]

In the British context, matters are even more complicated than they are in America. This is because the term 'think tank' was first used to denote the Central Policy Review Staff (CPRS), a 'central capability unit' established in the Cabinet Office in 1970–71 by the then Prime Minister, Edward Heath. Even after its abolition by Margaret Thatcher in 1983, the CPRS continued to be popularly known as '*the* Think Tank'.[25] Hence, for most of the past 25 years, the term has usually been synonymous in Britain with one particular 'policy planning and research unit' *within* central government.[26] As the 1980s progressed, however, 'think tank' acquired a quite different meaning and was increasingly applied to those outside, ideologically-charged, free-market bodies which provided a kind of 'private army' for Margaret Thatcher in her efforts to shift public policy towards 'a different conception of both political economy and social policy'.[27]

Most commentators would accept that (with the partial exception of the IEA) the New Right groups that came to prominence during the 1980s are best described as 'advocacy tanks' in the sense outlined earlier. As William Wallace notes, the new 'think tanks' that sprang up alongside the IEA in the 1970s were 'small, passionately committed and concerned only with providing arguments for those already half-persuaded'.[28] Staff at the CPS 'were already committed to the new economics of the market and monetarism' by 1974; rather, 'their task was to change other people's minds'.[29] However much the IEA may *aspire* to be a 'university without students', it is important to recall that the Institute was 'formed by people who were safe in the knowledge that they had already discovered the Holy Grail – the free market'.[30] In short, *none* of the New Right groups that became prominent in Britain during the 1980s has fulfilled the role of more 'traditional' Anglo-American 'think tanks', that of 'searching for policies and ideas'; instead, their primary task has been to evangelise.[31]

The British 'think tank' Tradition

This brings us to a further source of confusion that has crept into the British debate on 'think tanks'. The prominence of New Right groups during the 1980s has led some commentators to argue that 'think tanks' have only recently appeared in Britain.[32] In fact, it is possible to trace a long British tradition of groups which have sought both to bring about specific changes in society and to effect 'a more general change in the prevailing intellectual climate'.[33] The line started with the Utilitarians, or 'Philosophic Radicals', who worked under the leadership of Jeremy Bentham and James Mill in the early nineteenth century. As the tasks of government became more complex, the expertise and diligence of the Philosophic Radicals ensured a far greater influence than their numbers would suggest, particularly over legislation such as the 1834 New Poor Law. Mill's son, John Stuart, maintained this tradition through his writings and his brief membership of the House of Commons.[34] Through their journal *The Westminster Review*, the Philosophic Radicals reached a relatively wide audience of informed opinion. The trend continued with the English disciples of Auguste Comte. While the English Positivists were not as influential as their Utilitarian predecessors, they did help to transform the law relating to trade unions.[35] Last in the line of nineteenth-century 'philosophical-political ginger groups' or 'think tanks' was the Fabian Society, for whose tactic of 'permeation' there were already 'plenty of precedents'.[36]

A second generation of 'think tanks' emerged in the first half of the twentieth century, most of them in the inter-war years. The Royal Institute of International Affairs (RIIA) received its royal charter in 1926 and became 'the model of a foreign policy think tank which was received in country after country after 1919'.[37] The RIIA emerged after the Versailles Peace Conference and soon established itself after acquiring Chatham House in 1923. Its membership grew throughout the inter-war years, and endowments, gifts and individual contributions to its finances enabled the Institute to establish a journal (*International Affairs*), appoint a full-time Director of Studies and set up a library.[38] During the 1930s, the RIIA sponsored studies of questions such as nationalism, monetary policy and international investment. Other activities during the 1930s included an annual *Survey of International Affairs* and a parallel series of *Documents*.[39]

The 1930s also saw the establishment of Political and Economic Planning (PEP) and the National Institute of Economic and Social Research (NIESR). In February 1931, a new periodical, *The Weekend Review*, ran a pioneering article by Max Nicholson outlining a 'National Plan for Great Britain'. The article stimulated so much interest that the decision was taken to set up a research organisation to advance the principles of planning. Like the Fabians before them, the founders of PEP aimed to collect information and 'permeate' the Establishment with their ideas. In the 1930s, PEP produced reports on several basic industries, as well as on housing, the health service and the location of industry. Their influence was limited in the 1930s, but 'helped to prepare high-level opinion for the changes of the 1940s'.[40] After 1945, the political and intellectual climate was more favourable to the kind of ideas PEP fostered than in the 1930s and its influence increased. It has been claimed that, in the decade leading up to the merger of PEP and the Centre for Studies in Social Policy (to form the Policy Studies Institute in 1978), PEP's work had a major impact in half a dozen main sectors of policy and made a significant contribution 'across the wide range of its economic, social and political research'.[41] While this judgement may be over-stated, Alan Budd has noted that PEP's 1960 pamphlet *Growth in the British Economy* closely anticipated the approach of the National Economic Development Council and the later Department of Economic Affairs.[42]

The decision to set up the NIESR was taken at the end of 1937 and a certificate of incorporation was issued in June the following year. The motive, according to a press release of 5 January 1938, was the observed inadequacy of the facilities available for research in the social sciences compared with those in the natural sciences and the need for a national organisation for the pursuit of independent economic research (a public statement about a national institute of economic research had already been agreed by mid-1936). The NIESR was the first organisation to produce and publish economic forecasts and make available for the first time in Britain a systematic view of economic developments and likely world trends. It has also played an important educational role and has influenced the way economics is taught at British universities. The NIESR has also received extensive media coverage, both for its *Review*, which first appeared in 1959, and for longer-term studies.[43]

Thus the notion that 'think tanks' have only recently appeared in Britain is clearly mistaken. The tradition is well established, and British 'think tanks', like those found in the United States, range from scholarly research institutes on the one hand to ideologically partisan groups on the other; a further parallel is that the more partisan bodies in both countries tend to be those which have been established since 1945 (see Figure 1). Despite the differences of style and emphasis that exist between them, however, all of the groups commonly referred to as 'think tanks' in Britain have broadly similar objectives and engage in similar activities towards those ends. There are two main objectives that *all* 'think tanks' seek, 'albeit with varying degrees of emphasis'.[44] The first is to influence the 'climate' of elite opinion within which, it is assumed, political actors are bound to operate; the second is to inform actual public policy decisions. It remains for us to examine the extent to which these goals have actually been achieved by New Right groups in Britain during recent years.

FIGURE 1
TWENTIETH CENTURY BRITISH THINK TANKS

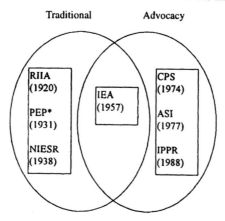

Note: For the purposes of this model, 'traditional' includes both 'universities without students' and 'contract research organisations'.

* now Policy studies institute, following merger with Centre for Studies in Social Policy in 1978.

RIIA – Royal Institute of International Affairs
PEP – Political and Economic Planning
NIER – National Institute of Economic and Social Research
IEA – Institute of Economic Affairs

CPS – Centre for Policy Studies
ASI – Adam Smith Institute
IPPR – Institute for Public Policy Research

An Intellectual Counter-Revolution?

For 20 years after the formation of the IEA in 1955, the advocates of economic liberalism found that their ideas remained out of favour with policy-makers. As one observer wrote in 1973, for example, 'the Institute of Economic Affairs might just as well never have existed' for all the influence its ideas had on the subject of inflationary control.[45] However, the election of Margaret Thatcher in 1979 promised to fulfil the ideals of the IEA and its free-market allies in the CPS (founded in 1974) and the Adam Smith Institute (1977). After 16 years of Conservative rule, the agenda of market liberalism appears to have triumphed, whatever the immediate fortunes of Mrs. Thatcher's party. The Labour Party is now receptive to the case for the market to an extent which would have been difficult to imagine in 1983. Debate over the details of policy continues, and it may be premature to speak of a new 'consensus' in British politics, but the interventionist approaches of the 1960s and early 1970s appear to be dead, at least for the time being.

According to Richard Cockett, the New Right 'think tanks' played a vital role in bringing about an 'economic counter-revolution'. Cockett claims that these bodies 'did as much intellectually to convert a generation of "opinion-formers" and politicians to a new set of ideas as the Fabians had done with a former generation at the turn of the century'.[46] This begs an obvious question about the true influence of the Fabians. In his excellent study *Fabian Socialism and English Politics*, Alan McBriar takes full account of the problems involved in such an assessment.[47] McBriar's careful analysis concludes that Fabianism helped the public to accept the end of *laissez faire* politics; however, the Society was divided, and its record is one 'of errors and self deception' as well as success.[48] Disappointingly, Cockett does not follow McBriar in providing a methodological framework for appraising the impact of New Right groups. Since his main sources were highly-skilled self-publicists, this omission was always likely to prove seriously damaging to his work. Indeed, his book is characterised by inconsistency. For instance, he credits the IEA with placing 'monetarism at the heart of British politics', yet within five pages he agrees with Milton Friedman's view that the acceptance of monetarist ideas was not primarily due to the IEA's 'intellectual arguments'.[49] After all, the monetarist experiment began under Labour Chancellors (Jenkins and Healey) who remained highly sceptical, even though their hands were forced by the International Monetary Fund (IMF). This is not the full extent of Cockett's ambiguity: while the prevalent tone of his book echoes the 'triumphalism' of the last Thatcher government, he suddenly concedes in the closing chapter that 'economic liberalism as applied in the 1980s effectively wiped out a large part of Britain's manufacturing industry, and ... left as many people unemployed as there were in the 1930s'.[50] As the first substantial work on the British 'think tank' scene in the post-war period, Cockett's book is to be welcomed. However, without a deeper analysis of 'think tank' influence it remains unsatisfactory. Perhaps the most unfortunate aspect of the work is that because it fails to subject 'think tank' claims to sufficient scrutiny, it invites critics to over-react, and to underrate the impact of these groups.

Whatever the evidence for a major change in the agenda of senior politicians and some prominent journalists, an examination of political and economic opinion (and the views of the wider public) shows that the victory of economic liberalism has been incomplete. In the early 1970s, a survey of British economic opinion found that 'well over 75 per cent of the economists who took part' subscribed to a distinct policy outlook which the survey co-ordinator, Samuel Brittan, termed the 'liberal economic orthodoxy'. This embodied a belief in competitive markets and pricing, but also in income redistribution and the effectiveness of the 'Keynesian' techniques of demand management and fiscal policy which the New Right groups vigorously opposed.[51] The prevalence of opposition to monetarism was publicly attested by 364 university economists in March 1981. A more recent survey (published by the IEA) confirmed that this trend has continued. Indeed, the results showed that, by international standards, British economists are more redistributive than those of any other country and also more 'Keynesian' in the sense of accepting at least a short-run trade-off between unemployment and inflation. There were few takers for the 'simon-pure' monetarist prospectus.[52] Rather than 'converting' the orthodox economic establishment, the IEA and its allies have been forced to 'by-pass' it.

If academic economists refused to abandon central Keynesian assumptions, the case for the market has also failed to win anything like universal acceptance among Conservative politicians. The historian of the free-market 'think tanks', Richard Cockett, concedes that economic liberal ideas 'never captured the hearts, let alone the minds, of more than a small minority of Conservative MPs, during the heyday of Thatcherism in the mid-1980s'.[53] Survey evidence supporting this assertion continues to mount, despite the problems caused to John Major by Thatcherite MPs such as John Redwood. Philip Norton has calculated that only 72 Conservative MPs (or 20 per cent of the parliamentary Party) could be classed as convinced ideological allies of Margaret Thatcher.[54] Moreover, the findings of a recent survey of Party members suggest that grass-roots Conservatives are much more 'progressive' than conventional wisdom would have us believe – even if affection for the former leader remains strong. There is still significant support at constituency level for incomes policy, strong regulation of markets, and social welfare spending – all of which are 'anathema to dyed-in-the-wool Thatcherites'.[55] Overall, these results suggest that the Conservative Party has not been converted to Thatcherism, despite the election victories of the 1980s.

Among the wider public, the free market message has fared no better. In his study of attitudes under Thatcher, Ivor Crewe rightly concludes that there was no cultural counter-revolution in the thinking of the electorate.[56] Between 1983 and 1987, for instance, those who thought that a government should be 'caring' during a recession increased by 16 per cent.[57] It is fashionable to treat this kind of poll finding with scepticism, but one can at least feel confident in assuming that if Mrs Thatcher had persevered with the general post-war political settlement her policies would have aroused less opposition. The sweeping changes introduced by the Conservatives can thus be seen as a mirror-image of the so-called 'ratchet effect', whereby post-war governments supposedly became increasingly interventionist regardless of what voters really thought. Maurice Cowling has written of 'about fifty people' who were fired by zeal for economic liberalism; one is forced to conclude that, in terms of true belief, the great free-market counter-revolution never extended much further.[58] This is very distant from the original aims of the New Right 'think tanks'.

In their article on 'Anglo-American Think Tanks Under Reagan and Thatcher', Hames and Feasey observe that there are no examples of legislation on either side of the Atlantic during the 1980s that were 'entirely and uniquely due to one individual think tank'.[59] Since active members of 'think tanks' rarely play a formal role in the passage of legislation, this lack of decisive influence is unsurprising. Judged by more realistic criteria, however, the record of the New Right groups in the 1980s is still disappointing, given the opportunities for access which apparently existed. As yet we lack authoritative studies of 'think tank' input for specific policies, and conclusive verdicts will always be hazardous because while ministers might not object to attributing failed policies to outside organisations, they are understandably reluctant to disclaim responsibility for radical plans which achieve their goals.

In the case of the Thatcher governments, the desire of some ministers to prove their ideological loyalty might have had the opposite effect, resulting in the serious consideration of 'think tank' ideas which such 'Career Thatcherites' would not normally have entertained. However, from the available evidence it emerges that the role of 'think tanks' was mainly restricted to the provision of intellectual legitimacy for the Thatcher governments; in addition, they undoubtedly helped to sustain the radical momentum of Thatcherism by reinforcing the sense of a collective crusade.

Geoffrey Howe's memoirs provided an excellent example of this ideological reinforcement; although he pays a handsome tribute to the value of the IEA's work on exchange controls, he previously indicated that the abolition of controls was 'an ambition that a number of us had long cherished'.[60] Ironically, a movement which has become associated with the view that there is no such thing as society depended crucially on this spirit of community among its most energetic adherents, and perhaps the greatest enthusiasts were those, like the ex-Communist Alfred Sherman, who had once been vehement opponents of economic individualism. For many of these activists, even the radical nature of Conservative Party policy during the 1980s was insufficiently bracing, and disillusionment was common.[61]

An important reason for this sense of lost opportunities was ambivalence about Mrs Thatcher herself. As early as 1969 Geoffrey Howe had confided his worries about her to Arthur Seldon of the IEA; in Howe's opinion, Thatcher might hamper the economic liberal case through 'over-simplification' of the message.[62] Years later the veteran Conservative writer T.E Utley made a curious remark in a *Times* article, implying that Thatcher was likely to rehearse complex IEA arguments in her speeches without translating them into words which would appeal to her audience.[63] This evidence is exquisitely double-edged; it implies that Thatcher was open to IEA influence, but that she was incapable of bringing their ideas down to earth in a manner which would make them suitable for propaganda purposes. According to Richard Cockett, key economic liberals realised that 'for all her other qualities, Mrs Thatcher was not a "strategic" thinker' early in her premiership.[64] From Cockett's account, one is left with an unmistakable sense of a counter-revolution that was 'betrayed', and that much of the responsibility for this lies with the leader. In reality, however, the disappointment of the free-market zealots points to a surprising failure of their own: a tendency to overlook the pressures of public office, which prevent the full-blooded pursuit of ideological purity. Given that 'think tank' enthusiasm for economic liberal measures was so narrowly shared, one cannot wonder that the Prime Minister was initially reluctant to follow their ideas very closely.

This is not to say that the Thatcher Governments failed to implement any of the cherished schemes of the New Right groups. However, many of their ideas got no further than the pamphlet stage. Education vouchers, negative income tax and prohibition of strikes in essential public services were all endorsed by the 'think tanks', but were rejected by responsible ministers. In addition, those policies that were enacted were often implemented for reasons other than the advocacy of 'think tanks', and in forms that did not satisfy their preferences. Privatisation was introduced piecemeal, and in some cases merely led to the substitution of private for public monopoly.

The proliferation of quangos to regulate these industries (and many public services) was preferred to the introduction of greater competition. The ASI originally claimed a pivotal role in the gestation of the Community Charge, since an article on the subject had appeared under the name of its director, Madsen Pirie, in October 1981.[65] However, this has been disputed by recent research (although it is interesting how many individuals who had once been associated with 'think tanks' took part in the planning of this measure).[66]

While 'think tank' influence over the Community Charge has been exaggerated, the ultimate fate of this policy was similar to that of other ideas which were strongly advocated by the New Right groups. Monetarism was a major plank of the 'think tank' programme, but this had been effectively jettisoned by 1985.[67] The ambitious plan to reform the state pension system (SERPS) in 1986 owed much to the background work of the CPS, but this policy proved to be equally ill-starred.[68] In the first years of Mrs. Thatcher's premiership, the ASI published several attacks on the culture of quangos; by 1989 it was publicly claiming credit for Government culls of these non-elected bodies.[69] The recent increase in quangos must be attributed at least in part to the relative *failure* of the New Right attempt to 'convert' either policy experts or the wider public: apart from the need to regulate privatised industries, the fact that 'think tank' enthusiasm for radical reforms in education and health was not widely shared means that ministers have to rely on a select band of ideological supporters to implement their ideas, at least in the short term. Ironically, then, even if one accepts the ASI's claim to have inspired many recent reforms, it has to be recognised that this has conflicted with the other important goal of reducing bureaucracy. This evidence suggests that much 'think tank' work has been opportunistic, rather than strategic.

Any appraisal of the impact of 'think tanks' on policy-making must take into account the relative poverty of these groups, and the countervailing pressures on British ministers (who, unlike members of 'think tanks', are subject to re-election). If the above account seems unduly harsh, it is proportionate to the exalted aims of the 'think tanks' themselves. By their own standards, the record of the 1980s must be rated disappointing. However, there are two achievements which must compensate in some degree. These are the prestige accorded to 'think tanks' by the media, and the rise of new bodies (even if in many cases this is a rather mixed compliment for the New Right 'think tanks', since the best-known new groups are associated with the political left).

The oxygen of publicity is essential to 'think tanks', and the ability to impress journalists with the news value of their findings can at least ensure that these are widely discussed. The New Right 'think tanks' have proved remarkably adept at this exercise in public relations. A much-cited article by Ronald Butt of *The Times* in January 1976 illustrates their skills; Butt claimed that 'a good deal of the most influential economic thinking comes from economists published by the IEA'.[70] An article of this nature was bound to receive more publicity than any survey showing that the economic establishment continued to resist monetarist thinking. The relationship between the media and 'think tanks' is mutually beneficial; the 'think tanks' get their views across, and newspaper (or television news) editors are provided with interesting (and often provocative) items.[71] This is particularly the case at times when other political news is in short supply – when parliament is in recess, for example. 'Think tanks' can also expect that their ideas will make more impression during the party conference season, when the shape of future policies receive unusual attention.

In the week between 20 and 27 September 1995, for example, three reports (by 'Healthcare 2000, Demos, and the Policy Studies Institute (PSI)) featured prominently in national newspapers.[72] Thanks to the skills of 'think tank' personnel, any kind of speculation or survey evidence now receives vital credibility through public association with a 'think tank', which inevitably lends the findings a greater impression of 'objectivity' than if identical results had been produced by pressure groups. The importance of the language-games played with think-tank reports is neatly illustrated by the publicity given to the 'Healthcare 2000' inquiry into the National Health Service, which was published on 19 September 1995. BBC Television news described the report as the work of '*the* think-tank Healthcare 2000'; if the bulletins had spoken of '*a* think-tank' (or 'an independent body') the news value would have been diminished. By contrast, *The Guardian* newspaper referred to 'the controversial findings of an independent inquiry', and helpfully produced a membership list; however, by that time the importance of the findings had already been established by the coverage given by other media.

The emergence of non-Thatcherite 'think tanks' in recent years is further evidence that the New Right 'think tanks' are at least perceived to be important players in the policy process. The Institute for Public Policy Research (IPPR) was set up in 1988, and Demos appeared in 1993. The Social Market Foundation (1989) is closer to the Conservative Party in its sympathies, but preaches a message which opposed the rigorous individualism of the New Right groups. If these 'think tanks' were hardly characterised by the ideological certainties of the IEA and the ASI, this only illustrated the success of the New Right agenda in at least forcing opponents to re-examine their pre-suppositions. At the same time, however, the emphasis on 'community' in the work of the new 'think tanks' has ambivalent implications; in part, it recognises that New Right ideas have fostered individualism, but it also indicates that this has been far from an unmixed blessing in its effects on society. The work of both the IPPR and Demos has been given wide publicity, although whether their effect will filter through into the policy process remains to be seen. Like the New Right groups, the 'think tanks' identified with the Labour Party may find that their researches are encouraged in the knowledge that political leaders can always deny responsibility if the public reacts adversely.

A final development which might be regarded as a success for the 'think tanks' has been the tendency for leading figures to win election to the House of Commons. One obvious reason for this is the media's belief that 'think tanks' are too lofty to care for cheap political point-scoring; as a result, eloquent members of these groups make excellent panel pundits on programmes such as *Question Time*, creating a public profile for them even before becoming a candidate for election. A background in 'think tanks' ensured that both John Redwood and David Willetts were regarded as potential ministers from the time that they entered parliament; Redwood has since tacitly endorsed the value of 'think tanks' by setting up his own group (the 'Conservative 2000 Foundation'). However, on closer inspection this evidence might carry a contrary message, implying that membership of a 'think tank' is not enough to ensure that one's ideas are put into practice. Redwood's case actually suggests that an apprenticeship in a 'think tank' can be a barrier to the highest ambitions; an excessively cerebral image can easily be mocked by a media which was once grateful to receive any 'think tank' output.

Since 1990, the fickle nature of the media has also been revealed by a series of articles claiming that the influence of the New Right 'think tanks' is declining.[73] In a recent study of the Major governments, both Dennis Kavanagh and Anthony Seldon have cautiously expressed a similar view, although Seldon indicates that there has been a limited revival since 1992.[74] By contrast, the irrepressible Madsen Pirie has argued that he now enjoys more personal contact with John Major than he ever did with Margaret Thatcher, and certainly his ASI influenced Major's policy venture of a 'Citizen's Charter'.[75] Despite the different ethos of the Major Governments – so clearly at odds with the frenetic New Right activity of the late 1980s – the actual direction of policy has remained fairly constant. On this reading, ministers are plundering the work of the 'communitarian' 'think tanks' for their rhetoric, while acting on the guidelines laid down by the IEA, the CPS and the ASI. In truth, the situation is as difficult to judge now as it was in the 1980s; all one can predict with much confidence is that if the media spreads rumours of the death of New Right 'think tanks', their long-term prospects of survival cannot be good.

Conclusion

The academic study of British 'think tanks' is developing, but as scholars struggle to assess the legacy of the 1980s a generation of new bodies is springing up to confuse the picture. Detailed studies are needed to prove the point, but it appears that it is more valuable to investigate the impact of 'think tanks' on the 'climate of opinion', which in turn affects government, rather than trying to trace decisive influence over specific policies (see Figure 2). This work can only be profitable once a clearer notion of a 'climate of opinion' has emerged; in the light of the British experience since 1979, it is particularly important to establish how it was that economic liberalism won favour from key political actors, despite the fact that it was opposed by most qualified experts and a clear majority of the electorate.

FIGURE 2
THE INFLUENCE OF THINK TANKS ON UK GOVERNMENT DURING THE 1980s:
A MODEL OF THE 'CLIMATE OF OPINION'

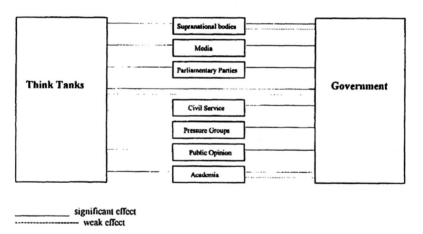

——————— significant effect
----------------------- weak effect

Note: This model ignores significant and weak effects between the intermediate actors.

At present, it is possible to conclude that 'think tanks' have won themselves an enviable reputation with the media, and are now seen as promising sources of political recruitment. They are also valuable to political parties, since their ideas have a 'deniable' status, but at the same time their prestige allows even controversial proposals to be treated with respect. In this way, they can act as political shields, making the public more willing to accept policies which might be badly received if they were first mooted by a government spokesman.

All this means that the emergence of 'think tanks', which was originally a response to the growing complexity of government and a corresponding need for expert advice, might soon be regarded as potentially unhealthy in a democratic system. Both 'think tank' members and their patrons (whether political parties, industrial concerns or private individuals) could be tempted to exploit their privileged status in public debate – for example, by distorting the likely impact of specific policies.[76] Madsen Pirie has claimed that 'think tanks' are 'part of the constitution now', but their role is ill-defined.[77] Sometimes 'think tanks' seem to regard themselves as something like a shadow civil service, without even the pretence of overall ministerial responsibility to keep their activities in check; as civil service departments continue to be transformed into semi-autonomous agencies, this resemblance is likely to grow.[78]

Unlike the civil service, however, the 'think tanks' do not have to deal with the results of their ideas; the tone of their work during the 1980s reflected an assumption that if mistakes were made they occurred at the stage of policy implementation, rather than design. In this sense, at least, the 'think tanks' have an interest in bringing the results of democratic elections into discredit; they also contravene Maurice Cowling's warning against the belief that 'those who write but do not rule would be rather better at ruling (if they had the chance) than those who do.[79] Although this is no place for a proper discussion of the relationship between the philosophy of economic liberalism and democracy, the doctrines of the New Right 'think tanks' added to the dangers, since they asserted that the activities of elected governments are usually negative in their economic effects. If this account exaggerates the dangers of excessive 'think tank' influence over public policy, the 'think tanks' can only blame themselves for producing this effect through their own publicity. Such an outcome would be very different from the original aims of even the most zealous ideologues in post-war British 'think tanks': however, it would not be the first time that good motives have led to unintended consequences in political life.

NOTES

1. See Paul Dickson, *Think Tanks* (New York: Ballantine Books, 1971); James A Smith, *The Idea Brokers* (New York: Free Press, 1991); David M Ricci, *The Transformation of American Politics* (New Haven: Yale University Press, 1993).
2. See Richard Cockett, *Thinking the Unthinkable: Think-Tanks and the Economic Counter-Revolution 1931–1983* (London: HarperCollins, 1994); Andrew Denham and Mark Garnett, 'The Idea Brokers: A Reply to Simon James', *Public Administration*, Autumn 1994; Radika Desai, 'Second-Hand Dealers in Ideas: Think-Tanks and Thatcherite Hegemony', *New Left Review* 203, 1994; Simon James, 'The Idea Brokers: The Impact of Think Tanks on British Government', *Public Administration*, Winter 1993. See also Tim Hames and Richard Feasey, 'Anglo-American think tanks under Reagan and Thatcher', in Andrew Adonis and Tim

Hames (eds.), *A Conservative Revolution? The Thatcher-Reagan Decade in Perspective*, (Manchester: Manchester University Press, 1994), and Dennis Kavanagh and Anthony Seldon (eds.), *The Major Effect* (London: Macmillan, 1994).

3. See Andrew Denham, 'Think Tanks of the New Right: Theory, Practice and Prospects', unpublished Ph.D. thesis, University of Southampton, 1992.
4. Hames and Feasey, 'Anglo-American think tanks', pp.226–7, 233–4.
5. Forthcoming titles on this subject include Andrew Denham, *Think Tanks and British Politics* (London: UCL Press), and Diane Stone, *Capturing the Political Imagination: Think Tanks and Public Policy* (London: Frank Cass).
6. Smith, *The Idea Brokers*, pp.xiii–xiv.
7. Ricci, *The Transformation of American Politics*, op. cit., p.21.
8. R. Kent Weaver, 'The Changing World of Think Tanks', *P.S: Political Science and Politics*, Vol.22, No.3 (Sept. 1989), p.564.
9. Hames and Feasey, 'Anglo-American think tanks', p.216.
10. Weaver, 'The Changing World of Think Tanks', op. cit., pp.564–8.
11. Diane Stone, 'Old Guard versus New Partisans: Think Tanks in Transition', *Australian Journal of Political Science* 26 (1991), p.201.
12. Ricci, *The Transformation of American Politics*, p.20.
13. Alice Rivlin, in Carol Weiss (ed.), *Organisations for Policy Analysis: Helping Government Think* (London: Sage, 1992), pp.22–3.
14. Ricci, *The Transformation of American Politics*, op. cit., p.20.
15. Smith, *The Idea Brokers*, op. cit., p.205–6.
16. Hames and Feasey, 'Anglo-American think tanks under Reagan and Thatcher', op. cit., p.217.
17. Jeremy Richardson (ed.), *Pressure Groups* (Oxford: Oxford University Press, 1993), p.1.
18. Stone, 'Old Guard versus New Partisans', op. cit., p. 201.
19. Hames and Feasey, 'Anglo-American think tanks under Reagan and Thatcher', op. cit., p.217.
20. Ricci, *The Transformation of American Politics*, op. cit., p.21.
21. Dickson, *Think Tanks*, op. cit., p.28.
22. Rivlin, in Weiss (ed), *Organisations for Policy Analysis*, op. cit., p.22.
23. Andrew Denham and Mark Garnett, 'Rethinking think tanks: A British Perspective', in Joni Lovenduski and Jeffrey Stanyer (eds.), *Contemporary Political Studies 1995* (Exeter: Political Studies Association, 1995), Vol.I, p.326.
24. Margaret Thatcher, *The Path to Power* (London: HarperCollins, 1995), p.252.
25. See Tessa Blackstone and William Plowden, *Inside the Think Tank* (London: Heinemann, 1988); Peter Hennessy *et al.*, 'Routine Punctuated by Orgies: The Central Policy Review Staff 1970–83', Strathclyde Papers on Government and Politics No. 31, 1985; Simon James, 'The Central Policy Review Staff 1970–1983', *Political Studies*, 34 (Autumn 1986).
26. See Michael J. Prince, *Policy Advice and Organisational Survival* (Aldershot: Gower, 1983).
27. Peter Hennessy and Simon Coates, 'Little Grey Cells: Think-Tanks, Governments and Policy-Making', Strathclyde Analysis Papers 6 (1991), p.2.
28. William Wallace, 'Between Two Worlds: Think Tanks and Foreign Policy', in C. Hill and P. Beshoff (eds.), *Two Worlds of International Relations* (London: Routledge and LSE, 1994), p.149.
29. Cockett, *Thinking the Unthinkable*, op. cit., p.239.
30. *Ibid.*, p.326. For the IEA's aspirations and self-perception in this respect, see Hames and Feasey, 'Anglo-American think tanks under Reagan and Thatcher', op. cit., p.217.
31. Cockett, *Thinking the Unthinkable*, op. cit., p.139, 239, 326. For some people at least, this suggests that the term 'think tank' is actually a misnomer when applied to 'Thatcherite' groups. See Desai, 'Second-Hand Dealers in Ideas', op. cit., p.62.
32. James, 'The Idea Brokers', op. cit., p.492. As we have argued elsewhere, this exaggerates the novelty of 'think tanks' in the UK and is curiously at odds with the inclusion of long-standing bodies in the author's definition of 'think tanks' (p.493) and in his subsequent review of the British scene (pp.494–5); see Denham and Garnett, 'The Idea Brokers: A Reply to Simon James', p.482.

33. Ian Bradley, 'Intellectual Influences in Britain: Past and Present', in Arthur Seldon (ed.), *The Emerging Consensus ... ?* (London: Hobart Paperback 14, IEA, 1981), pp.174–5.
34. Royden Harrison, 'The Fabians: Aspects: Aspects of a very English socialism', in Iain Hampsher-Monk (ed), *Defending Politics: Bernard Crick and Pluralism* (London: British Academic Press, 1993), p.73. See also William Thomas, *The Philosophic Radicals* (Oxford: Clarendon Press, 1979), and Bruce L. Kinzer, Ann P. Robson, and John M. Robson, *A Moralist In and Out of Parliament: John Stuart Mill at Westminster, 1865–1868* (Toronto: University of Toronto Press, 1992).
35. See Terence R. Wright, *The Religion of Humanity* (Cambridge: Cambridge University Press, 1986). For the Positivists and the law relating to trade unions, see Royden Harrison, *Before the Socialists* (London: Routledge & Kegan Paul, 1965), pp. 277-306.
36. Harrison, 'The Fabians', p. 79. Alan M. McBriar, *Fabian Socialism and English Politics 1884-1918* (Cambridge: Cambridge University Press, 1962) remains the best overall account of Fabian influence before 1918. For the continuation of their tradition in the inter-war years, see Elizabeth Durbin, *New Jerusalems* (London: Routledge & Kegan Paul, 1985).
37. Wallace, 'Between Two Worlds', op. cit., p.140.
38. Richard Higgott and Diane Stone, 'The limits of influence: foreign policy think tanks in Britain and the USA', *Review of International Studies* 20 (1994), p.18. See also William Wallace, 'Chatham House at 70: To the 1990s and Beyond', *The World Today* 46 (1990), pp.75–6.
39. Wallace, 'Between Two Worlds', p. 141. See also Roger Morgan, 'To Advance the Sciences of International Politics: Chatham House's Early Research', *International Affairs* 55 (1979), pp.240–51. Chatham House's role in developing the discipline of international relations in Britain in the inter-war years is demonstrated in Bill Olson and John Groom, *International Relations Then and Now* (New York, 1991).
40. Paul Addison, *The Road to 1945* (London: Quartet Books, 1977), p.39. See also Arthur Marwick, 'Middle Opinion in the Thirties', *English Historical Review* (April 1964), pp.285–98.
41. John Pinder, '1964–1980: From PEP to PSI', in John Pinder (ed.), *Fifty Years of Political and Economic Planning* (London: Heinemann, 1981), pp.155–6, 157. The role and impact of the PSI during the 1980s is discussed by Bill Daniel, 'PSI: a Centre for Strategic Research', *Policy Studies*, Vol.44, No.4 (1989), pp.24–33.
42. Alan Budd, *The Politics of Economic Planning* (London: Fontana edition, 1978), p.86.
43. Kit Jones, 'Fifty Years of Economic Research: A Brief History of the National Institute of Economic and Social Research', *National Institute Economic Review* (May 1988), pp.36–59.
44. Ricci, *The Transformation of American Politics*, op. cit., p.1.
45. Maurice Peston, 'Conservative Economic Policy and Philosophy', *Political Quarterly*,Vol.44, No.4 (Oct.–Dec. 1973), p.421.
46. Cockett, *Thinking the Unthinkable*, op. cit., p.5.
47. McBriar, *Fabian Socialism*, op. cit., p.ix.
48. *Ibid.*, pp.348-9.
49. Cockett, *Thinking the Unthinkable*, op. cit., pp.150, 155. None of the high-profile political and media figures who explained their abandonment of the Labour Party in the volume *Right Turn* mentioned the power of economic liberal arguments as a reason for their action: see Patrick Cormack (ed.) *Right Turn: Eight men who changed their minds* (London: Leo Cooper, 1978).
50. *Ibid.*, p.328.
51. Samuel Brittan, *Is there an Economic Consensus?* (London: Macmillan, 1973), pp.20–22.
52. Martin Ricketts and Edward Shoesmith, *British Economic Opinion* (London: Research Monograph 45, IEA), p.10; Nigel Lawson, *The View from No.11: Memoirs of a Tory Radical* (London: Corgi edition, 1993), pp.505–8.
53. Cockett, *Thinking the Unthinkable*, op. cit., p.325.
54. Philip Norton, 'The Conservative Party from Thatcher to Major', in Anthony King (ed.), *Britain at the Polls 1992* (New Jersey: Chatham House, 1993).
55. Paul Whiteley et al., 'Thatcherism and the Conservative Party', *Political Studies* 42:2 (1994), p.202; see also Paul Whiteley *et al.*, *True Blues: The Politics of Conservative Party*

Membership (Oxford: Clarendon Press, 1994), pp.126–60.

56. Ivor Crewe, 'Values: The Crusade that Failed', in Dennis Kavanagh and Anthony Seldon (eds.), *The Thatcher Effect* (Oxford: Oxford University Press, 1989), p.241.

57. Ivor Crewe, 'Has the Electorate Become Thatcherite?', in Robert Skidelsky (ed), *Thatcherism* (London: Chatto & Windus, 1988), p.46.

58. Maurice Cowling, *Mill and Liberalism* (Cambridge: Cambridge University Press, 2nd edn., 1990), p.xxxvi. See also Norman Barry, 'Ideas and Interests: The Problem Reconsidered', in Andrew Gamble *et al.*, *Ideas, Interests and Consequences* (London: IEA Readings 30, 1989), p.53.

59. Hames and Feasey, 'Anglo-American think tanks under Reagan and Thatcher', p.231.

60. Geoffrey Howe, *Conflict of Loyalty* (London: Macmillan, 1994), pp.141, 140. The mood at that time can be gauged from the reminiscence of the IEA's Lord (Ralph) Harris: 'How we rejoiced together in 1979 when Sir Geoffrey Howe as Chancellor confounded the faint-hearts by sweeping away exchange controls which looked set to last forever!', Ralph Harris, 'Seldon Man', in Martin J. Anderson (ed.), *The Unfinished Agenda* (London: IEA, 1986), p. 9. By contrast, although Norman Fowler mentions the CPS in his memoirs, its role in the campaign to abolish the Dock Labour Scheme goes unrecognised. See his *Ministers Decide* (London: Chapman's, 1991), pp.93, 303–9.

61. Cockett, *Thinking the Unthinkable*, op. cit., p.314.

62. *Ibid.*, pp.171–2.

63. Article of 26 April 1988, re-printed in Charles Moore and Simon Heffer (eds.), *A Tory Seer* (London: Hamish Hamilton, 1988), pp.142–3.

64. Cockett, *Thinking the Unthinkable*, op. cit., p.315.

65. Michael Crick and Adrian van Klaveren, 'Mrs Thatcher's Greatest Blunder', *Contemporary Record*, Vol.5, No.3 (Winter 1991), p.407.

66. See David Butler, Andrew Adonis and Tony Travers, *Failure in British Government: The Politics of the Poll Tax* (Oxford: Oxford University Press, 1994), pp.32, 41–69.

67. See David Smith, *The Rise and Fall of Monetarism* (Harmondsworth: Penguin, 1987), pp.123–8.

68. On SERPS, see Andrew Marr, *Ruling Britannia:The Failure and Future of British Democracy* (London: Michael Joseph, 1995), pp.143–50.

69. Adam Smith Institute, *The First Hundred* (London: Adam Smith Institute, 1989), p.2.

70. Quoted in Cockett, *Thinking the Unthinkable*, op. cit., p.301.

71. For a brilliant account of the inter-dependence between media and 'think tanks', see James Cornford, 'Performing Fleas: Reflections from a Think Tank', *Policy Studies*, Vol.10, No.4 (1990), pp.22–30. In the words of Hames and Feasey, 'the think tanks are important because the media believes they are important and the media believes in this importance because the think tanks tell them they are', 'Anglo-American think tanks', op. cit., p.233.

72. 'Dorrell discounts NHS crisis report', *The Guardian*, 20 Sept. 1995; 'Can we really afford to grow old?', *The Independent*, 25 Sept. 1995; 'The disturbing figures that point to a social disaster', *Daily Mail*, 27 Sept. 1995.

73. See articles in *The Economist*, 25 May and 7 Nov. 1992, and *Financial Times*, 22 Sept. 1993.

74. See Dennis Kavanagh and Anthony Seldon (eds.), *The Major Effect* (London: Macmillan, 1994), pp.16–17, 156.

75. Quoted in the *Guardian*, 21 Nov. 1994.

76. See, for example, the discussion of IEA survey findings on taxation and the Welfare State in Hugh Stephenson, *Mrs Thatcher's first year* (London: Jill Norman, 1980), pp.20–23.

77. The *Guardian*, 21 Nov. 1994.

78. Interestingly, Sir Robin Butler has responded to ministerial requests that civil service personnel should address 'think tanks' by stressing that those who choose to accept such invitations can only do so 'on their own account', and not 'normally' in the company of ministers. Reported in The *Guardian*, 10 Oct. 1995.

79. Maurice Cowling, *The Nature and Limits of Political Science* (Cambridge: Cambridge University Press, 1963), p.1.

The Social Market Foundation

LEWIS BASTON

The Social Market Foundation began its life as an attempt to define the David Owen Social Democratic Party. It defines its ideology as favouring the primacy of the market but understanding the social underpinnings of the market, in distinction to the 'free' market. It was relaunched in 1992 with the aid of large donations; it has grown in size and influence since. It targets policy formers and media commentators. Like many think tanks, the SMF is managed collectively and informally. It has an ambivalent relationship with the political parties. While its leading figures have close connections with the Conservatives, and its work has tended to be directed toward the right, it has tried to cultivate some influence with 'New Labour'. The true relationship of the SMF to the parties can only be tested by the election of a Labour government.

The Birth of the Social Market Foundation

The origins of the Social Market Foundation (SMF) are to be found in the murky wreckage of the end of the Social Democratic Party (SDP) and its dream of a realignment of the party system. The SMF was a diminutive phoenix that arose from the ashes of the fragment of the SDP associated with David Owen.

The Alliance lacked an associated think tank – the SDP's Tawney Society was modelled on the Fabian Society and was at least nominally a national organisation open to all members.[1] The years of David Owen's leadership of the united SDP saw the start of the attempt to define a distinctive Social Democrat project, in contradistinction to the Conservatives, Labour and, of course, the Liberals. The rhetoric of 'tough and tender' was matched with more philosophical discussions about the 'social market' as opposed to neo-liberalism and socialism. Ideological coherence was never the strong point of the ramshackle Alliance, but the Owenites found themselves, a smaller unit, with a more pressing need to define where they stood and defend the SDP's relevance as the fifth largest party in national politics. They considered that Owen was raising issues and questions that needed the underpinning of serious thought.

The Social Market Foundation was aimed at filling the gap. Owen hoped that it would become an SDP equivalent of the Centre for Policy Studies, to shift the SDP more towards free market thinking. Lord Kilmarnock and

Lewis Baston, Institute of Contemporary British History.

Robert Skidelsky set up a rudimentary think tank operation in 1989, run from Kilmarnock's personal premises in the House of Lords and Regent's Park Road. Skidelsky, Professor of International Studies at the University of Warwick and biographer of Keynes and Mosley, brought an intellectual spark to the process – brilliant but unpredictable. For the first three years it had no staff, but Kilmarnock was designated Director and the Viscount Chandos the first Chairman. It rapidly achieved charitable status, requiring formal independence from the SDP.

The initial aims were 'to research, publish and gain acceptance for policies based on the concept of "the Social Market".' They gathered in a few sympathetic colleagues from the old SDP, Danny Finkelstein and Nick Bosanquet among them. Many had been collaborators on a 1987 book, *The Radical Challenge*[2] aimed explicitly at an Alliance audience. The SMF ball was set rolling by Skidelsky's pamphlet *The Social Market Economy*[3] and a collection of responses from various points on the political spectrum.[4]

The Skidelsky Agenda 1989–92

Skidelsky started by facing the ambiguity of the ideological label he was claiming by stating a clear position on economic management:

> The use of the phrase 'social market economy' signifies a choice in favour of the market economy ... It means our first instinct is to use the market, not to override it, and that we are not afraid to apply the logic of this to matters of thought, expression and behaviour which most governments, not least Mrs. Thatcher's, have an incurable urge to control.

Neither of the two main political parties believed in the market by 1975.[5] Skidelsky's vision, while extravagant in its praise for the virtues of the market in terms of liberty, efficiency and morality, was far from implying a minimal conception of the state. The social part of the label implied:

The state's role is essentially threefold:

> (a) to create and maintain an appropriate legal framework for market exchange;
> (b) to limit and supplement the market where necessary; and
> (c) to ensure that the market is politically acceptable.[6]

Perhaps the most intriguing aspect of the Skidelsky paper was that 'certain market outcomes may be efficient and yet be socially unacceptable, and thus weaken the system which produces them'.[7] It rejected the dichotomy between social organisation and market economics, stating that society's norms affect the shape of the market system and induction through pure rationality was never going to be enough. This was a clear point of difference between the Social Market Foundation and 'free market' thinking.[8]

Social market thought was partly about converting the left to the virtues of the market, by saying that some left wing objectives could be fulfilled in a market system, and about making markets work acceptably for people with legitimate concerns about society. Fairness, Skidelsky points out in his reply to the discussion he inspired, is not something smuggled in by statist political theorists, but a part of the human condition.[9]

Skidelsky went on to flesh out these areas of justifiable state activity, providing a more extensive list than, say, any prospectus of the Adam Smith Institute. He concluded that the National Health Service could be defended on the grounds of market failure in dealing with insurance, and displayed a concern for equality and justice – the 'initial distribution' taken as given by right wing market theorists. He wrote approvingly of Rawls's theories of justice.

Skidelsky saw the roots of social market theory in post-war German economic thought, in the tradition known as Ordo-Liberalism. It was a contrast, at least in emphasis, to the purist free market Austrian school and Hayek.[10]

Skidelsky concluded by sketching out a list of current policy concerns, and suggesting possible social market approaches to them. He was met with respect, if not approval, from his interlocutors such as Frank Field and Graham Mather, who saw him as belonging to the other side. The next set of SMF papers, on a European currency, the NHS, education and telecommunications, sought to use the social market approach on these policy issues. In the public services, the general line that emerged supported the government's approach of introducing internal markets and sought to influence policy in specific ways. Two of its papers[11] were much more ideological statements of free market belief. One, which was not given the full status of a paper, extolled the virtues of strong local government for the social market[12] which was in contrast to the government's philosophy.

The SMF does not have a line, it has an approach. The parameters of the social market are set sufficiently broadly to accommodate statements of faith reminiscent of the Institute of Economic Affairs, and technocratic analysis that would command a wide political consensus. It makes clear that the opinions in its pamphlets are those of the authors alone, and not those of the SMF corporately. It tolerates a range of opinions, and direct contradictions between different SMF papers. The flexibility inherent in the definition of the aims of the SMF was to be tested during its relatively short life to date.

In 1990–92 the SMF was a think tank in search of a role. The Owenite

SDP had collapsed ignominiously in 1990, and the SMF was left, like many of its leading figures, in political limbo.[13] Towards the end of 1991 an internal review looked at the future of the SMF; it and the Conservative election victory of April 1992 provided an answer to the question 'Whither the SMF? Or wither the SMF?'

The Relaunch of the Social Market Foundation 1992

The review concluded that, though there was no future in an organisation looking backward to the SDP, there was a core commitment of former members to the values outlined by Skidelsky of a market economy underpinned by social consent and institutions. It also identified a gap in the coverage of British think tanks for one that took the social market philosophical position and was interested in public service reform. It also took note of the interest the Major government had shown in SMF publications.[14]

A political home was found in the Conservative Party for a group of minor luminaries from the former SDP, including Danny Finkelstein, via a carefully staged stunt during the 1992 election campaign. The prospect of five years of Conservative government, and the seeming probability that the Conservatives had a freehold on power, led the SMF to target its attempts at influencing the agenda mainly on the right.

The organisation was relaunched after some large donations from David Sainsbury and charitable foundations. Sainsbury offered a large grant to get things going, and considerable money from two more years. It moved into new offices, in Palmerston's town house, 20 Queen Anne's Gate in Westminster. In its new role, closeness to the centres of power was considered important. It acquired a permanent staff, Danny Finkelstein being appointed Director and Roderick Nye Editor. It had to worry about money rather less than most think tanks because of the breakthrough in raising start up funds.

Central to the relaunch was the instant credibility that the SMF could acquire from the intellectual capital of its backers. Lord Skidelsky – elevated to the House of Lords in 1992 – took a prominent role in establishing it in the consciousness of the British policy elite. David Willetts, newly elected Conservative MP for Havant and formerly of the Centre for Policy Studies and the Number 10 Policy Unit, joined the Board and became involved in its work. The board was chosen to add to the credibility of the new SMF. The new SMF is closer to the classical definition of a think tank;[15] it fits all the criteria identified by Simon James for qualification as a think tank, save for the contestable issue of partisanship.

The statement of aims was revised to read:

> The Foundation's main activity is to commission and publish original papers by independent academic and other experts on key topics in the economic and social fields, with a view to stimulating public discussion on the performance of markets and the social framework within which they operate.

The Social Market Foundation 1992–

The issues the SMF addressed started to concentrate on the overlap between the Skidelsky proposals and the agenda of the Major government. Reports followed on schools and pensions,[16] mixing thoughtful analysis with conclusions which went further than, but fell within the conceptual framework of, the Major government's ideas. They followed the emphasis found in the Citizen's Charter that there were services which had to remain more or less within the state sector, and attention should be given to market-driven internal reform in those areas. Insiders were invited to write on these issues; Howard Davies's SMF paper on the management of the public services, and Sir Peter Kemp's paper on the future of the civil service[17] were influential. The general thrust of SMF publications in this period was to offer constructive and friendly comment about the Major government's domestic agenda and public service reforms. It studiously avoids constitutional, 'moral' and European questions.

In 1994 and 1995 the SMF made successful sallies into wider philosophical questions. The high point of public attention was the publication in June 1994 of two important contrasting statements about the effect of the market on society, by John Gray and David Willetts. Gray argued that the market was destroying the interests and institutions that were the basis of conservatism, while Willetts thought the increased role of the market would lead to a revival of civic values.[18] Conservative commentators were more impressed by Willetts,[19] and *Civic Conservatism* has become one of the definitive statements of modern Conservative thought. The ideas of John Gray, on the other hand, have proved an insight into the contemporary problems of Conservative government.

The Organisation of the SMF[20]

As its finances and credibility have grown, so has the size of the SMF's staff and the range of its activities. In 1992 there were three members of staff – Finkelstein, Nye and a secretary. In 1994 and 1995 a fully qualified office manager was appointed and the research staff expanded greatly. Andrew

Cooper, another former Owenite, came in as Research Director. The advertisement for the position of research officer attracted 400 applications in spring 1995. The staff are generally young, and the prevailing management style relaxed and informal. The informality derives from the fact that most of the principals have been friends since the days of the SDP, or even from university.

There are four patrons – Lords Chandos, Flowers and Owen and David Sainsbury. They have had a role in selecting a new Director, and the Foundation extends an open door to them, but they are rarely involved in its business.

There is a nine-member Advisory Council which hardly ever meets as a collective body. As individuals its members feature in the SMF's list of authors and speakers, and are called upon to read all proposed papers.

Lord Skidelsky and Lord Kilmarnock are still very much involved. Kilmarnock is Editor of all publications, and scrutinises them in fine detail. He also oversees the company financial arrangements.

The Director is the external face of the SMF and its main representative to outside conferences, seminars and the media at large. From 1992 until summer 1995 this post was filled by Danny Finkelstein, working with Deputy Director Roderick Nye in a rather collective leadership. Since then Nye has been Acting Director. The appointment of a new permanent Director takes place on 13 December.

The SMF Business Forum is an important source of funds. Affiliates are entitled to the run of publications, attendance at SMF events and access to research services. This link has often led to further co-operation, for instance by joint arrangements for conferences. Pamphlets tend to be expensive, up to £12 for fairly slim volumes. This is because the purchasers are mainly institutional and the price elasticity of demand is low. Another source of income is ticket sales for conferences.

The Range of SMF Activities

SMF published output comes in several forms, the most significant being the series of regular Papers (23 to date). Output is commissioned through a rather informal network of staff, in association with Skidelsky. There is a steady inflow of unsolicited material, some of which is of use, and often Council members will send in arguments they have been working on. There are also Occasional Papers; these are usually reprints of speeches and papers given at SMF sponsored seminars. Memoranda concern more technical issues of policy, and are the main means of addressing questions of interest to the left. There is a series of reports called 'Hard Data' that tries to use figures to make what its press material calls 'counter intuitive' points. The most notable of these was a mischievous costing of the supposed implications of the promises of 'Today' programme interviewees.[21] The SMF is proud of being one of the most prolific among British think tanks. It also has an effective publicity machine which has ensured national press coverage for nearly all of its output.

The SMF also works through public seminars and conferences. It often co-sponsors seminars with other groups and opens its platform for the more ruminative public statements of government figures including Lord Mackay and Peter Lilley. One conference on cities in 1995 was addressed by the Prime Minister. It is a cost and labour effective way to keep the SMF in the public consciousness.

It also attempts to create networks within the policy elite by private seminars and social functions, and to associate lively conversations and meetings with the SMF imprint. David Willetts plays an important informal role in attracting senior government figures, and as its reputation has grown it finds it easier to assemble interesting groups.[22]

The International Role of the SMF

The SMF has an international side. It has taken an interest in the situation in Eastern Europe, and has published several papers on transition, including a defence of abrupt change to a market economy by Jeffrey Sachs, one of the most prominent exponents of 'shock therapy'.[23] It regards Eastern Europe as a promising area for its pragmatic free market principles, and in spring 1996 is co-sponsoring a conference with the European Bank for Reconstruction and Development in Russia. It has sponsored the creation of the autonomous Centre for Transition Economies which deals with this area.[24] International work has led to a shift in emphasis from the German social market model, to recognising the particular cultural and historical factors that affect the shape of the market economy in different countries.[25]

Danny Finkelstein and Andrew Cooper in particular have taken an interest in American debates on the size of the state and the various brands of American conservatism. It has informal intellectual links with a broad range of US think tanks, but is particularly close to the Manhattan Institute which specialises in urban problems and policies and takes a similar general approach. Robert Skidelsky also serves on the board there. They have organised two joint conferences in London. The Foundation has established links in Sweden and appropriately enough with the Konrad-Adenauer-Stiftung in Germany.

Effects of SMF Activity

The SMF, despite its occasional philosophical work, is basically at the detailed policy end of the think tank spectrum. Its links with the Majorite political establishment and technocrats like Davies and Kemp give it considerable opportunity to affect the policies of government. It targets the policy makers and newspaper columnists regarded as authoritative and has built up relations with *The Times*.

It is perhaps invidious to single out individual policies as resulting from particular think tanks, as – especially at the level of technical detail the SMF works on – origination is difficult to untangle. But government policy on health, education and other public services, the Private Finance Initiative and retirement, shows signs of working with ideas associated with the SMF. Some policy development in the Labour Party has also been affected by SMF work, in its approach to investment for example. The visit of New York Police Commissioner William Bratton under SMF auspices introduced new ideas about order in cities to the British debate, having a profound effect on Jack Straw.[26]

The Politics of the SMF: 'We are not a right wing think tank'[27]

Since the SMF lost its partisan mooring with the Owenite SDP in 1990, its relationship with the party system has been more ambivalent than that of other think tanks. It strongly resists the idea that it is a Conservative think tank; some of its members are happy with the label 'right wing' while others insist that 'independent' is the only name tag that fits.

From 1992 to 1995 it has adopted positions close to the Conservative leadership, while maintaining a distance from the purist free market outfits further to the right. Skidelsky and Finkelstein joined the Conservatives, and the thrust of its policy and philosophical contributions has been to inform Conservative debates. It has been a friend of the Major government's approach to public services – favouring not privatisation, but internal market reforms. It has published two important contributions to conservative thought in the Willetts and Gray pamphlets of June 1994. Its council of nine contains a Conservative MP (Willetts), a right-wing former Conservative MP (Michael Fallon), and a former Conservative special adviser to Chancellors Lawson and Major (Andrew Tyrie). While John Willman and Alex de Mont are associated with Labour they are much more marginal figures in that party than Willetts and Fallon are in theirs.

The think tanks of the unambiguous right were thrown into some disorder by the ousting of Thatcher in 1990, and Conservatives themselves were looking for the intellectual foundations of post-Thatcher Toryism. The SMF occupied the right sort of ideological territory for this. The appointment of Danny Finkelstein to the office of Director of Conservative Research in summer 1995 showed that SMF principles are still favourably regarded at high levels of the Tory Party.

However, to describe the SMF as a Majorite think tank is to simplify the story too far. Of the Patrons, Chandos is a Labour spokesperson in the Lords and Sainsbury has expressed sympathy for Tony Blair's positions. The facts that the Conservatives are in government, and that think tank activities are generally directed at government, make for an appearance of partisan Conservatism which may only reflect an impatience to affect policy now. In 1994 and 1995, Danny Finkelstein emerged clearly as the public face of the SMF and this in turn gave a blue tinge to the organisation, as it was well known that he was an active Conservative.

One also has to deal with the changes that have taken place in the Labour Party since Tony Blair was elected leader. The phrasing of the new Clause IV is reminiscent of social market language, and even the right-wing thrust of Nick Bosanquet's *Public Spending into the Millennium*[28] accords in part with the Blairite emphasis that lower income tax cuts are an effective way to increase equality as well as help people back to work.

Especially through the Memorandums, the Social Market Foundation has entered a dialogue with New Labour. The impending accession of Tony Blair in 1994 led to the production of a paper aimed at confronting Labour with some quite extreme policy challenges; this was followed up by another set of ideas one year on.[29] Stephen Pollard is a link between the SMF and the Fabians, and the SMF has published some of his work that was less than joyously received at the Fabian Society.[30] While the SMF may have shifted to the right since 1989, the entire political spectrum has shifted even further.[31] The only member of a political party on the staff at the SMF has been in the Labour Party since the 1980s.

The probability of a Labour victory at the next general election will pose a test for the Social Market Foundation. The guiding concept of the social market is certainly broad enough to be compatible with the Blair agenda, and unlike unapologetically right-wing think tanks, it stands a chance of conserving influence under a Labour government. The problem that its social and intellectual links tend to the Conservative Party is one that can be faced. One of the reasons is, somewhat strangely, the bitterness surrounding the break up of the SDP in 1987. Ex-SDP activists who have found a political home in the two main parties have preserved rather good personal relations with each other, while those who joined the Liberal Democrats are considered beyond the pale. The bonds of shared ridicule and adversity have proved strong. There is still a feeling of distance from the Liberal Democrats; formal relations are maintained but not regarded as very important.

If the SMF can resist the temptation to march rightwards in step with the Conservatives, and reorient its nuts and bolts policy work to issues that a

Labour government could pick up on, it could be a rare case of a think tank whose influence can survive a change of government. The verdict on its long term partisan stance will have to be delivered after the election.

NOTES

1. Ivor Crewe and Anthony King, *SDP: The Birth, Life and Death of the SDP* (Oxford: Oxford University Press 1995). Perhaps significantly, the whole saga of the Owenite SDP 1987–90 rates only an afterthought, the SMF nothing at all.
2. Alastair Kilmarnock (ed.), *The Radical Challenge: The Response of Social Democracy* (London: André Deutsch, 1987). Of incidental note is the discussion on p148 after Bosanquet's contribution, in which it is said that 'some of the New Right were saying to us that we should be with them in five years.' The uncanny accuracy of this prophecy is in contrast to contemporary New Right suggestions that Britain would run a permanent budget surplus and the poll tax would be popular.
3. Robert Skidelsky, *The Social Market Economy*, SMF Paper 1 (London: SMF 1989)
4. Sarah Benton et al, *Responses to Robert Skidelsky on The Social Market Economy*, SMF Paper 2 (London: SMF 1989).
5. Skidelsky, op. cit., pp.1, 7.
6. Ibid.
7. Ibid., p13
8. Author's interview with Roderick Nye, 1 Dec. 1995.
9. Skidelsky in Benton *et al.*, p30.
10. Robert Skidelsky, *The World After Communism* (London: Macmillan 1995), p.76.
11. Deepak Lal, *Fighting Fiscal Privilege*, SMF Paper 7 (1990) and Samuel Brittan, A Restatement of Economic Liberalism, SMF Paper 10 (1990).
12. George Jones, *Local Government and the Social Market* (London: SMF, 1991)
13. Simon James, The Idea Brokers: The Impact of Think Tanks on British Government, (*Public Administration* Vol.71 (Winter 1993).
14. Danny Finkelstein, interview with author, 29 Nov. 1995.
15. James, op. cit.
16. David Willetts, *The Age of Entitlement*, SMF Paper 14 (1993); Evan Davis, *Schools and the State*, SMF Paper 15 (1993).
17. Howard Davies, *Fighting Leviathan: Building Social Markets that Work*, SMF Paper 13 (1992); Sir Peter Kemp, *Beyond Next Steps: A Civil Service for the 1990s*, SMF Paper 17 (1993).
18. David Willetts, *Civic Conservatism*, SMF Paper 20 (1994); John Gray, *The Undoing of Conservatism*, SMF Paper 21 (1994).
19. See for example leader comment, *The Times*, 4 July 1994; Noel Malcolm, 'When a philosopher can't see the good for the grief', *Daily Telegraph*, 23 June 1994.
20. This section with thanks to Andrew Cooper, author's interview, 1 Dec. 1995.
21. Andrew Cooper, *Costing the Public Policy Agenda: A week of the Today Programme*, Hard Data 2 (London: SMF, 1995) and Leo McKinstry, 'How to Bankrupt Britain over Breakfast', *The Spectator*, 1 April 1995. The treatment this received was not a source of joy in the SMF, as the McKinstry article and cover artwork made a paper with a fairly serious point appear abusive and right wing. Interview SMF 6.
22. This section owes much to the Danny Finkelstein and Andrew Cooper interviews.
23. Jeffrey Sachs, *Understanding 'Shock Therapy'*, Occasional Paper 7 (1994).
24. Robert Skidelsky (ed.), *Russia's Stormy Path to Reform*, CTE Paper 1 (London: SMF, 1995).
25. Author's interview with Rick Nye, 1 Dec. 1995.
26. Interview, SMF 4.
27. Marc Shaw interview with author, 27 Jan. 1995.
28. London: SMF, 1995.

29. Ron Beadle *et al.*, *A Memo to Modernisers*, Memorandum 8 (London: SMF, 1994) and John Abbott *et al.*, *A Memo to Modernisers II*, Memorandum 15 (London: SMF, 1995); 'In the Market for Ideas, Tony?', *The Independent* 25 July 1994; author's interview, SMF 5.
30. Stephen Pollard, *Schools, Selection and the Left*, SMF Memorandum 16 (London: SMF 1995).
31. Shaw interview.

'Blueprint for a Revolution'? The Politics of the Adam Smith Institute

RICHARD HEFFERNAN

Elite centred, its target audience decision-makers in Whitehall and Westminister, the Adam Smith Institute is as much a political actor as it is a genuine think tank. It has no wish to study the world in a detached scholarly fashion but offers instead normative policy recommendations based upon strict partisan world view. An organised advocate for the free market the Institute attempts to adopt a neo-liberal ideological position. It is a policy advocate a 'political' as opposed to an 'independent' think tank and an eager participant within a conservative movement. As an out-rider and not a political insider, the Adam Snith Institute has been a determined cheerleader for both the Thatcher and the Major governments, one prepared to make a variety of recommendations to advance the neo-liberal cause but able only to encourage and support political actors from outside government.

The Adam Smith Institute was conceived in 1976 by three graduates of St Andrews University, Madsen Pirie, Eamonn Butler and Stuart Butler. Following a year long period of preparation the Institute was finally established on 31 August 1977 when it moved into offices in Great George Street, WC1, close to the Palace of Westminster. The year 1976 had been the bicentennial of the publication of Adam Smith's The Wealth of Nations, hence the name adopted by the Institute. The principal figures of the Adam Smith Institute are two of its founders, Madsen Pirie and Eamonn Butler. Together, Pirie as President and Butler as Director, they run the Institute as a team. The functions both men play appear to overlap but the general impression is that Butler is involved more with the day to day running of the organisation while Pirie is the ideas man. Stuart Butler is now a senior official with the Heritage Foundation, a Washington based think tank, which enjoys friendly relations with the Institute. As the 'youngest, most aggressively ideological and self confessed enfant terrible of the British think tanks',[1] the Adam Smith Institute has been a keen supporter of the efforts of the Thatcher and Major governments to turn back the so-called collectivist tide.

The origins of the Institute lie in St Andrews University in Scotland.

Richard Heffernan, Department of Government, London School of Economics and Political Science.

Adam Smith was himself Scottish and had been born not more than 50 miles from the St Andrews Campus; naming the Institute after him was simultaneously an affirmation of faith in market liberalism and homage to the founders Scottish associations. St Andrews' track record of producing conservative public figures throughout the 1970s and 1980s has bestowed the University with a reputation as a centre of economic liberalism. In addition to the Butlers and Pirie, the St Andrews Conservative Association has spawned a number of right wing Conservative MPs among them Michael Forsyth, Secretary of State for Scotland since July 1995. Many of these were founder members of the avowedly Thatcherite 'No Turning Back' group in 1988 with which the Institute has enjoyed close links. Other figures on the right of the Conservative Parliamentary Party such as Michael Portillo and John Redwood have written pamphlets published by the Institute.

Neo-liberals rather then neo-conservatives, Pirie and the Butler brothers have long track records of political activity on the political right. All were early versed in the literature of the Institute of Economic Affairs and were long established enthusiasts of economic liberalism. In 1971, the St Andrews University Conservative Association delegation to the Tory Conference numbered among its members Madsen Pirie and Eamonn Butler. They produced a mock-up front page of the *Daily Telegraph* for June 1981 which heralded the success of various right wing ideals. Among other things, Pirie, Butler and their colleagues 'predicted' the privatisation of telecommunications, and the sale of council housing. They also ventured that the free market Rhodes Boyson (not an MP in 1971 but already a leading right wing educationalist) would be appointed as Minister of Education (he became a Minister of State but never entered the Cabinet) and suggested that Ronald Reagan would be elected to the US Presidency in the autumn of 1980. It is hard to imagine that this student jape was taken seriously by fellow Conference delegates in 1971 but it is an illustration that this particular group of free market radicals were very early prepared to 'think the unthinkable'. As Pirie suggested of the Institute in 1987: 'We propose things which people regard as on the edge of lunacy. The next think you know they are on the edge of policy.' From the position of determined outriders the Institute founders claim they are now part of the process of government; for Pirie, think tanks such as the Adam Smith Institute are now 'part of the constitution'.[2]

Madsen Pirie and Eamonn Butler read for doctorates in philosophy. Both appear to have early conceived of themselves as active political scholars rather than engaged political actors. The Institute is fiercely libertarian in its political outlook. It campaigns for the free market in almost every sphere of life from the deregulation of licensing laws to the privatisation of the prison service. Uniformly critical of the public sector (Madsen Pirie is on record as having described it as 'inherently evil'[3]), the Institute has been particularly active in promoting privatisation across a range of services at the level of national and local government. This is a consistent theme of its work, one it is increasingly seeking to promote at the international level where many countries are eager to learn from the British experience. Firm supporters of the principle of deregulation and contracting out, the Adam Smith Institute remains committed to the privatisation of both the National Health Service and the Welfare State. Essentially, it is in favour of a night-watchman state, one that exists to enfranchise the free market and allow the 'magic hand' of free competition full rein. In its view the role of the state should be confined to setting the framework for social and economic activity and defending the rule of law: No other function is permissible because political institutions exist only to maximise individual freedoms.

Organised Advocates for the Free Market

The Institute is nominally run by a six member management board chaired by Sir Austin Bide comprising Pirie and Butler, Sir Ralph Bateman, Sir Robert Clark and Sir John Greenborough. The four lay members of the board have an impressive track record in industry and in public service but both Pirie and Butler remain the driving forces behind the organisation. In addition to the Institute proper, two new arms, the Conference Division and an International Division, were established in 1992. Each division is run on a separate basis from the others. Each has its own board (under the supervision of the board of management) and the finances of each division are ring-fenced. Pirie and Butler are the only individuals on the board of all three divisions.

The new International Division was given separate premises and charged with the task of overseeing the overseas work of the Institute. Headed by Peter Young (a former chair of the Federation of Conservative Students) and Paul Reynolds it marks an attempt by the Institute to capitalise on the growing trend of marketisation. It claims to have conducted projects in over 30 countries world-wide and its literature carries endorsements from past and serving ministers in Moldovia, Poland, Mongolia, Equador, Lithuania and Trinidad and Tobago. Here, the Institute is seeking to establish itself as a policy consultant prepared to offer advice and instruction in the general field of economic liberalisation. The establishment of the Conference and the International Divisions mark something of a departure perhaps signalling a shift toward policy consultancy which may eventually boost the income and turnover of the organisation.

On the domestic side the Institute employs not more than three or four full-time members of staff supplemented by a number of young interns and students on short term contracts. A 'low cost, no cost' operation,[4] the Adam Smith Institute is dependent upon corporate and individual support for its funding. Unlike the Institute of Economic Affairs it is not a charitable organisation although it does organise a small associated charity for educational purposes. The Adam Smith Institute (the trading name of its holding company ASI (Research) Ltd.) describes itself as 'independent and non profit-making'. Its modest funding is drawn from a variety of sources, among them 'subscriptions from companies, foundations and individuals' which 'contribute approximately half its income, the remainder coming from sponsorship and the sale of publications'.[5] Records filed at Companies House show that in the five years to September 1994, the Adam Smith Institute recorded an average company turnover of some £107,000 with donations of £99,000 received in 1993–94. More interestingly, in that same year the Institute claimed that it had spent £118,707 on administrative expenses and declared accumulated losses brought forward totalling some £122,862. It also recorded an operating profit of £6,729 and declared current fixed assets of £23,451. As with all other similar UK 'think tank' this compares unfavourably with counterparts in the United States such as Heritage and the American Enterprise Institute which command a vast budget and employ staff in their hundreds.

Conceived to advocate free market politics, the Adam Smith Institute was based on several organisations that emerged in the United States in the mid 1970s. After graduating from St Andrews, Pirie, Eamonn and Stuart Butler all spent a number of years in the States working in both academia and for Republican Congressional staffs on Capital Hill. Both Eamonn Butler and Pirie were variously employed by the Republican Study Committee, a conservative faction organised by the staff member of a Illinois Republican Congressman, Edwin J. Feulner. The Republican Study Committee was initially set up to promote policy proposals for right wing Republican Congressmen. Pooling legislative staffs and arranging conservative legislation, the Committee organised to block Democratic (and liberal Republican) proposals while advocating its own alternatives to the supposedly liberal policies of the Congressional majority and the Nixon and Ford administrations. While working in the Republican Study Committee, Feulner helped set up the Heritage Foundation in 1973, a conservative think tank modelled upon the Washington based Rand Corporation and the Brookings Institute. These two organisations, examples of non-party, non-government private research institutes, were deemed to carry greater intellectual authority and more likely to influence public debate than any Capital Hill-based political committee.

Feulner, Executive Director of the Heritage Foundation since 1977, has had a significant influence on the St Andrews graduates: Pirie's 1988 book *Micropolitics* is dedicated to him. Heritage sought to operationalise the conservative school of 'Public Choice Theory' developed by James Buchanan and Gordon Tullock in the University of Virginia and roll back the frontiers of the 'collectivist state'. Arising from their experiences in the US, both Pirie and Butler saw the Adam Smith Institute as a vehicle through which they could become 'scholar activists' and suggest specific policies to put their ideas into practice: Only though detailed policy proposals could the objectives identified by the Virginia Public Choice School be realised. Adapting the *modus operandi* of the Heritage Foundation and the work of the Virginia School, the Institute suggests that government failure could be a failure of 'policy engineering', not just intellectual nerve.6

Message and Audience: Addressing 'Decision-Makers'

A child of its time, the product of the right wing backlash of the mid 1970s, the Adam Smith Institute claims that it has no power, its only resources the power of its ideas. Pirie and Butler argue that of themselves anti-collectivist and free market ideas are not enough; they will not necessarily penetrate political and administrative institutions. The Adam Smith Institute thus distinguishes itself from the Institute of Economic Affairs whose long established working method has been to fight and win the intellectual battle of ideas. In the General Theory, Keynes famously suggested that the world is ruled by ideas:

> Practical men, who believe themselves to be quite exempt from any intellectual influences, are usually the slaves of some defunct economist. Madmen in authority, who hear voices in the air, are distilling their frenzy from some academic scribbler a few years back.[7]

This observation, mounted and framed, takes pride of place in the entrance hall of the Institute of Economic Affairs but does not find favour at the Adam Smith Institute where the very reverse is believed to be the case. In its own terms the Institute is not so much concerned with popularising ideas (which may be defined as ends) as it is seeking to communicate suitable methods (which could be defined as means) to enact designated ideas in practice. Pirie contrasts the role of the scientist and the engineer, as the Adam Smith Institute acts as 'policy engineers', complementing 'pure scientists' such as the Institute of Economic Affairs.[8] As a result, the Institute is more likely to mount and display the observation of Karl Marx that 'Philosophers only interpret the world, the point is to change it' than it is to endorse the Keynes quotation favoured by the Institute of Economic Affairs.

From inauspicious beginnings in 1977, the Adam Smith Institute has sought to apply ideas in the real world as 'policy engineers' willing to translate theory into practice: 'Whereas the Institute of Economic Affairs, or even the Centre for Policy Studies, might establish the theoretical case for denationalising British Steel, the Adam Smith Institute would provide the detailed, step by step proposals to show how this could be done in practice'.[9] As Pirie has argued, it is engineers who follow pure scientists to make the machines which alter reality. To win the intellectual battle methods must be devised to apply theoretical ideas in the real world: 'The idea at the core of micropolitics is that creative ingenuity is needed to apply the practical world of interest group politics the concepts of free market theory'.[10] Only through the application of 'practical ideas' can real change be effected: 'In several cases the success of the policy has led to the victory of the idea rather then the other way around'.[11]

The Institute of Economic Affairs disseminates an endless series of publications and seminars targeted at Hayek's 'second hand dealers in ideas', those opinion-formers (journalists, academics, writers, broadcasters, and commentators) who can determine the intellectual thinking of the nation. In contrast, the Adam Smith Institute shows little interest in Hayek's dictum; its chosen *modus operandi* is to address decision makers and persuade them of the suitability of a particular policy. It is elite centred, targeting decision-makers first and opinion formers second. Its primary audience is to be found in Whitehall and Westminster, among them ministers, civil servants and political opinion formers. Its objective to exert influence within the policy arena rather than win the battle of ideas; to frame policy options and have certain decisions taken. While the stance of the Institute is wholly determined by its ideological orientation, its choice of issue is often influenced by the preoccupations of decision-makers. In an opportunistic fashion the Institute attempts to find an opening into the heart of government; Madsen Pirie likens its efforts to 'pushing on a number of policy doors' until it finds one that may open. This strategy almost always involves positive advocacy as opposed to negative criticism; it is hard to find an example where the Adam Smith Institute has been openly critical of any particular aspect of the policy of the Conservative government. Unlike other actors on the political right it has never once joined the chorus of disaffected 'Thatcherite' criticism of the Major government.

In seeking to enter the corridors of Whitehall and Westminster the Institute spends as much time lobbying decision makers than it does in research and education. The objective of the Institute is to persuade decision-makers of the efficacy of various proposals and not to convince the general public of their suitability. The Institute's public work (which includes monitoring political developments, undertaking research projects, organising seminars and conferences, issuing books and reports) is devoted not to popularising ideas but in communicating suitable methods to secure desirable ends. Its publications are not an end in themselves but a means to address their chosen audiences; ministers, politicians and administrative officials.

The *modus operandi* of the Adam Smith Institute is remarkably similar to organisations such as Greenpeace, Shelter or even the Terrence Higgins Trust, the major difference being that it is not a single issue pressure group.[12] The media is the transmission belt by which decision-makers are indirectly targeted. Research papers, books and pamphlets are not intended for the general public who will have little or no opportunity to buy or read they. They are designed to access the media which is the vehicle through which decision makers may be addressed. Each public statement is designed to attract maximum exposure to ensure a high profile for its ideas; of themselves they have a limited and transient appeal. The media interest generated by a publication is the initial sign of its success, the first step in the long journey to impress the political elite; public relations, press contacts, where possible media manipulation, are all techniques designed to promote the discussion of a chosen issue. Targeting advice requires the skill of a political lobbyist prepared to use the media to indirectly press home its particular case. In addition to indirect lobbying the Institute organises a number of seminars and conferences at which ministers and key officials often agree to speak; these meetings are not intended to offer the decision-maker the opportunity to speak to the Institute but rather to enable the Institute to speak to the decision-maker.

Despite its limited size and budget, the Adam Smith Institute, compared with other think tanks, has generated a considerable media profile. In 1980, the Institute published a paper on Contracting Out Local Government Services. This received limited press coverage but was the subject of a detailed article in James Goldsmith's short-lived magazine *Now* (Goldsmith was an early financial supporter of the Institute). This article was taken up by the then head of Mrs Thatcher's Policy Unit in Downing Street, Sir John Hoskyns, who had copies circulated to Conservative local authorities up and down the country.[13] This is one example of 'hard policy', where the proposals of the Institute, publicised through the media, were taken up by decision makers at a number of levels. It demonstrates that the question for the Adam Smith Institute is not one of theory; they do not argue that market forces should be brought to bear on a political question but suggest the method by which they may be brought to bear. Its approach fosters a striving for originality as pace setting proposals (from privatising prisons to privatising the police) are adopted to retain a cutting edge and maintain a public profile: visibility is the lifeblood of the Institute.

This tactic is very similar to that employed by think tanks in the United States.[14] The Adam Smith Institute has certainly modelled itself on the Heritage Foundation. In November 1980, following the election of Ronald Reagan to the Presidency, Heritage issued Mandate for Leadership, a 1,000-page version of a 3000 page document which distilled nearly a year's work by some 250 conservative academics, writers and activists.[15] Heritage claimed that the report outlined the steps that the new President should take to seize the political opportunity offered the conservative movement by the 1980 Election. Whereas the 1980 Election provided a window of opportunity for United States think tanks such as Heritage to influence the public arena, so was the 1979 Election of the Thatcher government to prove the same for UK counterparts such as the Adam Smith Institute. In 1985, the Institute produced its own version of the *Mandate for Leadership*, *The Omega File*, billed in the media as a political guide for members of the Conservative government, a 435 page closely typed document to which some 100 'experts' contributed calling for a full scale programme of deregulation covering all government services.[16]

Independent Think Tank or Engaged Political Actor?

The Adam Smith Institute has long laid claim to the title of 'think tank', its charter describing its role as furthering 'the advancement of learning by research and public policy options, economic and political science and the publications of such research'.[17] The Institute certainly fits the usual definition of a think tank. Describing such an organisation as an 'entrepreneurial venture of a scholar activist', James Allen Smith suggests a think tank is 'a private, non-profit making research group that operates on the margins of a nation's formal political process'.[18] Through commissioned work (the overwhelming majority of the Institute's output is undertaken in house and much is written by Madsen Pirie himself), the work of the Institute is geared at persuading government to adopt a particular ideological position. Its members see themselves as out-riders and not as political insiders, counsellors rather than courtiers, prepared to work at the margins challenging received wisdom.

Its forward planning essentially opportunistic, the Institute decides its own priorities but has been prepared to follow the Conservative government when necessary. For all the claims made for it, the Adam Smith Institute is more a political actor in its own right than a genuine think tank. Simon James has defined a 'think tank' as an 'independent organisation engaged in multi-disciplinary research intended to influence public policy'.[19] While the Adam Smith Institute is certainly a 'privately funded and non governmental organisation ... intellectually independent from government',[20] it remains a very different organisation from the likes of such think tanks as the Policy Studies Institute and the National Institute for Economic and Social Research (or even the late Centre for Policy Review Staffs) . Unlike these well-established bodies, the Institute has no wish to study the world in a detached scholarly fashion. As a 'political activist' it does not undertake academic research for its own sake but offers normative recommendations based upon a strictly partisan ideological world view; its work is not 'independent' in the true sense of the word. Politically partisan, it reaches its conclusions in advance. Advocacy is more important than research; inadequate research would not deter the Institute from entering any public debate on any issue of public policy.

None the less, the Adam Smith Institute may be described as a 'research group' or a 'planning and advisory institution',[21] but if so it is one that is engaged first and foremost in political activity. Devoted to political propaganda rather than scholarship for its own sake, it may be best described as a policy advocate, a 'political' as opposed to an 'independent' think tank. As a 'political think tank', it seeks to advise decision makers through a combination of instruction and exhortation, offering practical prescriptions to demonstrate the feasibility of a certain course of action. If established practice defines things as either 'politically impossible', 'administratively impracticable' and 'socially unacceptable'. New Right think tanks such as the Adam Smith Institute have attempted to change the terms of references which underpin that practice. This perhaps is their *raison d'être*, part of their crusade (no other word suffices) to advance the cause of economic liberalism: Their drive for originality and their desire to maintain a public image gives advocacy the edge over explication.

The 'non-party political' Adam Smith Institute keenly prides itself on its actual independence from organised political groupings. Nonetheless, it is generally associated with the Conservative Party and with 'Thatcherism' in particular. As with fellow think tanks on the political right this reflects the ideological affinity they had with the Thatcher-led Conservative government. The Institute has had no direct or indirect association with the Labour Party. In theory, while its work should continue irrespective of the political colour of the government, the less friendly the particular party is to the ideological programme it advances, the less likely it is to influence those central decision-makers that matter. Conservative think tanks form only part of that right wing community which stretches across academia and journalism to encompass political actors, decision takers to take in a myriad of policy advocates. All made some marginal contribution to the efforts of the Thatcherite project to reorder British politics.

The Adam Smith Institute considers that it has successfully carved itself a niche within the community of conservative think tanks. One recent project undertaken by Pirie and Butler is the compilation of a 'Conservative Experts Directory', a resource that allows interested parties (specifically the media) to access leading neo-liberals across the entire think tank community. While safeguarding its own separate and distinct modus operandi the Institute enjoys good relations with other organisations, its management is in regular contact (both business and social) with other think tankers, most notably the Institute for Economic Affairs. Political issues that are likely to cause dissent within the organisation are particularly frowned upon, for example the question of the European Union is an issue on which Institute insiders claim strict neutrality given the divisions it can foster within conservative (and indeed other) political organisations.

It is mistaken to suggest that think tanks such as the Adam Smith Institute provided in themselves the ideas that gave intellectual weight to Thatcherism. Any direct impact that they had was at the margin of public policy rather than at the centre. Determined outsiders, proud of their independence from government and of closed political circles, the Adam Smith Institute certainly played a part in the New Right crusade to turn back the so-called collectivist tide. Keen supporters rather than involved participants, the impact of the Institute was that of a Thatcherite foot-soldier eager to make some contribution to the political work of the Conservative government. Never prepared to openly criticise government policy or Conservative ministers, the Adam Smith Institute was prepared to make the most of the election of John Major in succession to Margaret Thatcher. The guest speaker at the fifteenth anniversary dinner of the Institute, Major has been prepared to offer it his public support: 'We could not have had a more powerful advocate of privatisation and liberalisation than the Adam Smith Institute', an endorsement prominently featured in the Institute's promotional literature.[22] As would be counsellors of the Thatcher and Major governments, the Institute has sought to persuade ministers of the efficacy of certain proposals and the political impact they would have. Constantly using the media to push at the nearest Whitehall or Westminster door, making suggestions and offering advice, the objective of the Adam Smith Institute has been to advance the 'Thatcherite revolution' from outside the Whitehall village.

Several authors, most recently John Barnes and Richard Cockett, have rightly described the conservative think tanks as part of the 'outer circle' of the Conservative Party, organisations that in the Opposition years prior to 1979 'filled the void which was not being filled by the existing party machinery'[23] (they certainly played a significant role in the economic 'counter-revolution' which saw neo-liberalism sweep aside social democratic practice in the years after 1976[24]). What is less clear is the 'unique contribution' that think tanks made to the Conservative Party in government. Where Kenneth Baker, the Heathite turned loyal 'Thatcherite', remarks that they became 'an influential powerhouse of ideas and policies for 1980s Conservatism',[25] hard and fast evidence of direct think tank influence on government policy after 1979 is less forthcoming.

An Influential 'Thatcherite' Outsider?

Some commentators suggest that the number of policy initiatives specifically attributable to Conservative think tanks are relatively small: Tim Hames and Richard Feasey claim that 'There is virtually no example of any legislation on either side of the Atlantic that was entirely and uniquely due to one individual think tank'.[26] It is difficult to assess the specific motivations and (more particularly) the motivators that drives the Thatcher and Major governments. It is more difficult to consider the direct contribution an outside player such as the Adam Smith Institute may have made to its endeavours. The behind the scenes image cultivated by the Adam Smith Institute (and other Conservative think tanks) is not well reflected in the contemporary memoirs of those leading decision makers it sought to influence. In *The Downing Street Years*, Margaret Thatcher makes no reference to the Adam Smith Institute (and offers only one passing reference to the Centre for Policy Studies). Similarly, Nigel Lawson in *The View From Number Eleven*, also makes no reference to the Institute (and mentions the Centre for Policy Studies only in the context of his delivering a series of speech to it). Nicholas Ridley, the pre-Thatcher 'Thatcherite' in his memoir *My Style of Government* and the former Chancellor and Foreign Secretary Sir Geoffrey Howe in *Conflict of Loyalties* also make no mention of the Institute.[27] This might well be an example of the unwillingness of political actors to give credit to others where due but it surely illustrates the fact that out-riding political think tanks exercise only an indirect influence upon decision makers, one necessarily limited in effect whereby no single policy initiative may be attributed (in Hames and Feasey's phrase) 'entirely and uniquely' to the efforts of any one organisation.

Unlike other organisations and actors, the Institute has claimed responsibility for the poll tax (a claim less well publicised these days[28]). Madsen Pirie makes much of the fact that he first advocated such a tax in the *Daily Mail* in April 1981 (an article apparently ghost written by an Adam Smith Institute associate Douglas Mason[29]). That the invention of the Poll Tax has often been credited to the Institute has been described as one of the 'great myths' that have surrounded this subject.[30] According to Michael Crick and Adrian van Klaveren the Institute was in no way responsible for the initiative.

For most of 1984 and 1985, inside the Department of the Environment, a select team of civil servants and outside academic advisers, led by Environment Ministers, Kenneth Baker and William Waldegrave, had been at work in devising an alternative scheme to replace the rating system in local government. Their report advocating a per capita tax went to a March 1985 Chequers meeting comprising almost half the membership of the Cabinet. It was at this meeting that, in Margaret Thatcher's words, 'the Community Charge was born'; it was a policy devised within Whitehall and not one designed from without. The main publication of the Adam Smith Institute on the poll tax, 'Revising the Rating System' written by Douglas Mason, was published in April 1985, six months after the Baker and Waldegrave enquiry began.[31] The Institute did not publish a blueprint until after government ministers had reached their own conclusions.[32] Other non-governmental actors were far more important in launching the Poll tax flagship than any free-market think tank. One such individual was Christopher Foster, a director of Coopers and Lybrands and a former faculty member at the LSE, who played a key role in the Baker-Waldegrave review.[33] His practical involvement was probably far more directly important in the conception of the Poll Tax than any ideological crusade mounted from without by the Adam Smith Institute. The role which fell to the Institute and to other free market think tanks was to legitimise the efforts of the Thatcher governments to drive politics to the political right; as 'Thatcherite' shock troops they were simply urging ministers on from the sideline.

As political advocates seeking to influence the policy agenda, think tanks are a step removed form the process of policy formation. In the case of privatisation, Whitehall departments and the City of London (notably H.N. Rothschild) had far more direct impact upon the form of privatisation than any out-riding think tank. None the less, the Adam Smith Institute made a significant (although limited) contribution in a number of areas. By its own admission the Institute judges its long term influence by a harsh standard, its strike rate determined by those proposals that result in government action. Short term success is defined by its ability to generate media interest in its various initiatives, the first step in gaining the attention of the policy making community. Pirie and Butler privately claim that over 200 of the 624 proposals contained in the Omega File have been implemented by government and suggest that key elements of the 1988 Education Act were the result of their initiatives. The introduction of Freeports in 1983 owed much to an initial suggestion raised by the Institute. Having the ear of certain ministers allowed it to set out a number of the practical steps by which privatisation could be implemented. The Institute published an influential book, The Privatisation Manual, and sponsors a 'Privatisation Conference' in London each year. Certainly Whitehall insiders are prepared to recommend the Institute as suitable advisers to visiting officials of former Communist states keen to follow the UK's experience of privatisation.

More recently the Institute has claimed credit for the idea of 'empowerment', a concept which underpinned John Major's *Citizen's Charter* launched amid much fanfare in 1991. Here, claiming influence is altogether different from actually having influence. Sarah Hogg and Jonathan Hill, who played a significant role in the conception of the Charter as members of John Major's Policy Unit, observe that a great many think tanks have claimed credit for the initiative:

> It is a wise child that knows its own parent, and on 23 July 1991 the Charter seemed to have plenty. The Institute of Economic Affairs traced Charter ancestry back to a Hobart Paper they had published in the 1980s, on the notion of government by contract. Madsen Pirie, of the Adam Smith Institute, pronounced in tune with the arguments the ASI had been advancing. The Centre for Policy Studies noted that their director, David Willetts, had been a speaker at the June Chequers seminar [which had discussed the Charter]. The National Consumer Council traced the idea back to one of their publications.[34]

Despite this the Institute did invest a great deal of effort in fleshing out the initial proposals for the initiative: the Charter is most definitely something they are willing to support. Madsen Pirie sat on the Prime Minister's Citizen's Charter advisory panel (and was described by Sarah Hogg as a 'stalwart member' of the panel[35]) until he chose to resign his position earlier this year. His membership may not in itself demonstrate a role for the Institute any more than the appointment of the Chairman of Boots the chemist, Sir James Blyth, to chair the advisory panel indicates that his company was of any particular importance. Naturally any think tank is prepared to claim credit where ever it can: The more it is thought to influence government policy, the higher its reputation and the more likely it is to influence government policy in the future.

If not yet a part of the unwritten British Constitution, conservative think-tanks, among them the Adam Smith Institute, have had some impact on British politics, their neo-liberal appeal exercising a modicum of influence upon public policy. By its very nature this influence is difficult to assess: Pirie (who is said to enjoy a friendly relationship with John Major) claims that he sees the Prime Minister eight or nine times a year, whereas he saw Thatcher only once or twice.[36] But the influence his Institute wields is at the margin, it is at best able only to encourage and warn from the outside rather than advise or decide from the inside. In this capacity, as part of the political community which inhabits Whitehall and Westminster, conservative think tanks have none the less demonstrated some clout. The intellectual climate has changed in their favour and their efforts have showed some figures on the centre-left how best they may follow their example.[37]

The changed political circumstances of the 1980s gave these think tanks the space in which to pursue their ideas. Only when conventional thinking has been breached and some form of new paradigm established can practical ideas to enact policy in line with the new paradigm be successfully advanced. It becomes easier to demonstrate the chosen method in which a practical problem can be tackled. To return to the analogy of 'pushing at a series of doors', the Adam Smith Institute found it easier to push at a half open door than one which was firmly shut. The rise of neo-liberalism (and economic liberalism in general) and the abandonment (in practice if not yet in theory) of full employment policies in the 1970s was not based on the force of the intellectual arguments of the New Right. It was a product of a new demand for ideas within the Conservative Party that reflected the socio-economic predicament of the United Kingdom during the 1960s and 1970s. The Thatcher-led Conservatives were simultaneously a receptive audience and the champion of those ideas promoted by a neo-liberal political community which numbered within its ranks think tanks such as the Adam Smith Institute: Where that government and its successor led, out-riding conservative think tanks followed.

NOTES

1. Tim Hames and Richard Feasey, 'Anglo-American Think tanks under Reagan and Thatcher', in Andrew Adonis and Tim Hames (eds.), A Conservative Revolution? The Thatcher-Reagan Decade in Perspective, (Manchester: Manchester University Press, 1994), p.233.
2. Guardian, 21 Nov. 1994.
3. Dennis Kavanagh, Thatcherism and British Politics; The End of Consensus? (Oxford: Oxford University Press (2nd edn.), 1990), p.88.
4. Richard Cockett, Thinking the Unthinkable; Think Tanks and the Economic Counter-Revolution, 1931–1983 (London: HarperCollins, 1994), p.285.
5. Promotional brochure issued by the Adam Smith Institute, Summer 1995.
6. Cockett, Thinking the Unthinkable, op. cit., p.282.
7. John Maynard Keynes, The General Theory of Employment, Money and Interest (London: Macmillan, 1936), p.383.
8. Madsen Pirie, Micropolitics: The Creation of Successful Policy (Aldershot: Wildwood House, 1988).
9. Cockett, Thinking the Unthinkable, op. cit., p.283.
10. Pirie, Micropolitics, op. cit., p.267.
11. Ibid. p.269.
12. Critics may suggest that the Adam Smith Institute is indeed a single issue campaign, a fervent crusader for economic liberalism, where all too often 'the recital of the free market prayerwheel [is] a sufficient substitution for reasoned argument': Simon James, 'The Idea Brokers: The Impact of Think tanks on British Government', Public Administration. Vol.71 (Winter 1993), p.503.
13. Kavanagh, Thatcherism and British Politics, op. cit., p.88

14. See James Allen Smith, *The Idea Brokers: Think Tanks and the New Policy Elite* (New York: Free Press, 1991).
15. Ibid., p.195.
16. The forward to the document claims the Omega File is an initiative 'designed to research new ideas, to develop new policy initiatives, to analyse the obstacle to change and to bring forward into public debate new options which could overcome the conventional difficulties'. Some 98 named individuals are acknowledged for their assistance, many of them identifiable Conservative and neo-liberal activists and numbered among them are three serving members of John Major's Cabinet: Michael Forsyth, Michael Portillo and Peter Lilley.
17. Promotional leaflet issued by the Adam Smith Institute, Summer 1995.
18. Smith, *The Idea Brokers*, op. cit., p.xv.
19. James, 'The Idea Brokers', op. cit., p. 492
20. Ibid., p.492.
21. Smith, *The Idea Brokers*, op. cit., p.xiii.
22. Promotional brochure issued by the International Division of the Adam Smith Institute, Summer 1995.
22. John Barnes and Richard Cockett, 'The Making of Party Policy', in Anthony Seldon and Stuart Ball (eds.), *The Conservative Century: The Conservative Party since 1900* (Oxford: Oxford University Press 1994).
24. See Cockett, *Thinking the Unthinkable*, op. cit.
25. Kenneth Baker, *The Turbulent Years: My Life in Politics* (London: Faber & Faber 1993), p.162.
26. Tim Hames and Richard Feasey, *Anglo-American Think tanks under Reagan and Thatcher*, op. cit., p.231
27. Margaret Thatcher, *The Downing Street Years* (London: HarperCollins 1992); Nigel Lawson, *The View From Number Eleven: Memoirs of a Tory Radical* (London: Bantam Press 1992); Nicholas Ridley, *My Style of Government* (London: Hutchinson 1991); Geoffrey Howe, *Conflict of Loyalties* (London: Macmillan, 1994).
28. *Guardian*, 21 Nov. 1994.
29. Michael Crick and Adrian Van Klaveren, Mrs Thatcher's Greatest Blunder, *Contemporary Record*, Vol.5, No.3 (Winter 1991), p.407.
30. Ibid., p.406. They suggest that 'the Adam Smith Institute itself has been quick to take responsibility for the Poll Tax' and that 'left wing critics may like people to believe the poll tax was foisted on ministers by a mysterious right wing body'.
31. Ibid., p.407. 'Nobody involved in government work on the tax in 1984 and 1985 believed that the Adam Smith Institute had any influence at all. 'Never heard of him', says one of the leading officials of Douglas Mason, though others were vaguely aware of his ideas'.
32. David Butler, Andrew Adonis and Tony Travers, *Failure in British Government: The Politics of the Poll Tax* (Oxford: Oxford University Press 1994), p.286.
33. Ibid.
34. Sarah Hogg and Jonathan Hill, *Too Close to Call: Power and Politics -John Major in No 10* (London: Little, Brown 1995), p.103
35. Ibid., p.104.
36. *Guardian*, 21 Nov. 1994.
37. As the foundation of the Institute for Public Policy and Demos aptly demonstrates. The founders of Demos, Martin Jacques and Geoff Mulgan, were greatly influenced by the way in which the Adam Smith Institute was organised. Indeed Demos appears to have literally copied its *modus operandi* from the Institute and Jacques sought detailed advice from Pirie and Butler on how to establish his think tank.

The Institute of Economic Affairs: Undermining the Post-War Consensus

CHRISTOPHER MULLER

The Institute of Economic Affairs was founded in 1955, as a research educational charity, to examine the role of 'markets and pricing systems as technical devices for registering preferences and apportioning resources'. The IEA is financed by a series of voluntary contributions, sales of publications and conference fees, but has ensured that it is not over-dependant on a particular source of income to guarantee academic independence. The IEA began to publish regularly in 1957, with much of its work based on micro-economic analysis. Whilst remaining conspicuously free of any political organisation, the Institute has been able to provide a consistent alternative analysis to the collectivist macro-economic hegemony, which existed from the 1950s to 1970s. Much of the success of the IEA came during the 1970s, when politicians began to question the role of the state in economic life. Through publications IEA authors had caused the prevailing intellectual climate to be re-considered, with the benefits of markets being more understood. During the 1980s much of the IEA's philosophy was adopted in practical terms, with the political and economic agenda having shifted away from Keynesian collectivism, and towards classical liberalism. The end of the 1980s brought difficulties for the IEA, both internally and externally, and the 1990s has seen a far broader intellectual outlook in its analysis, not least with public choice economics.

Introduction

The Institute of Economic Affairs is unusual among the other think tanks discussed in this volume, partly because its early history has been recorded in some detail by Richard Cockett[1] and partly because of the length of time it has been established. Many of the other think tanks considered are relatively new creations, indeed often in response to the work of the IEA.[2] Having been established to conduct a war of ideas against the political and economic consensus, it has seen in recent years both an explosion of think tanks leading to an almost suffocating environment in which to proffer ideas, and a decline in the perceived popularity of many of the main tenets of Thatcherism, although the Institute would reject the journalistic appellation 'Thatcherite'.[3] Furthermore, the familiarity and acceptance of broad liberal economic ideas, not least by Tony Blair and 'New Labour', has meant that much of the philosophical agenda of the IEA is no longer novel, and detailed solutions in the form of implementation are far more

Christopher Muller, St Dunstan's College.

sought, something which the IEA intentionally avoided. It should also be noted that the IEA itself holds no corporate view, but seeks to convey public understanding concerning the role of markets in the political and economic sphere. In this respect, unlike many of the recently created think-tanks, the IEA was not established to search for an idea, but to promote one: market philosophy.

This study of the history and influence of the IEA will attempt to show that much of its strategy was largely successful, and that it has been relatively instrumental in inducing a genuine change in political thinking and expectations, although it will be concluded that the change occurred through the failings of that consensus, as well as through an outright intellectual victory.

The Historical Background

After the 1945 General Election popular support for collectivist ideas and policies seemed unassailable. The Conservative Party won only 213 seats. The Liberal Party was all but wiped off the political map: the Labour Party, however, was committed to the establishment of the welfare state as had been advocated by William Beveridge in 1942; the nationalisation of many major industries; and government planning of the economy. The political agenda, it seemed to many commentators, had changed for good.

In academic circles the arguments between the proponents of economic liberalism and Keynesian intervention had also tilted decisively in favour of Keynes. In his criticism of the market mechanism, Keynes had shifted ideas concerning macro-economic analysis away from the liberal economic approach towards a far wider role for the government in economic affairs. In social policy too, The Beveridge Report had laid the foundation to extend state intervention in areas such as housing, welfare and pensions.

The government's ability to plan and run the economy had been tried and tested in exceptional circumstance of war. For many, the idea of an unfettered free market seemed both out-dated and out of date. The post-war electorate still possessed strong memories of the severe and prolonged unemployment and poverty of the 1930s and vehemently sought a 'New Jerusalem' for the soldiers and families who had suffered so much before and during the war. In such areas as health, education, employment, and the economy, the government was believed to have a moral and political duty to intervene and organise. With such feelings prevalent amongst the populace, social and economic collectivism flourished.

The argument for greater state intervention had been gaining progressively more ground throughout the Second World War, despite the fact that many liberals had become increasingly concerned as to the direction of policy. Aware of the growing consensus, F.A. Hayek, at the time a little-known political philosopher at the London School of Economics, attempted to highlight many of his own fears for the future within an academic environment in his short book *The Road to Serfdom*, published in 1944. However, his warnings had little political impact, although the book itself was remarkably popular and was to some extent adopted as a source of intellectual guidance by the Conservative Party before the 1945 election, the party itself being too pre-occupied with the war to establish a counter-balance to the new thinking of the time.

However small the electoral impact had been, Hayek's analysis was shared by the small number of economic liberal academics and politicians. For many of them he had articulated their own suspicions and concerns as to the extension of the role of the state in individual lives, and the destruction of prosperity by the progressive collectivist ideas.

Among Hayek's readers was a young RAF pilot, Antony Fisher who had read the *Reader's Digest* condensed version of Hayek's work in 1945. Fisher was born in 1915 and educated at Eton, then Trinity College, Cambridge. During the war he had become unusually interested and concerned about the intellectual advance and political acceptance of socialism. His instinctive fears were reinforced on his reading of the *Road to Serfdom* and ,being well-educated and moderately well-financed, seriously considered entry into politics, in order to halt, as he saw it, the march of socialism.

By chance Fisher had decided to seek out Hayek himself in order to ascertain what Hayek thought would be the best possible course of action. He advised Fisher that his entry into politics would prove to be a waste of his time and effort. Drawing on Keynes's dictum that it was ideas, not vested interests, which caused political change and challenged intellectual consensus,[4] Hayek suggested to Fisher that he might establish a scholarly, research foundation, intended to promote and extend the ideas of the free market and the free society. Hayek at the time correctly believed that the current economic and political consensus had shifted strongly against liberalism and it would be at least another twenty years before that consensus could be thoroughly and practically challenged. The research institute would be created to influence the 'academic scribblers' and intellectuals who shaped, promulgated and even advertised ideas in an attempt to advance not only the abstract philosophical principle of liberalism but also the application of markets to practical affairs within the current economic and social sphere. Fisher had insufficient funds to create such an institute in 1945,[5] but the idea did not leave him. In 1947 he happened to hear a speech at a Conservative Political Centre weekend conference given by a young man, called Ralph Harris, who at that time was an Education Officer for that department. Fisher was impressed and soon struck up a friendship, mentioning the proposed institute to Harris, who was both keen and interested should anything arise.⁶ Whilst Harris went away to teach economics at St Andrew's University, Fisher worked hard at establishing his business, as well as campaigning against subsides in farming, the Egg Marketing Board, and the Milk Marketing Board. His financial fortunes were transformed in 1952 by a trip to the United States for the purpose of examining the work and method of the Foundation of Economic Education. During the trip he was shown a new farming method at Ithaca. Fisher, impressed both by the revolutionary method of broiler chicken-farming and the work of the FEE, was thus equipped with both the means and method of establishing a research institute when he returned back to England.

The Liberal Heritage

In order to acquire practical advice on establishing such an institute, Fisher sought out Oliver Smedley. Major Smedley was an activist for the cause of liberalism, believing passionately in the beneficial effect of markets, and at the time was himself running a large number of free-trade campaigns. Unlike Fisher, who was a Conservative, Smedley was a Liberal Party member, but was convinced of the necessity to persuade the intellectual elite of the advantages of markets and the dangers of planning.⁷ Fisher had met Smedley at an organisation called 'The Society of Individualists'. Smedley, having viewed with dismay his own party becoming ever more keen to accept and embrace the concept of collectivism, was singularly disillusioned at the time and therefore highly receptive when Fisher approached him with his idea of establishing a research institute to examine the theory of the price mechanism and the application of markets.

Smedley was not the only disillusioned liberal who was attracted to Fisher's cause, and much of the new thinking behind economic liberalism from the 1950s to 1970s was driven not by Conservatives but by former members of the Liberal Party, among whom were Arthur Seldon, and two LSE academics Jack Wiseman and Alan Peacock who had also become similarly dis-spirited with the political course taken by the Liberal Party.⁸

In the embryonic stages of the Institute's formation Smedley had two key roles. First, he allowed the new institute to use the services of his own organisation, Investment and General Management Limited, in particular its accommodation and facilities. This was to prove essential if the new institute was to survive and flourish. Second, he provided the name for the new institute. Thus on the 9 November 1955, a legal charitable entity, called the Institute of Economic Affairs, was created.⁹

Initial Strategy and Finance

The motives and aims of the IEA had thus been thought-out and considered, over a ten year gestation period.[10] Smedley and Fisher were drawing on Hayek's advice that the process of creating an intellectual change would be long and drawn out. They both saw that it was vital to ignore the immediate political climate and to refuse allegiance with any particular party. The IEA, therefore, sought to avoid any direct political attachment and, through the diversification of financial support, the accusation of being locked to one vested interest, an important consideration both for the intellectual honesty of its work and for its charitable status.

Furthermore, the decision to consider and analyse the role of markets on micro-economic topics and exposing them to the critique of the price mechanism, enabled the Institute in its early years to pursue a slow, scholarly and steady course of influencing the climate of ideas at a time in the 1950s and 1960s when the Keynesian macro-economic analysis was dominant and virtually. unquestioned. In this role the IEA could, it was hoped, achieve the task of explaining the workings and blessings of the free-market to Hayek's 'second-hand dealers in ideas', such as journalists, broadcasters, teachers, students and political commentators.

The exact early financing of the IEA appears to be in a some doubt, and in recent years has been the subject of dispute. Richard Cockett has suggested that the three trustees, Antony Fisher, Oliver Smedley, and Smedley's colleague J.S Harding each contributed £100 to the Institute's first capital. The initial working capital was provided by Fisher together with the founder of the fund raising organisation, the British United Industrialists, Sir Robert Renwick who each contributed a sum of £500. Upon the move from the City office to Hobart Place, Fisher privately promised Harris to cover expenses up to £10,000, but explained that he would rather use such capital in his business, if funds could be raised elsewhere. Although demands on this scale were not regularly made upon him, the Trustees in 1960 thought it prudent to insure Fisher's life, to cover the possible loss of the Institute's chief guarantor. Inevitably there were financial difficulties in the early years, and the minute book from 1959 confirms that frequent meetings took place to consider the financial problems. This is best conveyed by the documents from July to December 1961, showing expenditure at £4,250 and income at £1,352. Further meetings noted that printing bills were high, and the bank overdraft was increased from £1,000 to £2,500. By December 1960 Fisher was contributing £1,000 per month, and it was minuted in a Trustee's meeting that 'Mr Fisher accepted responsibilty for providing whatever proves necessary' to Fisher himself added by hand before formally signing 'within an annual limit of £30,000'. By the time, Fisher's financial support was reduced due to financial difficulties in the 1960s, the IEA leadership had been able to ensure that funding was forthcoming from a growing number of diverse companies. A multiplicity of contributions was essential from the beginning as it enabled the Institute to pursue subjects disinterestedly and independently.

An Advisory Council was also established which consisted of Lord Granchester, who had previously founded the International Liberal Exchange, the economists George Schwartz, Graham Hutton, and Colin Clark, the financial journalist Sir Oscar Hobson and Professor Eric Nash.[11]

The reaction from the outside world to the new Institute was muted. Indeed only one MP took any interest in its formation, Major Freddie Gough,[12] a neighbour of Fisher's in Sussex. However public awareness had begun to grow already, by July 1955, four months before its formal creation, with the publication of *The Free Convertibility of Sterling* by George Winder, which was the first pamphlet commissioned under the auspices of the IEA Fisher had wisely commissioned an economist to write about his specialised subject, thus ensuring academic validity, and had placed it in the hands of a sympathetic journalist on completion, Henry Hazlitt. This favourable review by Hazlitt in *Newsweek*'s 'Business Tides' column ensured that the publication was far more popular than it might have been and the event was an important lesson for the future success of the IEA.

The Importance of Harris and Seldon

If the IEA was to survive in what would soon become a full time exercise in persuasion then some permanent staff had to be found. Fisher realised that with a full-time job at Buxted Chickens, he himself was not equiped for the required task and therefore began to search for a, initially, part-time Director. Smedley had admitted that he was 'doing more than he could'[13] and Fisher had already considered whom he wanted. Consequently Fisher wrote to Ralph Harris at St. Andrew's to offer him the job of Director, which, after several reassurances of the seriousness of the offer and the initial success of the IEA, he accepted, and was duly appointed on 5 July 1956.[14]

Harris was the 'intellectual salesman' that Fisher and the new Institute needed. Committed to the cause of economic liberalism, his contacts in the world of academe formed from his time at St. Andrews and his journalist work with the *Glasgow Herald* would prove invaluable in finding support both intellectually and financially for the Institute. As a partner to Harris, an Editorial Director was sought who would oversee the activity of publication. Arthur Seldon was recommended by Lord Granchester who had come to know him through Seldon's work on *The Owl*, the journal of the International Liberal Exchange. Seldon had been educated at the London School of Economics, where he was taught by Lionel Robbins, Arnold Plant and Hayek. Both Harris and Seldon were equally convinced that the method suggested by Hayek in causing intellectual change had to be adopted and were well aware that the fruits of their labour would not necessarily come about until another ten or twenty years. Seldon himself was also concerned that the fight for economic liberalism should be conducted in as rigorous an academic manner as possible, without creating confusion and incomprehension through needless economic jargon.[15]

The first publication of the IEA under their directorships, *Pensions in a Free Society* was written by Seldon himself in 1957 as a response to a Labour Party's proposal to extend the state pension and it argued for personal and private savings to be used for retirement.[16] The publication highlighted the strategy of the IEA until the 1970s; namely to focus upon micro-economic issues rather deal with the macro-economic consensus. It was effective because it enabled specialist economists to pursue particular fields of interest with academic rigour as well as exposing the current practical economic problems of the day to the market analysis and offering alternative solutions. Furthermore, by ensuring that the pamphlets were readable and cheap (highly important in the crucial market of university and 'A' level students) the IEA could hope to reach as wide a market as possible.

Influence during the 1960s

The IEA's publications grew more frequent as each year passed, but it was not until after 1960 that the IEA began to be seen by some economic and political commentators as a potential source of thoughtful and respectable comment and criticism.[17] The first, published as a Hobart Paper, which caused not only press comment but was the possible motivation of government action was Basil Yamey's *Resale Price Maintenance and Shoppers' Choice*.[18] Yamey argued for the abolition of the Resale Price Maintenance and made his case highly effective politically by pointing out that its abolition would save the average shopper £3 10s a year. Surprisingly its abolition was brought about in 1964 by the then President of the Board of Trade, Edward Heath, who at a lunch at the IEA in the same year had made it quite clear in his view where the impetus for such a policy had come from.[19]

The second was the publication of a book, important not so much for its impact but as a guide as to the kind of individual who was becoming more prepared to write for the IEA Whilst never a conventional party politician, Enoch Powell had nevertheless been a Financial Secretary to the Treasury only two years before and would be soon be a Cabinet Minister.[20] His IEA book *Saving in a Free Society* was also well-publicised and favourably reported, not least by the *Financial Times*, declaring that it 'was of interest to all men of affairs'.[21]

The third significant publication of 1960 was an attempt by the IEA to challenge the prevailing macro-economic consensus and was the first of a long line of publications linking the supply of money to the rate of inflation. The IEA's *Not Unanimous* was a critique of a report of a committee on monetary policy chaired by Lord Radcliffe in 1959 and was the beginning of the attempt to assign a much greater role of responsibility for inflation to government through its manipulation and expansion of the money supply. Indeed, as it will later be shown, the importation of the theory of monetarism through its most eloquent advocate, Professor Milton Friedman of the University of Chicago, to Britain, rests largely with the efforts of the IEA.

Assessments of the influence upon the government, its thinking, and its decision-making process by external sources are inevitably problematic because of the inaccessibility of government files and documents, and the IEA is not an exception to this difficulty. Moreover this task is made more difficult because the IEA engaged less in offering practical solutions and means of implementation to government and rather sought to change the climate in which government thinking was taking place. However fresh research provides an understanding both of the response by government officials to the work undertaken by the Institute at this time and of the alleged weaknesses which were present, certainly in the early part of its history, in many of the publications produced.[22] At almost the very beginning of its inception the IEA had commissioned a number of Research Reports, which would base its study around empirical research within economic analysis, leading to recommendations for policy. The first of these was in 1959, with the 'Survey of Large Companies' conducted by Harris himself and a new recruit to the IEA Michael Solly. However, the most interesting and in many ways the most important was 'Choice in Welfare' published in 1963.[23] The report was an attempt to deploy in market research which, it was argued, demonstrated that 'a majority of the adult male population favoured a switch of public welfare towards a concentration of benefits for those who need them and a development of private alternatives for those who wish them'.[24] The report was read in August of 1963 by Otto Clarke, a second permanent secretary in charge of the public sector group, who, together with John Boyd-Carpenter, the Financial Secretary, established an inquiry to discuss the reports findings.[25] Boyd-Carpenter himself declared at a meeting on 24 October 1963 that he was not personally keen on the report's conclusions, although Clarke was attracted to the idea that people might pay for the use of public services. The departmental reaction was hostile: the Department of Health did not even reply to the document in writing, whereas the Education Department dismissed it as running 'counter to half a century of history'.[26]

However, it was the Treasury itself, potentially the most keen of all the government departments to reduce expenditure, which produced the most devastating critique of the report suggesting that in general the universal benefit system was electorally popular, fair and efficient and in particular the report failed to take account of the 'danger of free riders'; namely that if individuals were allowed to opt out of the national insurance scheme, some would probably make no contribution at all, but simply rely on the state scheme. It was also thought that health vouchers were unable to provide sufficient guarantee of care for those consistently unwell.

The idea of education vouchers was seen to be more favourable by the Treasury, but it was noted that a voucher system would offer a subsidy for those in private education, thus making the idea to be more expensive. All agreed that the IEA had highlighted some important considerations concerning public ignorance about a 'free' welfare system, but much of the report condemned itself because the research had not been conducted sufficiently widely and academically to warrant serious study. The report *Choice in Welfare* serves to show that by 1963 in the Treasury at least there was an interest in re-examining the role of the state and in particular its effect on public expenditure, but the evidence produced by the IEA at that time was not deemed of sufficient calibre to provoke any change, and certainly not strong enough to counter the enormous political backlash which would have occurred should a policy of selective benefits be proposed.

The General Election of 1964 brought an end to the Conservative government and an opportunity for both former members of the government and new MPs to re-consider their ideas and policies. The influence which the external think-tank had upon an organisation as inherently suspicious of intellectuals as the Conservative Party was at that time limited, but there were certainly a number of younger MPs, most notably Geoffrey Howe and Keith Joseph,[27] who were genuinely keen to examine an alternative approach to the economic problems of Britain and were prepared to look to the IEA for answers. By this time the IEA had published a whole range of documents, many examining the traditional problems of the economy and 28 Hobart Papers which sought to offer market solutions to long standing economic problems; solutions to problems, it was believed, which were rarely examined in universities. However, whilst the names of Joseph, Howe and during this period Powell were seen as rising stars of the Conservative Party and even possible Prime Ministers, the leadership from Macmillian to Heath viewed the ideology of the IEA as irrelevant and out-of-date. Indeed, both Heath and his shadow Chancellor, Iain Macleod, saw a need for government intervention in the economy.

Furthermore the critique offered by the IEA was damning not only of socialist intervention but also of Tory paternalism, and therefore was unlikely to be embraced by a party which had sought in office to manage the economy and continued to believe that the government had a duty to intervene to prevent the more unpleasant side-effects of capitalism. The more free-market agenda, which was eventually adopted as policy in 1970 at the Selsdon Park Hotel, stemmed from a need to oppose the Labour government, in the hope of creating a decisive distinction from them. Thus the idea of an incomes policy was abandoned far more because the Labour government had had one, rather than through any intellectual acceptance that the price mechanism should be the means to settle the level at which wages were paid. Macleod ,himself, was sceptical of the free-marketeers in his party and of the notion that 'all things have a price', and he tentatively embraced market solutions only for political reasons. Macleod had flirted with the idea set forth by Professor Frank Paish in 1962 that inflation was caused by government's attempt to run the economy at full capacity,[28] and had therefore begun to question the link between inflation and employment. Paish was a member of the anti-collectivist Mont Pelerin Society and would write a Hobart Paper for the IEA in 1964 attacking full employment targets.[29] In 1966 Macleod called for a White Paper on employment to be published, but as soon as the Labour Government deflated the economy after 1967, Macleod ever the politician, immediately opposed their action.[30]

Whilst the Tory opposition showed little sign of adopting the free-market agenda in its purest IEA form, it was the Conservative-inclined press and Conservative politicians who began to move slowly in its direction. The new editor of the Daily Telegraph, Maurice Green saw himself as a 'very firm economic liberal' and was keen to examine the analysis of the IEA Moreover he was prepared to allow valuable space in the centre pages of the paper for writers of the IEA, in particular Arthur Seldon, to present their views and expound their ideas. Seldon wrote 47 articles for the *Daily Telegraph* and *Sunday Telegraph*.[31] Indeed it was through this medium of communication that the IEA was best able to pursue Hayek's original thesis of influencing the intellectual climate during the 1960s. Moreover, by being established in London, the authors and staff of the IEA were able to reach the key market of opinion journalists with ease through lunches and lectures, demonstrating to political commentators that neither they nor their ideas were cranks.

It was during the late 1960s that the IEA made some serious break-throughs in the economic consensus. Established in 1963, Eaton Papers were to 'examine the sources, utility and limitations of information and public economic policy'. The principle was a familiar one to economic liberals who had been taught by Hayek that 'without a structure of prices, no social system can know where resources ought to be used' and the papers were an attempt to demonstrate in practical terms the inability of government to acquire sufficient information at any one time to make informed choices. No other single piece government proposal therefore was more damned by economic liberals than the Labour government's National Plan. In 1965 the IEA published a paper by John Brunner called 'The National Plan: A Preliminary Assessment'. The Economist described the paper as an 'corrosive examination of the ponderous portmanteau questionnaire that the Department of Economic Affairs sent out to businessmen to help it prepare its plan'. Such was the severity of the attack, that Austin Albu, a Minister in the newly created Department of Economic Affairs felt obliged to respond to it. The IEA had at last begun to create shock waves through the established consensus.

Monetarism and the Trade Unions

Monetary stability and a reduction in trade union power had always been an objective of economic liberals and in particular of Hayek; the IEA did not diverge from this point of view. For the economic liberal the return to the market economy could only be achieved if the labour market became more fluid. Moreover, as inflation began to increase throughout the 1960s together with unemployment, an alternative, non-Keynesian analysis and response to Britain's economic problems began to be argued and sought. A number of the IEA's papers had already began to explore the link between the supply of money and inflation as early as 1964 such as Professor E. Victor Morgan's *Monetary Policy for Stable Growth*, but the whole theory which later became known as monetarism, was not fully developed until 1967/8, when Milton Friedman argued in the United States that inflation was always a monetary problem and government should seek to restrict the growth of the money supply in order to reduce inflation.[32] As interest in Friedman's theories grew in the academic world, the IEA invited Alan Walters, then professor of economics at the LSE, to write a Research Monograph entitled *Money in Boom and Slump* which would throw more light on the recent developments in monetary theory and policy for a far wider audience than had hitherto been familiar.[33] The press comment was considerable, and not all favourable, but by popularising the macro-economic work and thinking of free-market economists, the IEA had begun to pitch the argument at a higher and more intense political level.

Inevitably much of the interest was due to the very real problem, which had slowly begun to face governments, of rising inflation and rising unemployment, with the interest growing, not so much because of the validity of the arguments, but more because of the problem becoming ever more acute and the perceived incapability of orthodox economic methods to counter it. The most famous event in the history of the popularising of monetarism was the publication of Friedman's Wincott lecture *The Counter-Revolution in Monetary Theory* by the IEA.[34] The lecture itself in 1970 had been attended by both politicians and academics, including the former Labour Chancellor, James Callaghan and had therefore attracted a considerable public response. In attacking the Keynesian response and approach to economic difficulties and suggesting that inflation was always a monetary phenomenon it broke totally from post-war economic consensus. The IEA then pursued a publication programme on the macro-economic issue of inflation during the 1970s, very often written either by Friedman himself or Alan Walters.[35] The publications became increasingly high-profile, catapulting the IEA into far wider attention than had previously been experienced. The press began to report the IEA's short essays and lectures on aspects of business and the market economy which were published as Occasional Papers far more frequently and treated them more seriously.[36]

The Economist wrote of Friedman's *Monetary Correction* in 1974 that it 'contained a resumé of his always well reasoned views on how the conquest of inflation depends wholly on control of the money supply'. It was effective precisely because of the perceived inadequacies of the economic consensus which had been pursued by the Heath and Wilson governments. Through the medium of the IEA came a powerful critique of the causes of inflation based on scholarly empirical research which appeared to answer the problem of rising inflation and rising unemployment known as 'stagflation'. Political commentators, such as Samuel Brittan and Peter Jay, were often invited to lectures, lunches and publication launches by the IEA, to discuss and learn about the new economic theory. The fact that economics departments in very few universities, with the notable exceptions of Manchester and LSE, were prepared to reconsider their theories or, more often, thought that Friedman was wrong, provided the IEA a stronger foothold in the market of new ideas and ensured that the proponents of those ideas would be more willing to publish with the IEA It was not so much that the advocates of Keynesianism were on the defensive and unable to provide a response to the economic situation that the success of monetarism as an idea occurred, but rather that very few academics and left-inclined political thinkers took monetarism as a serious economic strategy.[37]

Hayek himself had been particularly concerned about the growing power and influence of trade unions in their ability to constrict and prevent

the workings of the market economy by distorting the price mechanism. For
Hayek it was vital to allow the economy to work freely at the micro-
economic level.[38] During the 1960s and the 1970s the trade unions were the
strongest political pressure group with their grasp and influence over their
membership causing commentators to believe that government could not
pursue its policies without their acquiescence. Their role in the workings of
the economy was conventionally seen as both vital and on the whole
beneficial. However, much of the work published by the IEA examined the
effect of union power at the micro-economic level, drawing attention to the
fact that fluidity and mobility of labour was being prevented or distorted by
the unions. Moreover, in an increasingly competitive world market, many of
the practices of the unions were highly damaging to the interests of the firm,
and therefore to the jobs of their members, whom they wished to protect.
Hence, with such perceived public support for the trade union movement, it
was a hostile atmosphere into which the IEA entered when this thesis was
first fully publicised.

Their first explicit attack concerning the way in which the unions
distorted the price mechanism and market was published as early as 1959.
In an attempt to offer 'friendly' advice to the National Union of
Railwaymen and to increase the impact of the book *Trade Unions in a Free
Society*, the IEA had ensured that the writer, Ben Roberts, was himself
sympathetic to the trade unionist movement and had benefited from it. The
reviews of one their first examinations of the workings of restrictive
practises, published in 1966, however, *Restrictive Practices in the Building
Industry* were mostly unfavourable and highly critical demonstrating that
the IEA had a long way to go if it were to achieve a change of political
opinion.[39] Moreover, the IEA did not confine itself to attacking the unions
for their restrictive practices, but also sought to expose the distortions of the
market which were occurring within the legal and accounting professions.
The research monograph written in the same year by D.S. Lees entitled
Economic Consequences of the Professions for the IEA exposed the distortions of the price mechanism that were taking place in the professions.[40] It
was evident therefore that the charge of class-based attacks could not be
levelled at the IEA. Nevertheless, it was a change in circumstance together
with growing public concern at the power and influence of the unions
during the 1970s which provided the IEA with an opportunity to publish
papers on the union issue that were highly effective and far more
sympathetically received. The fact that Hayek himself was the author of two
of the most widely discussed, *A Tiger by the Tail* published in 1972, and
Economic Freedom and Representative Government published in 1973,
ensured that the IEA was again succeeding in causing an intellectual change
within both the world of opinion formers and decision-makers.[41]

The Golden Age of the 1970s

The influence of the IEA increased steadily during the late 1960s and 1970s both among politicians and political commentators.[42] The perceived failures of the Conservative government of 1970–74 had created a far more determined group of politicians, eager to explore the alternative economic strategy as laid out by the IEA The accession of Margaret Thatcher, an instinctive economic liberal, to the leadership of the party in 1975 had given the IEA an indirect access, though unsought by the Institute itself, to the policy-making of the Conservative Party, which had previously been unthinkable.[43] The IEA therefore began to provide both the intellectual armour and armament for the economic liberals within the shadow cabinet. Although most of the party was unconvinced by the IEA market analysis (and is still to this day), nevertheless men such as Sir Keith Joseph and Sir Geoffrey Howe had been placed by Mrs Thatcher in vital economic policy positions, and their own convictions, much of which had been articulated by the IEA, now began to influence the policy and general economic strategy of the party.[44] It is well known and often recorded how Joseph made his own conversion to, as he called it, 'Conservatism' and a great part of the responsibility for that conversion lies with the work of the IEA.[45] The IEA, however, still remained independent of any political party despite the change of direction currently undertaken by the Conservative Party, due to the very real suspicions both Harris and Seldon had come to entertain about politicians in general and following the adoption and almost immediate abandonment of the 'Selsdon Man' manifesto of the Conservatives in 1970 in particular.[46]

Despite this detachment, the IEA was still keen to seek out opportunities for interested and sympathetic politicians to meet free-market academics and thinkers. In this respect the IEA established a series of lunches and dinners which enabled the potential policy makers to meet the policy thinkers.[47] The effectiveness of this policy lay in the role it played in keeping key figures, particularly Mrs Thatcher, well aware of the developments both in market analysis, and, perhaps more important for any incoming Conservative government at the time, in monetarist thinking.

It was also in the 1970s that the IEA's influence within the student campus began to be felt. In keeping with its original objective of providing a long-term assault on the economic consensus and creating a shift in ideas, the student market was seen to be essential. Arthur Seldon was able to ensure that economists wrote clearly and in plain, readable English without reducing the academic content of the publications. The financial accessibility of the pamphlets also ensured a wide range of readership for the IEA among the student campus. Many of those influenced during the 1970s have since either made their way into politics, such as Michael Forsyth who was promoted to the cabinet as Secretary of State for Scotland in 1995, or have decided to establish their own think-tanks in order to continue the battle intellectually against state intervention, such as Madsen Pirie, the founder of the Adam Smith Institute.[48]

The Social Affairs Unit

The intellectual consensus of collectivism, for so long contested by the IEA on the battle-ground of economics, had also been established in academic areas such as sociology. Arthur Seldon himself had realised that many of the economic arguments deployed by the IEA were being intellectually attacked not only by Keynesian economists but also by sociologists who were examining the very nature of society itself from a collectivist attitude.[49] During the 1960s and 1970s much of academic sociology had become dominated by Marxist thinking, ensuring another opponent against the drive for a free-market. The IEA therefore, after discussions with an academic from Nottingham University, Digby Anderson, established the Social Affairs Unit in December 1980, under Anderson's direction. Within a few years the Social Affairs Unit became independent from the IEA, acquiring its own premises. The Unit was created to provide an alternative academic analysis to the overtly collectivist outlook and thinking in areas such as education, health and law and order. Its conclusions were often unorthodox and it became especially successful in drawing attention to the problems which were dominant in education due to, it argued, left-wing influence. Its publications on teacher-training and its exposé of the left-wing agenda within the curriculum were well reported by the press.[50] The SAU publications attacked the nature of collectivism in its broadest manifestation from government health targets to policies on the environment.[51] It became a 'beacon of responsiveness' to the collectivist dogma of government in social affairs, with its director, Digby Anderson very often writing leading articles for national papers. One pamphlet argued that the GCSE had been hijacked by the left-wing educational establishment, and as a result had become less rigorous.[52] In 1995 the SAU attempted to analyse the nature of criminal activity in society and has highlighted the need for greater individual responsibility, calling for tougher measures to prevent crime itself and the social disintegration which it induces.

Thatcherism and the IEA

The dismay felt by Joseph after the 1974 General Election and his disillusionment with the performance of the Conservative government between

1970 and 1974 led him to reassess not only his political and economic views but also the need for the Conservative Party to establish a policy centre, modelled on the IEA. Unlike the IEA, which had sought to publicise the market analysis on a whole range of political areas to a wide public audience, the new organisation would be linked directly to a political audience, with the purpose of influencing the next Conservative manifesto. Much of the economic agenda accorded closely with the work of the IEA, but the motivation of the Centre for Policy Studies was directly concerned to map out policy for the Conservative Party, ensuring that there was not too much internecine competition for ideas between think tanks. Thus the IEA was able to continue to analysis markets with the unique advantage of being removed from immediate political pressures.

The advent of the 1979 Conservative government placed the IEA in an entirely new position from that which it had recognised and in which had been devised to survive. Much of its analysis had become accepted by the new government and many of the new economic ministers were believers in the beneficial effect of markets and in the necessity of monetarism. Therefore, the IEA found that often its articles and pamphlets were beginning not only to 'think the unthinkable' but also seemed to defend many of the policies of the government. Inevitably this change of agenda, through political circumstances and not through deliberate choice and association with a particular party, caused confusion with many of its sympathisers who began to view the IEA as Thatcherite. Indeed the creation of Ralph Harris as a Life Peer in 1979, reflecting the intellectual debt Mrs Thatcher herself believed she owed to the IEA and its work, caused some difficulty due to the political attachment that such an offer might entail, and the possibility that the IEA and its directors might no longer appear to be politically independent. In order to avoid any political compromise therefore, Harris took up his peerage as a cross-bencher.

In the early years of the Thatcher government, the IEA continued to provide intellectual support for the economic policies of the government and its publications tended to agree with and in many cases were ahead of the general direction of economic policy. Combined with this the publication programme maintained the policy of extending the market analysis to every conceivable subject. Recognising the minority in which the Prime Minister herself was in for much of the time, both within government and outside of it, Harris and Seldon would often invite Mrs Thatcher to the Institute in the sure knowledge that she was 'amongst friends'.[53] At crucial moments in economic policy the IEA was able to provide intellectual ammunition to counter the academic and political backlash which the government was encountering. This was most clearly demonstrated at the time of the 1981 Budget, after which 364 economists, some IEA authors, wrote to *The Times* urging a retreat from monetarist policies and declaring that the was no justification for the government's economic direction. Harris and Seldon then encouraged Patrick Minford to reply to the arguments and provide a clear and coherent response. For the moment government economic policy was broadly met with qualified approval by the IEA.[54]

The ease with which the IEA was able to obtain academic authors by this time provided the opportunity for the Institute to establish another medium through which the market analysis could be pursued. In 1980 *Economic Affairs* was launched as the official journal of the Institute. Edited by Arthur Seldon, the Journal enabled the Institute to publish the shorter writings of a larger number of academics on a more frequent and topical basis.

Privatisation was a central tenet of the Thatcher years, and although the policy was not pursued in earnest until after the 1983 general election, the IEA was necessarily supportive of it. However, whilst the actual method and means of privatisation were never explored by the IEA, the detail being left to other think tanks such as the Adam Smith Institute, the IEA did publish a number of pamphlets examining the shortcomings of political control over electricity, coal, post-offices and telephones.[55] The resultant government method of the privatisation has not been examined by the Institute, which has argued that competition is the best regulator, although the general principles have corresponded well to the IEA's approach of reducing the opportunity for government agency.

Hence economic liberalisation combined with trade union reform were seen to be largely successful features of the Thatcher governments by the IEA, in which much its own analysis had been adopted and applied. However, in the public services of education and healthcare, the Thatcher administrations proved to be no less timid than previous governments. As the market began to more accepted in economic policy, the welfare state was still considered by politicians to be beyond the market analysis. A new political consensus was beginning to be forged, one which continued to deny the use of markets in areas such as health, education and welfare. In response to this and learning from the success of specialisation in its early endeavours and through the establishment of the Social Affairs Unit, the IEA created the Health and Welfare Unit, to concentrate on these politically sensitive aspects of welfare. The Unit's authors took the view that the government's Health Service reforms were a betrayal of the very philosophy which the IEA had done so much to inculcate. In a pamphlet entitled *The NHS Reforms* published in 1990, David Green, Head of the IEA's Health and Welfare Unit, argued that the government ought to have ended the 'paternalism of providing services in kind, paid for by taxes'. He predicted that the reforms would not stop the cries for more funding nor provide the government with more votes. The Conservative government had, he argued, forgotten that it ought to 'reduce its power' and ' increase the power of individuals and families.'[56]

In education, perhaps the most personally disappointing of all areas of no market reform for the IEA, the government singularly failed to adopt the measures of education vouchers strongly advocated by Arthur and Marjorie Seldon, despite being highly sympathetic to the voucher scheme initially and despite the department being led by Sir Keith Joseph. By 1984 Joseph declared that he had failed to implement such a policy. For the IEA, the inability of its most sympathetic politician to establish market reform in education by means of a voucher system was confirmation of the analysis offered by the public choice school.[57]

By 1987 Ralph Harris, had resigned from the post of General Director and had become Chairman of the institute, a position he held until 1989. Arthur Seldon had originally retired as Editorial Director in 1981, but continued to serve as Consultant until 1988. The new General Director, Graham Mather was appointed in 1987. Mather had previously been with the Institute of Directors for six years, and had welcomed the opportunity of taking overall responsibility for a research institute. However problems began to occur over the general direction of policy and over Mather's belief that the former leadership were unwilling to release complete control to him.[58] Mather believed that the role of the IEA had to change from that for which it had been created, if it was to survive into the 1990s. The free market had been triumphant as political idea, a victory for which the IEA could justly claim credit, but a new agenda was needed. He also was prepared to take part in public debate on economic and policy matters. The change of agenda also required a change of audience, and therefore politicians had to be courted and lobbied, something which Mather felt was not contrary to the tradition of the IEA in the past. However, Harris and Seldon were still convinced of the need to maintain the IEA's original purpose of applying the market analysis to political problems and of the necessity to remain out of the overt political environment.[59] Hence they became concerned about the change of strategy and Mather's leadership.

In the meantime the IEA under Graham Mather pursued an intellectual agenda of law and the economy, the future of regulation, the application of public choice to bureaucracy, and the challenge of constitutional reform to support an ever increasing role of the market. The IEA also commissioned numerous surveys, not least amongst economic departments in universities throughout the country to gauge to what extend it had been successful in causing an intellectual change within academic circles throughout the previous 30 years. The results were disappointing as most of the departments still proved to be predominantly Keynesian in outlook, leading to the gloomy conclusion that the market ideology had not been as favourably received as it had been in the outside world. Although Hayek himself would not necessarily have been surprised by this finding.[60]

The dispute between the two styles of leadership continued, leading to much acrimony on both sides and often considerable press coverage. The battle for the leadership of the Conservative Party, with the eventual fall of Margaret Thatcher in November 1990 also created tensions within the Institute. Eventually Graham Mather resigned in 1992.

The New Agenda?

After the resignation of Mather the IEA employed a new General Director, John Blundell in January 1993, who had studied economics at the LSE and had learnt his free market lessons from IEA publications. A year earlier a new Editorial Director was appointed, Professor Colin Robinson. Robinson was the professor of economics at the University of Surrey, being both an IEA author of long standing as well as a member of the IEA Academic Advisory Board for the previous ten years. The direction of the IEA began to return to its former objective of consistently applying free market analysis to the changing and evolving political arena without overt political lobbying. There was a continuation of aspects of the Mather agenda, not least with public choice analysis and regulation. In this respect many of the former ideological battles have changed; away from the consideration of the benefits of markets compared with government economic planning, to the nature of the form of capitalism which ought to succeed socialism.

The IEA, therefore, has commissioned studies examining the notion of regulation in all its manifestations, with the view that competition is the best and most efficient regulator. With such a philosophy and analysis, the centre of intellectual gravity has moved into the spheres of environmental and European regulation, together with a sustained critique upon the ever-increasing size of public expenditure in maintaining a welfare state, fortified not least by the economics of politics critique as expressed in public choice analysis. The IEA has also benefited from specialisation and a realisation that a dry, economic analysis is not sufficient in an attempt to create a complete intellectual and political change. The success of the Social Affairs Unit, whilst no longer a part of the IEA, and the Health and Welfare Unit, has led to the further creation of units within the Institute, the Environmental Unit and The Education and Training Unit. The Environmental Unit was established in 1993 to apply the market analysis to environmental problems. Interestingly the harnessing of the price mechanism to combat environmental damage has met with broad approval from many other left-inclined think tanks. This flexiblity of response to the changing agenda has created new ground on which the IEA has been able to provide new solutions to new problems.

The IEA has also began to identify the thinkers of the future by targeting students with an effective Student Outreach Programme, taking note of the fact that many of today's thinkers and politicians were themselves influenced by the publications of the IEA as students. Much of the work, such as catering for working lunches and the organisation of the one-day conferences, is sub-contracted out. Publications continue to be core of the IEA work. The Editorial Director commissions, reviews and edits the writings in detail with the authors, and has the pieces refereed in the same way as other academic organisations, namely a blind refereeing process, in which the referees do not know the author and the author does not know the referees. He also arranges the Institute's expanding programme of conferences and lecture series.[61]

Conclusion

The IEA has had a remarkable political existence, learning from its mistakes and drawing on the wise advice of its intellectual founder, F.A. Hayek. It has been successful because of its chosen path of pursuing a micro-economic market analysis in the face of macro-economic collectivist dominance. Its attempt to maintain a continuing and unswerving line of principle based on the price mechanism and markets, and its willingness to reject political compromise to gain short-term political results, has enabled the institute to remain independent of party and flexible to deal with anyone interested in their ideas. Being located in a highly centralised capital has provided the Institute with the opportunity to reach the market of opinion formers through formal mediums such as lectures and meetings and informal mediums such as lunches with relative ease and immediacy. The dominance of Harris and Seldon, and the continuity of staff within the organisation created an atmosphere of loyalty and respect, vital for those who were to be in the intellectual minority for so long. The IEA has also benefited from being perceived to produce quality publications, which although not always offering a necessarily politically correct or popular solution to a problem and being unwilling to provide practical application of policy in terms of political reality, have nevertheless argued for the general market principle in terms which could be easily understood.

However, it was not all success. Indeed many of the problems which the early Thatcher government encountered in its application of monetarism were neither foreseen nor considered by the IEA authors. Ironically much of the difficulty arose due to a measure which also had been advanced by the IEA authors, namely the abolition of exchange controls, deregulation of banks and the development of the global financial market. Perhaps most remarkable was the fact that the future influence of Europe was rarely fully appreciated or explored by the IEA authors during the 1970s, when in fact much of its free market reforms could be nullified through the external legislation of the EEC, although there were two publications, one published in 1962 written by J.E. Meade, and the other in 1971, by W.R. Lewis, which did examine potential advantages and disadvantages of the then Common Market.

The IEA was notably more successful in the early parts of its career, when its policies were advocating abolition, for example, the Resale Price Maintenance, for which it was far more easy to create a consensus amongst economic theorists, than in the later part of its career when IEA authors began to advocate specific policy, about which it was inevitably more difficult to build consensus. Perhaps the best example was the IEA's advocacy of monetarism, about which the agreement on the necessity was as strong as the disagreement about its method of implementation amongst academic monetarists.

The IEA's political and intellectual success has been well noted both by its opponents, who have created their own think-tanks to emulate the strategy pursued by the IEA in their consideration of micro-economic analysis and by other proponents of free-markets who have cloned the IEA around the globe, establishing think-tanks throughout America, Eastern Europe and Africa.

In its attempt to apply the price mechanism to a vast range of subjects, political and economic, which were hitherto unexplored by the economics departments of many universities, and in its advocacy for a far greater role for the market as the most efficient means of supply and distribution, and as the strongest guarantor of individual liberty, the IEA authors, through their 'teaching' of the neglected theories of classical liberalism to politicians and journalists, can credit themselves with a part of the intellectual change in attitude towards economics and the reduced expectations of the role of the state, that have occurred throughout the 1980s and 1990s.

NOTES

1. Richard Cockett, *Thinking the Unthinkable. Think-Tanks and the Economic Counter-Revolution 1931–1983* (London: Harper Collins 1994).
2. Interview with John Blundell, 28 July 1995.
3. Interview with Arthur Seldon ,4 Aug. 1995.
4. F.A. Hayek, 'Intellectuals and Socialism', *University of Chicago Law Review*, Vol.16, No 3, (Spring 1949), provides a full account of this theory and and influence of intellectuals.
5. Speech given by Anthony Fisher at Twentieth Anniversary Dinner of IEA 6 July 1977.
6. Interview with Ralph Harris recorded by John Blundell published in *How to Move a Nation* (London: Reason Foundation).
7. Interview with Lord Harns of High Cross, 26 Sept. 1995.
8. Vernon Bogdanor (ed.), *Liberal Party Politics* (Oxford: Oxford University Press, 1983).

Andrew Gamble, in his essay *Liberals and the Economy*, notes how the Liberal Party chose to remain committed to Keynesian economics, whilst individualist liberals began to argue for the cause of economic liberalism, mostly outside of the party.

 9. Speech given by Anthony Fisher, 6 July 1977.
10. Speech given by Anthony Fisher, 6 July 1977.
11. Interview with Lord Harris of High Cross, 26 Sept. 1995.
12. Fisher himself saw the Institute as a cheap means to fight socialism, see letter to Gough, 7 June 1956 (quoted in Cockett, *Thinking the Unthinkable*) op. cit., p132-3.
13. See letter from Smedley to Fisher, 26 June 1956 (quoted in ibid., p.133).
14. John Blundell, *How to Move a Nation* (London: Reason Foundation, 1987).
15. Interview with Arthur Seldon, 4 Aug. 1995.
16. Arthur Seldon, *Pensions in a Free Society*, (London: IEA, 1957).
17. By 1970 the *Sunday Telegraph* had written in a review of the Hobart Paper 'Half a Century of Hobarts' that the previous decade had been 'enormously fruitful' for the Institute, showing that the 'market economy, so far from being obsolete, is highly relevant to many of the problems of life'.
18. B.S.Yamey, *Resale Price Maintenance and Shoppers' Choice* (London: IEA Hobart Paper, 1960).
19. A.Fisher, *Must History Repeat Itself?* (London: Churchill Press, 1974).
20. Powell had resigned as Financial Secretary in 1958 because of the proposed increase in government spending. In 1960 he was made Minister of Health by Macmillan.
21. The review of *Saving in a Free Society* by the *Financial Times* said 'It is even more interesting when his *Saving in a Free Society* turns out to be an economic credo. This is a very good book, of interest to all men of affairs.'
22. From unreleased Treasury Files: Social Service and Public Income/Outlay. Acquired by Rodney Lowe.
23. Arthur Seldon and Ralph Harris, *Choice in Welfare* (London, IEA, 1963).
24. Review of *Choice in Welfare* by David Hume in *Harpers Bazaar and Queen* (1970) (quoted in IEA catalogue of publications, 1986).
25. From Treasury Files, acquired by Rodney Lowe.
26. From Treasury Files, acquired by Rodney Lowe.
27. Joseph had been interested in the ideas of the IEA as early as 1964, but, despite many sympathetic meetings between himself and Arthur Seldon, he was unable to implement his ideas during his time in government between 1970 and 1974.
28. F.W. Paish, *Studies in an Inflationary Economy: The United Kingdom 1948-61* (London: Macmillan, 1966).
29. F.W. Paish and J. Hennessy, *Policy for Incomes* (London: IEA Hobart Paper, 1964).
30. Robert Shepherd, *Iain Macleod: A Biography* (London: Hutchinson 1994).
31. Arthur Seldon, *The State is Rolling Back* (London: IEA, 1994).
32. Milton Friedman and Anna, J. Schwatz, *A Monetary History of the United States* (Princeton, NJ. Princeton University Press, 1960).
33. A.A. Walters, *Money in Boom and Slump* (London: IEA, 1969).
34. The lecture was published by the IEA in December 1970 as an Occasional Paper and had run to its 5th impression by April 1983. It was very well received with 'The Director' commenting: ' It was a brilliant exposition of the theory which he had done so much to develop. In practical terms his message was one whose relevance was immediately apparent to the audience.'
35. In total the IEA published five pamplets written either by Friedman himself and two pamplets to which he made a contribution between 1970 and 1977.
36. Of Friedman's *Unemployment versus Inflation?* (London: IEA Occasional Paper, 1975) the *Daily Express* said: 'a standard piece of reading for all Chancellors'.
37. In his memoirs, Jim Prior, a shining example of the post-war economic consensus, said of the monetarists and monetarism: 'What began to stick in the gullet was the growing belief during our years in opposition (1974–79) that the only thing that really mattered was the control of the money supply ... I instinctively reacted against the dogmatic or simplistic answers to what I believed were very complex and deep-seated problems', Jim Prior, *A Balance of Power* (London: Hamish Hamilton, 1986).

38. F.A. Hayek, *1980s Unemployment and the Unions* (London: IEA Hobart Paper, 1980).
39. Of 'Restrictive Practices in the Building Industry' *Contract Journal* wrote in 1966: 'Betrays on almost every page how little the authors know about the industry'.
40. D.S. Lees, *Economic Consequences of the Professions* (London: Research Monograph, 1966).
41. F.A. Hayek, *A Tiger by the Tail* (London: IEA Hobart, 1972). The *Daily Telegraph* wrote that the book was 'incredibly apposite'. Peter Jay writing for *The Times* was equally favourable.
42. The reviews of the Hobart paperback *Not from benevolence* published in 1977 provide clear evidence of the respect in which the Institute was held by the late 1970s.
43. According to John Campbell, *A Biography of Edward Heath.* (London: Jonathan Cape, 1993) Heath himself would have no truck with monetarism nor with the free-marketeers, especially after the October 1974 election defeat. He was later prepared to criticise the Conservative government's policy in adopting it.
44. Keith Joseph, *Reversing the Trend: A Critical Reappraisal of Conservative Economic and Social Policies* (London: Chichester Rose, 1975).
45. Joseph himself admitted the importance of the IEA to his own thinking in a speech he delivered to the IEA's 20 Anniversary Dinner on 6 January 1977.
46. Interview with Arthur Seldo, 4 Aug. 1995.
47. Interview with Lord Harris of High Cross, 26 Sept. 1995.
48. Letter from Pirie to Fisher, 8 Oct. 1975 (quoted in Cockett, *Thinking the Unthinkable*, op. cit., pp.190–91).
49. Interview with Arthur Seldon, 4 Aug. 1995.
50. Anthony O'Hear, *Who teaches the Teachers* (London: SAU, 1988).
51. Digby Anderson, *A Diet of Reason* (London: SAU, 1986).
52. Shirley Robin Letwin, *The Anatomy of Thatcherism* (London: Fontana, 1992).
53. Interview with Lord Harris, 26 Sept. 1995.
54. Interview with Arthur Seldon, 4 Aug. 1995.
55. Michael Canes, *Telephones-Public or Private* (London: IEA Hobart Paper, 1966), and Ian Senior, *The Postal Service: Competition or Monopoly?* (London: IEA Background, Memoranda, 1970).
56. Dr David Green, *The NHS Reforms* (London: IEA, 1990).
57. *Economic Affairs* (Spring 1995). *The Witness of Keith Joseph.* (London: IEA, 1995).
58. Interview with Graham Mather, 12 Oct. 1995.
59. Interview with Lord Harris, 26 Sept. 1995.
60. Interview with John Blundell, 28 July 1995.
61. Interview with Professor Colin Robinson, 23 Aug. 1995.

The Number Ten Policy Unit

Edited by MICHAEL DAVID KANDIAH

This witness seminar on the Number Ten Policy Unit was held at the Institute of Contemporary British History's Eight Annual Summer School on 13 July 1995. It was chaired by Dr Anthony Seldon of the ICBH and the participants included Lord Donoughue, Andrew Graham and Sir John Hoskyns.

SELDON: The Number Ten Policy Unit has just had its twenty-first birthday. It seems therefore an appropriate time to discuss it, and in particular we are going to look at four questions amongst others: how it was set up in 1974 and how and why it continued in operation; how it operated, internally; how it related to the rest of the Whitehall machine and to Number Ten in particular; and fourthly what difference has it made, to what extent has it compensated for a perceived hole at the heart of the British political system in the advice to the Prime Minister.

Today's panel today includes Dr Andrew Graham, Fellow and Tutor in economics at Balliol College, and economic adviser to the Prime Minister from 1967 to 1969. He is going to talk in particular about the antecedents of the Policy Unit in the Wilson governments of 1964–66 and 1966–70: what was it that was doing the job of the Policy Unit before it was set up? He subsequently became a policy adviser to the Prime Minister from 1974 to 1976 (and most recently he has been chief economic adviser to the Labour leader John Smith between 1988 and 1994).

Lord Donoughue is an academic as well as a policy adviser, an author of several books including a biography with George W. Jones of Herbert Morrison[1] (1973) and a book on the 1974–79 government entitled *Prime Minister* (1988).[2] Lord Donoughue was Head of the Policy Unit, chief policy adviser to the Prime Ministers Wilson and Callaghan between 1974 and 1979. He is also very much the inspirer of this session today.

Sir John Hoskyns was chief policy adviser to the Prime Minister and Head of the Number Ten Policy Unit from 1979 to 1982. He will also talk about the work of the shadow Policy Unit from 1977 onwards.

Michael David Kandiah, Institute of Contemporary British History.

GRAHAM: I would like to start by just pointing out that I am rather unusual in the sense that I am both old enough to have managed to work for all of the Wilson administrations (from 1964 to 1970 and from 1974 to 1976) and young enough not yet to have died! Before talking about the post-1974 period I therefore want to say a few words about the forerunners to the Policy Unit. In particular, while Lord Donoughue undoubtedly created the first Policy Unit, I shall comment on the precedents which made it easier than would otherwise have been the case to establish this new unit.

The fundamental point is that the Civil Service was extremely suspicious of this animal. For example, when I returned to Downing Street in 1974 to work for Bernard, I knew that it was the time of year when the Treasury economic forecasts would have just become available. So I rang up somebody I knew in the Treasury and I said, using the right words, as you have to if you are operating in the British system 'Has the NIF (National Income Forecasts) become available?'. The person at the other end replied, 'Oh, yes, Andrew, how nice to hear you, yes, it has just been finished'. I said 'In that case could you send a copy across to Number Ten?'. My conversant replied 'well, Andrew, friends are friends, but outsiders are outsiders. I'll have to see about that.' In other words, one has to start from the presumption that the British Civil Service was not by any means unanimously of the view that they wanted outsiders brought in. In establishing the Policy Unit in 1974 it was therefore an enormous help to be able to refer to the office of Thomas Balogh which had preceded it.

Thomas Balogh had been the long-term friend, confidant and economic adviser of Harold Wilson before he came to power in 1964, and Wilson wanted to continue to use Balogh in some way or other. They did not, however, set up a Policy Unit in 1964. Instead, Balogh's formal title, which almost nobody gets right, was Economic Adviser to the Cabinet. This was partly because, while Wilson wanted Balogh available, he preferred him slightly at arm's length. In addition, the Civil Service did not know quite what to do with Balogh and they also were glad to keep him at arm's length. So he was given the title of Economic Adviser to the Cabinet, which meant that he need not be located in 10 Downing Street, but in the Cabinet Office. However, Tommy Balogh was not a man easily satisfied with this kind of arrangement and within about a year or so and after a great deal of manoeuvring between Tommy and Marcia Williams, his office was moved into Number Ten.

When I first went to work for Balogh (in October 1966) I was still located in the Cabinet Office and I used to have to go through the extra-ordinary rigmarole of visiting the office of the Permanent Secretary to the Cabinet to collect the key to go through from one office to the other. This was, of course, partly so that the Cabinet Office could keep tabs on who was moving about where.

Access to the Prime Minister means what is says. It depends upon the Prime Minister trusting the people working for him and upon them being *physically* close. People thought that Marcia Williams was making a rather trivial point when she complained that the Private Secretaries always caught the Prime Minister first in the gent's loo and she could not get in there, but actually the pressure at the top is so intense that being in the right place and knowing exactly what is going on and being able to intervene at the right moment is absolutely critical to the success or otherwise of policy advisers.

Balogh worked for Wilson full time from 1964 to 1967 and on a part-time basis during only 1968. He had at that time only two people working for him full time, plus two others on a part-time basis. It was, therefore, a very small outfit, supposedly dealing with economics, but Tommy Balogh was not somebody who thought that economics had a natural boundary. He did not see any distinction between economics and almost any aspect of policy you cared to mention: so he was involved with the Rhodesian affair, negotiations with the Americans, defence strategy, technology policy, anything you like. One of the first impressions that I had was of reading minutes on everything under the sun, a kind of machine gun-like approach to the whole of government policy.

At the outset Anthony Seldon asked us to comment on three questions: how are these advisers chosen, what effect did they have, and what is the justification for a Policy Unit? Let me make a brief comment about each of these. How are they chosen – the main point is that the key people have to have some kind of chemistry with the prime minister, if they do not have that it is simply not going to work, and the prime minister for his or her part has to make a judgement that the adviser has something to contribute. I think all of the advisers who have been effective at Number Ten have had both of those two things, a very considerable ability and a degree of natural chemistry with the people at the top.

Secondly, something about their effects. Very, very difficult in my view really to judge, because frequently when you thought you had succeeded in doing something, you might only have been pushing on a door that was already opening. It may have been that you were simply coinciding with advice coming from elsewhere. And, on the other side of the coin, if the Whitehall machine is headed firmly in one direction it is very difficult to stop. Nevertheless in my view the Policy Unit or its predecessor in the Balogh unit was able to be effective in two very different ways. First, when things really are at crisis point, then decision-making bubbles up from all over the Civil Service and it arrives in the prime minister's office. There are particular junctures in history when the crucial decisions really are just at the very top. At these moments, if you are good at it, and you have both analytical ability and imagination, you can intervene successfully and effectively. In my view the most successful intervention of all of the Policy Unit was during the pay crisis in mid-1975, and that was because everything had come to a head at that moment and because we had an alternative policy to suggest. Of course, not all of one's interventions are so successful. I recall in particular an occasion when the Treasury wanted public expenditure cuts of £2 billion to be prepared. At the time the Policy Unit was trying to develop a more rational approach to public expenditure and, since I knew the Treasury wanted *total* cuts of £2 billion, I proposed that cuts of £3 billion should be prepared so that a choice *between* cuts could be made. The Treasury agreed, but, once the package was prepared, the Treasury pressed for, and got, total cuts of £3 billion!

The second way that a Policy Unit can play an important role, especially over the longer term, is in keeping options open and indeed in opening up options that would otherwise not be considered. I shall come back to this under 'justification'.

What then about the justification for a Policy Unit. I offer three kinds. One is based on a theory of power. I believe in what I would describe as the 'up, across and down' approach to power. There are a lot of people in the Civil Service with good ideas, but they are too young to have reached a position where these ideas can get to the top, and you have to put down feelers everywhere to find the people with the good ideas. The Policy Unit and the Balogh unit before it had its people going out and being involved in the Whitehall decision-making process, and it helped good ideas to reach the top where they can be sent across to some other minister and go down again for further examination. But, of course, they are reinforced at that stage by having been projected from the prime minister's office.

Second, I offer a more philosophical justification. Anybody who has studied philosophy will know that there is the famous fact-value distinction. Civil servants, especially when they are being very civil service-like, try to maintain this distinction and use it to justify the neutrality of the civil service. Their job is to put forward the factual advice, the job of the ministers is to impose the values.

However, as I have argued elsewhere,[3] and as anybody who has looked at the real complexity of policy-making will know, this distinction does not and cannot hold. There are all sorts of decisions made at an earlier stage of the policy-making process which are quasi value-judgements. So a Policy Unit which knows what the values of the prime minister and of the party are, but also has technically competent professionally-qualified people, such as economists, sociologists and scientists, knowing the real constraints, can play an important part in that. Finally, Policy Units because they are not tied to the interests of a single Department can also play an important co-ordinating role. They can also play an important long-term role in shaking up thinking when the Civil Service has become bogged down. Overall I have no doubt that Policy Units can be effective and that they are justified.

SELDON: Thank you very much. Can I now introduce Lord Donoughue?

DONOUGHUE: Andrew mentioned the famous key from the Cabinet Office to Downing Street or the other way. Our rooms were right near that then green-baized door where they had to use the key. People going through had to ask for it and the Cabinet Secretary had to phone Number Ten and get permission to come through. And I always used to be so amused by this. I once acted as a regular adviser to the television series *Yes, Prime Minister,* and we did a whole programme on the key, and when the prime minister threatened to take away the Cabinet Secretary's key he nearly burst into tears.

The Policy Unit is, I believe, primarily an instrument for the prime minister's power and everything else we say is around that. When Mr Wilson asked me in 1974 to set up a unit, he said he felt that that was what had been missing in his governments of 1964–70, but he felt that they had the real seeds of what he needed, and that was really what Andrew has just described and what Andrew did. I do not think I have ever said this to Andrew, but Mr Wilson said 'you can recruit who you like, as long as they include Andrew Graham, because he is the best man there is'. And so I did. Before the first 1974 election I was doing opinion poll work for Wilson. I was politically what would then have been called an old unreconstructed Gaitskellite, that is to me almost indistinguishable from what I notice is now called the 'New' Labour Party. It was absolutely typical of Harold Wilson's tolerance that I had in fact been organising a campaign against Wilson in the 1960s, which he was well aware of, and had participated in all such matters, the Campaign for Democratic Socialism and so on, and he did not mind at all. One of his marvellous characteristics was his capacity to forgive nearly all enemies (there were about four exceptions).

Recruiting the Unit was the most stressful time I ever had, because to start with nothing in Whitehall, you do not get a lot of support, and the prime minister did not have any time, he just left me to it. Actually knowing that the people you recruited were going to be critical, and that if you did not get the best people the Unit was bound to fail, that I found very stressful. Andrew was very helpful to me in the recruitment. We had to define the functions, which was very important because I just knew that access was power, so I had long discussions with the Cabinet Secretary and we drew up a document that was unofficially called the 'Concordat' between him and me. Those who know late medieval religious history will see implications in that. It accepted and recognised the tensions between the two parts of Christianity, but it defined where we could go and where we could not go and what we could do, and it was absolutely essential because it gave us the basis of our access. So setting it up was a most stressful time, but by the summer we were fully operating.

The prime minister needs the Policy Unit in my view as an essential adjunct to some of his prime ministerial functions, not all; there are a lot of prime ministerial functions which the Unit does not often touch. But certainly his basic functions, his executive role as chairman of a Cabinet and Cabinet committees, and as head of the Civil Service running the administrative machine, that is where he needs the Policy Unit. Basically to help him in co-ordinating policy, and sometimes also to initiate policy decisions. He needs the Policy Unit in his political role, leading the ruling party in the country, helping with electioneering, helping with conference, leading the ruling party in Parliament, helping dealing with Parliamentary questions and debates. Linked to that is his image role of course, the presentation of the prime minister to the government and the party for mainly election purposes. The Policy Unit can be helpful in all of those roles, though all policy areas are possible, as Andrew mentioned.

We also dealt with every subject, or virtually every subject. I have said that we were not particularly interested in foreign policy, but in fact in the re-negotiations of Britain's membership of the EEC we were deeply involved in plans for re-negotiating in Europe. We were very involved at the beginning, though I do not know that Andrew knew any of that, on the Irish question, where a small group of us was thinking the unthinkable about withdrawal from Northern Ireland, to which Harold Wilson was quite sympathetic. But our main focus was domestic policy areas, economic policy, Andrew has mentioned the incomes policy affairs in 1975, and Joe Haines has written that up,[4] I have written that up in *Prime Minister*. Incomes policy certainly was an area where the Policy Unit's intervention actually changed the nature of a major British policy area and that was a good sort of laboratory example if you want to see what a Policy Unit could do.

After Andrew had gone, Gavyn Davies took Andrew's creation over and he had been properly tutored, and he played a central role in us negotiating over the IMF crisis in 1976. We were very involved in housing, where we got the Prime Minister and the Cabinet in principle to agree to the sale of council houses, which was later squashed by other people but which in my view would have made a major difference if the Labour Party had had that in its platform in 1979. We once came up after Andrew's time with a policy which we broadly called 'back to basics', which appears to be a Policy Unit weakness! I spoke to Jim Callaghan about it in 1977. I said to him 'we have had too much economics, you need to get the electorate off thinking economics and give them a new initiative full of principle and so forth', and I wrote him a little note on it. He sent for me and he said 'you know, Bernard, it is a very attractive idea, but I have been in politics a long time and, what I have noticed, is that it sounds the kind of idea that comes back and hits you on the back of the neck'. So we did not do it, but someone else did, and their neck was bruised for some time.

We also had a go at the professions, which I have always seen as the heart of the reactionary nature of our society. We tried to get reform of the law and got a Royal Commission set up, which Harold Wilson supported. I felt if we were going to deal with rip-off property speculators and so forth we might as well deal with the rip-off lawyers. But they blocked us on that. I learned a lot about true power in British society when the entire legal establishment moved in to stop that one.

You will be aware of course that the Prime Minister has no department or continuing responsibility, so in that sense it is not clear what the Policy Unit does, because in one sense the prime minister does everything or nothing. But what I think we found was that the opportunities of crisis are really what leads to the Policy Unit moving in, and there is no shortage of crises though you cannot predict what area they come in.

In terms of requirements for the success of the Policy Unit, then timing of intervention, which Andrew rightly mentioned, is absolutely critical. The right time to intervene. There is a right moment in the policy process; you must not go in too early nor too late, but there is a moment when the prime minister can intervene and stop something, and there is a moment when he is ready to listen. There is a stage earlier when he is not ready to listen. I think that is crucial, and whoever runs the Policy Unit, and the advisers, must have that sense.

Information is critical; you must have access to papers and people. I mentioned earlier the Concordat and relationship to Cabinet committees, and I was trying to negotiate that. You needed a Whitehall espionage system, and I think Andrew and Gavyn and David Piachaud ran the best Whitehall espionage system that I am aware of. We were able to find out what any department was planning to do well ahead, and many times we discovered what a department had discussed, what options it had considered, and we knew the option that they had chosen. Andrew or Gavyn or others were able to tell me what were the very attractive options which had not survived, and we were able to re-promote them. So information and knowledge of Whitehall is crucial.

Because access to the Prime Minister is crucial and I realised location was important I chose those rooms close to the Cabinet Room and close to the stairs to the study. Indeed on the evening we went with Wilson to

Buckingham Palace, when he was accepted to be Prime Minister, Joe Haines and I were with him, but our discussion was all about location, where should our offices be. And when we got into Downing Street, there were all kind of celebrations, we both shot off to claim our offices. I heard later that under Mrs Thatcher the Policy Unit moved to the third floor or something. That was much more elegant, but in my view it was a bit further away.

It is also very important that the prime minister should trust, should simply trust, who heads the Unit and who the advisers are. That is absolutely critical, that is the chemistry point that Andrew made. If the prime minister loses trust in the Policy Unit, there are so many pressures on his time, so many people clamouring for his ear, that he will just shut the Policy Unit out. One reason why he should trust them is because of the point about them needing to be of the top calibre, the expertise of the members of the Unit. They have got to win the arguments in Whitehall, they have got to have the facts and the figures as ammunition. They have to have credibility in Whitehall, the rest of Whitehall has to respect them. I thought the staff I had in the Policy Unit, I was very lucky, were absolutely first class. In all cases they were experts in their fields, and though one person was taking on a Whitehall department, that department knew that that one person knew what he was talking about and that they had to listen to him. It was also my view that they should not be civil servants; that principle was breached later under the Conservatives. I took the firm view that there would be conflicts of interest and responsibility, in that any civil servant in the Policy Unit is also thinking where he is going to be working next, and there may be times where that presents a conflict. So I personally prefer that they should all be independent, all the experts. But the credibility is key, the trust is important, you have to be able to work with the Civil Service.

Andrew mentioned the mistrust and suspicions. That was worse in the 1960s, a little less in the 1970s, and I think less later on. But you have to be able to work with the Cabinet Office, you have to be able to work with the Prime Minister's Private Office. We worked very closely with the Private Office and got on I think very well with them. If you get too isolated into a bunker in the Policy Unit, then your effectiveness in my view is much diminished.

The optimum number in the Unit is about six to eight people; more than that it begins to be unmanageable. You need to be a small, very effective, very cohesive panzer unit, all of whom know one another and are working together.

There are just a couple of what might be negative ingredients which are important to mention. You must not create mistrust among Cabinet colleagues. Cabinet colleagues will inevitably view the Policy Unit as a potential enemy, because you will be espionaging what their departments are up to and you may be briefing the Prime Minister against what they are going to say in Cabinet. It can never be a love affair, but the Policy Unit must try to maintain relations. I was very lucky, because half of the Labour Cabinet I had known as friends personally. It must be more difficult for someone who comes in not knowing them. I think it is also very important not to talk to the press. I read in the last couple of weeks statements of what the Policy Unit was thinking and proposing. I thought that was crazy; if anyone in the Policy Unit is briefing the press that is a disaster. Your job is to be anonymous. You are just a silent and anonymous extension of the Prime Minister. The moment the Policy Unit staff start having their own personalities and trying to project themselves, then the other ministers will hate them, other civil servants will be suspicious of them, even the prime minister will wonder can he trust telling them things? So I think that is very important.

Finally, I think the Unit has been successful. I suspect it is the most important Whitehall institution innovation in the last forty years. Credit is not just due to those of us who started it I may say, but to those who continued it after us, and there is no doubt that it has made a major contribution to the growth in the Prime Minister's power and his capacity to intervene effectively. I think it is better as it is and that there should not be a separate Prime Minister's department, which means more bureaucracy. The present set-up looks untidy but it works.

My final thought; what are the implications with Michael Heseltine in there now? If he is to send for the head of the Policy Unit, I think, had he sent for me, I would have consulted the prime minister first. I am not sure that two bulls in the bedroom necessarily create harmony.

SELDON: The story of the Policy Unit, and how it continued after 1979, will now be taken up by Sir John Hoskyns, Head of the Policy Unit until 1982.

HOSKYNS: I think the interesting point about the Policy Unit, unlike anything else in Whitehall, is that it has to reinvent itself each time a new Administration comes in. It has got to bring in new people and it actually has to rethink what the Policy Unit is for, because the political situation is obviously going to be different each time round.

My involvement started in 1975-6. I am a businessman; I am not an academic. I am not an economist. I am a sort of self-taught economist; Alan Walters once said I had already learned all I needed to know about economics by understanding the importance of the price mechanism, which many economists nowadays did not take very seriously. I am not sure whether that is true, but I was only self-taught in that sense. I met Keith Joseph in 1975,

I met Margaret Thatcher in 1976, and in 1977 I told Keith Joseph that I thought that the work that was going on at the Centre for Policy Studies, and also the work going on at the Conservative Research Department, was really a sort of circular debate which did not lead to any conclusions about what a government would do if it actually came in. The great point about Keith was that he had such intellectual self-confidence that he never felt he had to defend himself when he was faced with some alien species from the business world. He was immediately intrigued and talked to Margaret Thatcher about it and asked me whether I and Norman Strauss, who was then at Unilever and was working with me, would produce a paper for the Opposition about how it would win the election and what it would do if it did win the election.

The paper we produced was called 'Stepping Stones'. It puts the trade union issue at the top of the agenda and caused a great stir in Conservative Central Office. Peter Thorneycroft, the Party Chairman, said that all copies of the report should be called in to Smith Square and burned. There was a great division in the Shadow Cabinet about whether the unions were an issue which could be tackled at all, or whether to even talk about it. This attitude would have meant that they would never in fact have formed an effective government. In the end, particularly with the assistance of the Winter of Discontent of 1978–79, which caused tremendous problems which Bernard lived through and we observed, the mood in the Shadow Cabinet changed, and the 'stepping stone' thesis was accepted.

I want to talk about the Unit itself, and I will have to go back and forth a little because I want to weave that in with saying something about the strategy which we were pursuing. First of all, the Unit after the election in 1979 was very very small. It initially consisted of Norman Strauss and myself. I was not in fact anxious to recruit anybody else, because I just did not think we had the time. We were extremely sharply focused and we did not really need six people to help the prime minister screw it up, if two people could prevent her doing so. The government had a very short honeymoon period, like most governments, and all the indications and all the sensible assumptions from past experience were that within eighteen months it would be consigned to the footnotes of history, having failed to make any impression on any of the problems in front of it. So we were very sharply focused. I brought in one civil servant, although in principle I agree with what Bernard says about keeping it to true outsiders, I was lucky in this case. Peter Carey, Permanent Secretary at the Department of Industry, gave me somebody who had been Eric Varley's private secretary, a high flier called Andrew Duguid, who was wonderfully irreverent about Whitehall. In fact, he left Whitehall about two years after I left in 1982. He was completely *not* a part of the machine, he was a late entry, he had come in from the private sector, so he was a sort of counter-cultural change agent. And he was tremendously useful, as Peter Carey thought he would be, in helping us find our way around the machine quickly. We did not waste any time going to Question Time; I only went to the House of Commons about three times in the three years I was there, because I felt that was time wasted. We did get involved though in speeches and in censure debate responses and so on and we had to go to the House then, but I avoided it as far as I could.

To borrow from Clausewitz, 'strategy is simple but not easy'. Our aim was the stabilisation of the economy. We got off to a reasonable start with this very small team, Andrew Duguid moving very quickly up to speed, because we had been thinking about the sort of problems which would face an incoming Conservative government for the best part of two years before we started. We reflected on why previous governments had gone wrong, particularly the Heath government of 1970–74, with the single exception that it did indeed attempt to reform the trade unions. But it possibly went too far too fast (in fairness though it was incredibly unlucky, with the first oil shock and everything else coinciding with it). There is an analogy to explain how we regarded the difficulties of incoming governments. Imagine a bunch of builders coming along to refurbish or reconstruct a building only to find that it was on fire, and that actually the first thing you had to do was to switch into fire brigade mode and put the fire out, and that would take four or five years, then you could start rebuilding the building. What they did instead was to start rebuilding or refurbishing a burning building. Having a systems background the nature of the problem was very clear to me. A cybernetics man would say that the positive feedback from every problem was turning out to be the cause of other and greater problems, which in turn eventually, in a sort of circular process, fed back and aggravated the original problems. That sort of network of very powerful dynamics consisted of a number of things which you could link together in your mind much more easily than you can on paper.

Well, the linked problems were inflation; inflationary expectations; nationalised industries, which were at that time putting prices up all the time and at the same time turning to the government for massive subventions; trade union expectations in the face of inflation, which gave them a completely new role, a completely destabilising role; public sector pay generally; funny money budgeting, and a few other things of that kind, which all interlinked to produce a situation which burns the house down quite quickly. We therefore reckoned that stabilisation of the government finances (not of the real economy, that would come later) was all that we should be trying to achieve in the first four or five years.

That was a difficult message to get across, because when you talk to politicians they always think that when you talk about policies you are really talking about speeches. Words are deeds for politicians. Using a word like 'stabilisation' in a conceptual sense is acutely difficult. This was true even with Margaret Thatcher, because she was always thinking about how to communicate the message, which she was very effective at, and she would instantly retort 'but stabilisation is a very depressing sort of word, because it sounds like stagnation'. But to anybody who thinks in systems terms stabilisation is the absolute key issue. So that was understood, but there was an internal communication effort needed really to get that right.

One more thing on strategy, and that is that the whole of the stabilisation effort had to be conducted against a background of a very hostile trade union movement at that time. It is now in the hands, by and large, of much more sensible people and the whole thing has changed. It is difficult to remember how politicised and how economically-illiterate the trade union movement was at that time. It saw itself as having a micro role of looking after its members, who unless they secured large nominal pay increases actually had a cut in living standards, so you could sympathise with their problem. But their major, macro, role was actually to stop the Thatcher experiment in its tracks before it did damage and removed their powers and their role, their *raison d'être* indeed, in the way in which they feared it might. The result therefore was that the whole thrust of government policy was conducted against a background of strikes or threatened strikes, steel strike, civil service strike, a later National Health Service strike, a lot of disruption on railways, and then of course the final Battle of Waterloo, the miners' strike, in the preparations for which we were actually quite heavily involved. It was very difficult to get people to think about it, starting from within about six weeks of the 1979 election. It took a very long time plus the climb-down over pay claims and resistance to pit closures in the spring of 1981 before the government realised that it could not just pretend to itself that there would never be another miners' strike. That is all I would really like to say about the strategy.

I wrote my own terms of reference, to make absolutely sure that Mrs Thatcher understood exactly what we were going to do, and we did not stray from that brief. We did try to increase the Unit's size in late 1980; John Redwood was the man I was trying to bring in. To my exasperation the Cabinet Secretary managed to persuade Mrs Thatcher that we could not increase the size of this tiny Unit, which by this time had one other civil servant, making just four people trying to help the Prime Minister to think at a rather critical time. We were not allowed to take anybody else on and she was persuaded unfortunately by Robert Armstrong that she really had to practise the general rule of de-manning in Whitehall as regards the Policy Unit itself.

I left, in the early summer of 1982, because I really felt that we had done everything we could in the first term. The second term would require a bigger Policy Unit and a complete rethink. I thought it would really be about two things: privatisation, which is why I had tried to bring John Redwood in, because I knew he had done a lot of work on it; and the welfare state, which I knew was the next, much more complex and politically much more difficult, problem to be tackled, once the fire had been put out in the first term.

Let me just leave you with some final thoughts and a little anecdote about working in Whitehall. It is a strange place, it is a very lonely place to work for outsiders, and really you have to decide very early on whether you are actually going to provide what the present incumbents of Whitehall cannot provide. Civil servants cannot by definition (this is not a criticism, it is just a statement) provide leadership. That is not their job – they cannot very easily provide even the sort of pay-and-rations leadership to their own organisation. So it is difficult, as ministers have not got time to think, even those who are good at thinking, and not all of them are. Strategic thinking as anybody knows in business is the hardest thing you ever do, full of ambiguity, duality, exhausting work, very easy to just give up and say it is all too difficult.

Andrew Duguid was a very effective individual, because he was very tough-minded and had a very good brain. He told me a story when I was just about to leave. He said 'you know, after I had been working in the Unit for about six months, I had to go over to one of the big departments of state to find something out, talk to one or two people for you'. So he arrived and said 'I have just come over from the Policy Unit, John Hoskyns wondered whether you could let me have some information on such and such'. It was a miserable afternoon, the rain was pouring down outside and these two officials, quite senior officials, sat in this room, looked out of the window, and one said to the other 'Andrew, this fellow Hoskyns, do we tell him what we tell everybody else, or do we tell him the truth?'. And there was a pause, and Andrew said 'I think it would be a good idea if you told him the truth'. Andrew recounted this story to me and I was very gratified. But then I thought to myself, 'I wonder if Andrew is telling me the truth?'!

SELDON: Over to you ladies, and gentlemen, for questions. Brian Harrison.

HARRISON: From what you said, it seems to me that the Unit in 1979 was quite different from the Unit before 1979. Is there really continuity between these two Policy Units?

HOSKYNS: I said at the beginning that each Policy Unit is different and has to reinvent its own role. I do not remember seeing any Concordat setting out the Unit's role as described by Bernard. Obviously, Policy Units change bit by bit over a period, as for example during the Thatcher years and indeed the Major years, and is going to be slightly different. We had one big advantage, and I am not sure to what extent it was an advantage which Bernard did not have, and that was that we had been working with the colleagues, as they always called themselves, in Opposition full time for two years. That meant two things. It meant I knew all the key people really quite well, I always made a point of writing to them on first name terms, because I wanted completely to differentiate myself from any other part of the Civil Service. It secondly meant that, although it was a very slow, drawn-out process, really sometimes like walking through treacle, we had managed over the 1977–79 period to refine down absolutely in as crystalline a way as we could, and this is simply my business experience driving me in that direction, which of the things we were going to do, because we knew you can get deluged with paper. I remember getting papers about should old age pensioners have free television licences?

DONOUGHUE: We drew that paper up after 1974!

HOSKYNS: Yes, and in a rash moment I said 'you know, I think that sounds rather a good idea' and the Prime Minister said 'absolute rubbish, what on earth are you talking about?'. And I suddenly realised that quite apart from anything else I had wasted time talking about something that was not in the terms of reference I had drafted at my suggestion and which she had agreed. So we were very, very sharply focused on putting the fire out, because we felt that it was curtains for Thatcher and it very nearly was, because enough mistakes inevitably were made. The monetary policy, which was a central part of it, went completely wrong in 1980-81, producing a horrendous squeeze coupled with huge overspending, and therefore vast fiscal pressures which led to the 1981 budget which we were very heavily involved in. We had actually been pressing for something in that direction as it happens long before Alan Walters arrived, but Alan had all the technical knowledge in order to make that stick. So our terms of reference were very constrained.

DONOUGHUE: As John has said, and as I also observed, the Unit reflects the Prime Minister and his government, that's all. Mrs Thatcher's government to me was a quasi-revolutionary government, certainly very radical, and focusing on some defined areas. We were, as is usual with Labour, a much more conservative government, and we were managing decline across the broad front. And we had a Prime Minister who was very good at that, that was his approach.

NOTES

1. Bernard Donoughue and G.W. Jones, *Herbert Morrison: Portrait of a Politician* (London: Weidenfeld & Nicolson, 1973).
2. Bernard Donoughue, *Prime Minister: the Conduct of Policy Under Harold Wilson and James Callaghan* (London: Cape, 1987).
3. Andrew Graham, 'Impartiality and Bias in economics', in A. Graham and A. Montefiore (eds.), *Neutrality and Impartiality: the University and Political Commitment* (Cambridge: Cambridge University Press, 1975).
4. J Haines, *The Politics of Power* (London: Cape, 1977).

The Influence of Collectivist Ideas

ANTHONY SELDON interviews BERNARD CRICK

SELDON: We are looking at the influence of ideas, and specifically collectivist ideas, on British post-war policy making. I wonder whether you have any general comment about the extent to which British post-war policy has been ideas-driven?

CRICK: I am going to speak personally and one's age is important for one's perspective – having been a biographer, I make that point. I was 15 in 1945 and it took me a year to catch the spirit of the times and to change from a child Tory into a child socialist, and now a democratic socialist. I think reading one of Harold Laski's books by chance and a socialist schoolmaster had some influence. One certainly believed then that a new world was beginning after 1945, and that it was ideas-driven. It took one a long time to realise that a lot of the institutions of the welfare state were a product of the war and to learn and appreciate, this is later wisdom of course, Richard Titmuss' dictum that the war did more to accelerate social change than the rhetoric of the Labour Party (although he made his fair contribution to the rhetoric of the Labour Party). We inherited a lot of wartime assumptions, and were optimistic despite the general unhappiness of everyday life. I think it is a very good British trait on the whole: a sort of sardonic scepticism that we have somehow muddled through and can now do better.

It took us a little time to realise how well the war effort had been mobilised compared to that of the totalitarian powers. The morale and adaptability of a free people who agree to be led for the duration of an emergency is far greater than that of people only ever used to command and constraint. What I am getting at is this: we inherited a belief in the effective and beneficent workings of the central state, if it was controlled by the right people, and also in particular the doctrines then associated with the Labour Party (which Mr Blair now wishes to lose or de-emphasise) universal welfare provision, full employment and nationalisation. We did not see nationalisation as anything particularly novel, it seemed to be the common

Professor Bernard Crick interviewed by Anthony Seldon, ICBH, on 5 September 1995.

sense which had emerged from the war. The railways were working again and could be turned into a national system under national ownership, whereas before the war the four private companies had been on the edge of bankruptcy. It seems universally necessary to subsidise public services out of taxation for national priorities. The specific doctrine that we all talked about at the LSE was administrative, though I was always more interested in political ideas. One of the best seminars going was by a man called William Robson, a public lawyer, who studied 'the public corporation'.

This public corporation seemed to me a marvellous device, immune from direct ministerial interference and from the vagaries of the market. Now this may seem, in the light of my well-known interest in political ideas, to be rather an odd thing to say, but I am sure looking back on it that we were all vastly impressed by the nationalisation Acts. But in the mode of the Morrisonian 'public corporation', not the vague but passionate left wing dogmas of control by workers and trade unions.

So it was I think this old Fabian tradition, allied with the confidence of a civil service who before the war had viewed any planning as at best a necessary evil, but during the war had rather enjoyed it and done it well. They enjoyed managing and planning things, so the public corporation was just a concrete example of a general belief in planning, democratic planning, at that time. The economist Evan Durbin's *The Politics of Democratic Socialism* (1942) certainly had a great, though I do not know whether a direct, influence. I think we read him a bit later, but everybody was talking about him. So that was our belief: that there was a *theory of democratic planning*. Of course, if you try to look for the literature, you find that the 'theory' hardly exists. There was no *theory* of planning, there was a *belief* in planning.

SELDON: Could you define a 'political idea'? What is an idea and how does it differ from any other category?

CRICK: I think ideas are of two kinds, and in life they are very often conflated and a great deal of confusion arises because of this. We can mean principles, and sometimes we do, or we can mean general perceptions that shape our view of reality. For instance, I can not see any moral content, any ideal content whatever, in the concept of Parliamentary sovereignty. But it is in fact an extremely important concept, both as an organisational concept and because it affects people's perceptions. In 1776 Lord North said 'Sovereignty cannot be divided', when compromise proposals were brought to him by American merchants. He was as thick as they come really as a speculative mind, but he had this great big presupposition of 'sovereignty'. As I was saying about planning, that was a dominant political idea: we thought the world could be planned and had been planned. But to turn that into a moral principle would seem to be wrong, or rather then one is talking about a different kind of idea, as when people say 'Ah, but nationalisation should not be any end of its own, only a means towards an end'. The end was supposed to be egalitarian, but also a free society, an egalitarian, liberal society. But the implementation is frightfully more complicated and difficult than the annunciation.

A few years ago I wrote a pamphlet with David Blunkett called *Labour's Aims and Values*. It was one Neil Kinnock should have written, but somehow he never got round to it, so rather than waste my work as a 'ghost', I persuaded David Blunkett to come on board and for us to make an 'alternative statement' in our voices. We said 'aims *and* values', because both of us saw that one can talk about 'aims' as moral objectives, but one must also talk about 'values' – how one pursues these aims; as when one says 'Well, does the end really justify the means?' or 'There are these objectives I ought to pursue, but my values prevent me from pursuing them in this particular way'. So I think we both had reasonably clear aims and values. The interesting thing about the post-war British Left is that whatever muddle people sometimes stumbled into, clearly the aims were socialist and egalitarian, but the values have been liberal in a good old-fashioned sense of not willing to coerce people or to remove possibilities of choice.

SELDON: In making that statement, are you describing the reality of, let's say, the first twenty-five years of the post-war Labour Party, or are you really describing what you would have liked it to have been like?

CRICK: No, I think that was the reality. One can illustrate the general point by introducing another commonplace of political thought -the idea of preconceptions. Very often people are idea-driven, but they are often not aware of how much they are idea-driven, the preconceptions that they have. In a very simple sense, the public corporation that dominated thinking about the running of Britain in the 1940s and 1950s did not change with the fall of the Labour government, the Conservatives carried it on afterwards. The Conservative preconception, the dominant Conservative preconception at that time, was that it mattered vitally *who* governed, but it did not matter all that much *how* the government was conducted. There was not this modern Thatcherite/Keith Joseph-like old-fashioned Liberalism. There was not that kind of prejudice against state intervention as far as people on the Right were concerned as long as the right kind of people sat on the public boards; people on the Right were after all gentlemen, a traditional governing class with a strong sense of history, a strong sense of national integration. It was a very real preconception.

Now that sounds boringly sociological, but in fact it could be justified in moral terms (as I often have to remind my students), because after all it was the Burkian doctrine of experience: things were done best by people who had learned how to do them from actual experience. Oakeshott later said that the belief that certain things can be taught from books – like cookery, sex and politics – was ideology. We do not learn such things from books, we learn them by experience and by modifying the experiences. So my general feeling is that people are ideas-driven even when they are not aware of it. One could go on to the Thatcherites, where it becomes explicit.

SELDON: So that is the difference, that Thatcherism is more clearly traceable to particular texts, and articulated to a greater degree by the influential figures who capitalised on that process like Joseph and Howe? It was more of a muddy amalgam than the Labour Party's experience post-war?

CRICK: Yes, a muddy amalgam in a sense. But those two tendencies have been with the Conservatives for a long time, one saw that big business began to move to the Conservatives after 1886. The connection grew through the 1900s – Joe Chamberlain and all that. As big business came into the traditional party of the small gentry, the aristocracy, the big landowners, one had this amalgam of the Burkian experience and the enterprise culture and beliefs of the market. But it was remarkable, looking back, how rarely free market principles were invoked by English Conservatives in the late 1940s and really throughout the 1950s. There was a little bit, but most old Tories were very ill at ease with American Republicans. Then there was this gradual quantitative change if you like, that became a qualitative change. Most free-market ideas were there already, but not as the major theme, certainly not in print. We all know the paradox of the old Conservative Burkian doctrine: a suspicion of setting things down too rigidly, indeed almost of setting things down in print at all. We found it extremely difficult to find books to assign to our students on Conservatism, we had to go back to Robert Cecil and a book by L.S. Amery written in the late 1920s.

SELDON: Why do you think the dominant elite in the Conservative Party changed its ideas towards greater absorption in and articulation of free market ideas?

CRICK: I think because of the changing character of the Conservative Party in having to compete more aggressively: it had to go in for a degree of party organisation. That is not a slur, I think it is sociologically accurate. After all, why not have organisation in the suburbs, so people can come and talk suburban rather than landed experience, or rather big business. There was a curious alliance in the country of the big men at the very top of the business classes and the old land-owning class, but gradually more and more people came into Conservative seats whose experience was not of that kind. I mean, many had been to Public Schools, brought up to have the manners of the 'gentle tradition', an altruistic tradition, which has had a tremendous effect on culture etc. I simply think that there came a time when this pressure within the party, this impatience with the old guard, was I suppose symbolised in Macmillan.

Here, of course, one has come to a very paradoxical figure, because Macmillan held himself up as a very model of a successful entrepreneur, somebody standing in the entrepreneurial tradition going back to his grandfather and the great publishing family. In fact, 'Mac', marrying into the Cavendishes, appeared the very epitome, the archetypal image, of the very laid-back person who had in fact a heart of steel and great determination when the time came – the sort of Baroness Orzcy myth of the British aristocrat. I think that some of the younger businessmen and some of the younger and middle generation of Conservative MPs got a bit impatient with all that benign old foolery. Now, had he succeeded politically of course, of those two tendencies of the Conservative Party, the old one might have continued much longer.

There is a lot of luck and contingency in this. But then, once a contingent event opens the door to a set of ideas, then the ideas become very powerful. There is a lot of political contingency as to what ideological road to take. If Willie Whitelaw had been more energetic he could have beaten Thatcher for the leadership and the old guard's control continued, 'One Nation' Conservatism might have continued. Look at the difference between the way Major is dealing with the Scottish question and the way both Macmillan and Heath dealt with the very much more minor Welsh question. There was a bit of a panic in the 1960s when Plaid Cymru won some extra seats. Macmillan and Heath threw money at the problem and bought off Plaid Cymru by giving them Welsh television and entrenching the language in the education system of North and West Wales. They were shrewd old devils, those sceptical old Tories, because they saw through the nationalist rhetoric and saw that that was what they really wanted, the culture. Much more important and the dreadful threat to nationalists, when you come to think of it, was that a Welsh Parliament such as Labour promised would have a majority of Neil Kinnock-type Welsh – non-Welsh speaking. Heaven forbid, thought the Nationalists, that they should be under a majority of non-Welsh speaking Welsh! The old Tories saw this. The new Tory instinct is, in contrast, very ideological: it believes in general rules like 'market principles everywhere' and a comprehensive British nationalism. It has a sense of heritage but no sense of actual history, and talks about the Union, viewing

Scotland as a threat, as if Britain is a centralised state, whereas the old Tories always knew that if it was a centralised state it was a most peculiar kind of centralised state, with a different local government system, a different legal system and even a different established church in Scotland – somewhat similarly Wales, Northern Ireland.

SELDON: So the change in the 1970s is social change within the party, combined with a degree of contingency and the availability of these other ideas, which have always been latent but which now become active?

CRICK: Exactly. If one is dealing with ideas in politics, it means of course dealing with the behaviour of political parties, and the behaviour of political parties is very much affected by the behaviour of the other parties. So I think there was a sense not merely in the Conservative Party but in the country at large, that the Thatcherite cry about Britain being over-governed made a good deal of sense, especially when Labour's policies under Michael Foot appeared to lurch so far to the left. On the one hand we desperately want governments to do things for us, on the other hand we desperately want governments to keep off our back in certain areas. Public opinion perpetually oscillates between these two poles. Either extreme is ludicrous. But there was a general feeling growing not merely that the state was taking too much, but that it was not really able to deliver the goods by doing so – a kind of powerlessness of state power. There were the series of balance of payments crises, or the strange prestige Harold Wilson attached to not devaluing the pound; dreary stuff, but these were very powerful national symbols which discredited the idea that the state could control the economic environment. Wilson spoke about being 'blown off course', and I think he was opening the door, perhaps realistically, but he was certainly opening the door: we now have a most incredible state of affairs, compared with when I was young, in which the state is able to persuade most of the country that it has no responsibility for levels of unemployment, or that it has virtually no responsibility for levels of poverty.

SELDON: Could we just come back to ideas in either or both senses, and pinpoint the ideas of the post-war Labour government? You have said that these were essentially Fabian ideas?

CRICK: I find it very difficult to remember when we first started to say 'Alas! There are no thinkers now'. In the Labour government in the 1950s, after all, people who were in their forties and fifties, had been reading books of the late 1920s and early 1930s. So they were still talking about Tawney, Laski, Cole, Brailsford, and even Kingsley Martin. Even Orwell I think begins to fit into this picture, perhaps not as a direct influence, but he was very typical of the kind of socialist moral argument abounding. But it is very difficult to think of anybody post-war, there seemed to be no writers. So, 'Oh dear, Evan Durbin tragically killed in a bathing accident in 1946', many of us said, 'supposing that had not happened he would have been a major thinker'. Of course that was slightly daft. In a way we were thinking of 'thinkers' as people who write books. Because the subject is taught in universities, you have to turn to books. I found it very difficult to look at the general ideas of public and political opinion of that era. There was not a book until Tony Crosland's *The Future of Socialism* in 1956.

SELDON: Was this saying anything new, or was it just a succinct reformulation of the ideas of different formulae?

CRICK: I think it was saying something that was new altogether in one book. It angered the New Left very much, they thought it was a breach from socialist tradition, but of course the young *Marxissant* New Left did not understand our British socialist tradition. Most of the people who had written big pre-war books, Tawney, Laski, Cole and so on. had been on the Left, but there was also a whole generation in the 1930s of pre-war economists who were Labour by persuasion, who were Keynesians, but none of them – except Evan Durbin – happened to write a popular book. But that buzz was all there. Those ideas became Fabian after the war. Crosland was in that tradition. We got through the war with incredible public expenditure but without inflation, in fact afterwards Britain was virtually bankrupt. So, those Croslandite ideas of socialist values coexisting with and modifying a market economy were always there. But I am speaking now very much like the Cambridge historians with political ideas of the school of Quentin Skinner: not just to look at the relative accident of big books of political ideas, but to look wherever general ideas are found: state papers and documents, newspapers, speeches – even the results of the more intelligent opinion surveys. All this suggested a more pragmatic democratic socialism in a market context.

SELDON: What do you think were the ideas that especially influenced the 1964–70 Labour governments? To what extent was that an ideas-driven government?

CRICK: I think the actual government was remarkably un-ideas-driven, this was the paradox of Wilson. I ca not remember if 'the white-hot blaze of the technological revolution' was his phrase or Tony Benn's (Wedgewood Benn as he was in those days); but it was a fine bit of rhetoric because it seemed to be saying that Labour can do more for productivity in Britain than the gentleman's party of Macmillan and Douglas-Home: 'We are really concerned with getting back to enterprise and productivity; socialism can co-operate with business'. I think the contrast was between that and Alec Douglas-Home and Macmillan, their almost ludicrous pretence to be people with anything to say about reversing economic decline. Wilson played the economic card in rhetoric, but it did not work out in practice. The attempt to steer the economy through a Department of Economic Affairs broke down partly through the Treasury's opposition; but the breakdown was also through lack of ideas for policy. The Department was a product of 'drafting instructions' and political rhetoric, but policies were not there. Wilson, flying by the seat of his pants, was a superb party manager, but I do not think he had any dominant ideas except to show that Labour could appear to be an effective party of government. Oddly, that is a precondition of effective policy, but it is not actually a policy.

So the public and the press did not like his pragmatism or what determined his policies, and they did not like the rhetoric of either social democrats or democratic socialists. This was the time, after all, of Marxism, and it hardly felt respectable to be a member of the Labour Party amongst what one would have thought would have been the natural generation of supporters, the students and recent students – a kind of British intelligentsia. They could not find any exciting ideas, they had to go to the alternative Left, and Wilson's first government had very few intellectuals who were seen to be 'young' intellectuals as members of the party.

SELDON: And when Heath began to look effective against Wilson?

CRICK: There was a remarkable return of the young Left wingers who said 'We will not touch Labour, it is not the true party of the working class, it is not an authentic party of socialism. We have all read Ralph Miliband, and he tells us that Parliamentary Socialism will never deliver Socialism'. A lot of them actually flocked back into electoral work to try and keep Heath out, and some of them, perhaps in the short run unfortunately, stayed and worked in the Labour Party. They found to their surprise that there was very little organisation and numbers were very thin on the ground. So all over the country these quasi-Marxist young began to take over, and you have got the beginnings of the drafting of what Denis Healey called the 'longest suicide note in history' – Michael Foot's election programme.

SELDON: So that was happening in the late 1960s? What about the ideas informing Jenkins' reforms at the Home Office? Homosexuality, divorce laws... .

CRICK: Well, that is good, straight, liberal-radical stuff, is not it? It is easy to take those achievements for granted, or rather not to remember at which point one really starts defending them against repeal rather than advocating them. The death penalty too; security of employment; married women's rights, all saw considerable real changes. The odd thing about that though is that there would have been considerable support amongst Heathite Conservatives for many of these generally speaking liberal reforms. My memory is not of clear ideological lines, the lines were never as clear as the Leaders were trying to draw them in rhetoric, the lines certainly were not as clear as in Heath's day. Roy Jenkins as Home Secretary was the old liberal part of Labour's two-headed appearance, but it did not satisfy most the rank and file of the party, who were talking up an egalitarian project, not simply a liberal one: they wanted to talk about planning, whereas Jenkins seemed to want to make, possibly, a decent society, a sort of Orwell-like concept. Yes, Jenkins was going for 'a decent society', but he did not seem to be interested in public expenditure, redistribution of income or control of industry, as the Left were demanding.

SELDON: Why did the Thatcherite/Joseph right not draw on Orwell?

CRICK: Some of them tried to. It has happened more in the US than in Britain because, after all, here people had a real memory that he had been literary editor of *Tribune*, that he had fought in the Spanish Civil War on the republican side, in the anarchist-Trotskyite ranks. Whereas in the USA people knew nothing about all this, so it was much easier to take his anti-Communist stance as an endorsement of free market ideology, which was certainly not in his text. Orwell insisted on the spelling 'democratic Socialist' – small 'd' and big 'S'. But Americans did not catch this. Most American commentators were exactly like the Russian commentators: they drew no distinction between Communism and socialism.

SELDON: But on one reading *Nineteen Eighty-Four* and *Animal Farm* are straight libertarian texts.

CRICK: No, not straight libertarian texts. I think controls are quite important in the narrative. After all, the animals wanted an egalitarian society, but the pigs violated it. Theirs was a war of, if you like, class liberation against a ruling class. It is quite clear that Orwell favoured individual liberties but thought they could only flourish for all in an egalitarian society. So they are not straight libertarian texts unless you are an anarchist, although you can read them that way. Norman Podhoretz, the editor of *Commentary* in New York, wrote in 1984 that if Orwell were alive today he would have been on the radical Right. I find this unlikely – either ignorance or ideological body-snatching.

SELDON: Who have been the political philosophers writing after 1945 actually influencing the decisions and directions of government policy? Oakeshott?

CRICK: Most unlikely. I think if Oakeshott's ideas had any influence at all, they would have considerably modified Thatcherism, or rather treated it as a form of rationalism. I think she perfectly fits the specifications for rationalism of his essays *On Rationalism*. Indeed, there he jibes at Hayek. Some of Oakeshott's disciples, of course, who like many of us who were both thinkers and politicians, have tried to have it both ways: traditional hierarchy and a free market. Somebody like Ken Minogue tries to say the new liberal thing as well as the traditionalist. But these two things just do not square, or rather, they are a matter of political compromise, not a coherent intellectual position. John Grey has come to see this. No, I think the intellectual sources of Thatcherite policy were the old economists, like the then common misreading of Adam Smith; and, of course, Hayek's writings.

SELDON: To what extent do you see a breakdown of a Keynesian, social democratic consensus in the late 1970s?

CRICK: I would go back to my earlier distinction between aims and values. I do not think the consensus ever governed the aims of the two parties, which were quite different. I think there was a consensus about values, and those values were expressed as belief in parliamentary democracy, some kind of welfare state, taxation sufficient to keep every citizen in employment through – when necessary – public investment. The reasons why it broke down? We all have our different theories, but my impression is that the activists in the Labour Party frightened the public. As membership in *both* parties declined, militants got hold of the megaphones. Labour activists sounded too Marxist and theoretical and completely unrealistic about the actual texture of British society. They wanted to reform British society, but really could not cope with what was needed to have it actually work. There was a real lack of realism, and also a lack of any kind of interest in the national character and changing national feelings. So they had not got anything to fight the Thatcherist individualist: this strange mixture of individualism and patriotism, which falls under free market ideology as against Keynesianism. There is a tremendous amount of that in books and it has been popularised. Keith Joseph did a brilliant job of popularising complex free-market themes, which was exactly what the

Labour Party had hitherto always prided itself on: he took theoretical ideas and simplified them to political effect. The new Marxist Labour Party intellectuals of the 1960s and 1970s were poor popularisers. Kinnock was beginning, however, to make very interesting moves. He thought a lot about the need not to scorn individualism but to put forward a radical view of individualism. I think he had a sense for the sort of South Walesian respect for self-made man or woman, who rises by talent in society but does not forget his or her roots. I feel that myself, I think that is something the Labour Party neglected in its thinking. You can find it in Tawney; in Orwell; I would call it the radical ideology of the Welsh, Scottish and Northern lower-middle class, but it was not what people look back to.

SELDON: And by the 1960s and 1970s?

CRICK: I was critical of the mess the New Left led the Labour Party into in the late 1960s and throughout most of the 1970s, but I think now perhaps with the collapse of the Soviet Union, perhaps with three successive Conservative governments, and all that kind of thing, a greater realism, Hobsbawm's version of realism, becomes extremely convincing and influential. Many of those people of the New Left abandoned Marxist high theory and, almost comically, rediscovered democracy. An old colleague and former Marxist Althusserian called Paul Hirst gave his inaugural lecture at Birkbeck on democracy. We were all sitting purring with pleasure and waiting for something original for some time, when the lecture suddenly ended. He had, thank God, reinvented the wheel. Now very few were, in the old Communist sense, defending political authoritarianism or the Soviet Union, but most of them were then defending the authoritarianism of 'true theory' – an abstraction of 'reason' rather than the free activity of reasoning. Lots of them had decided that the biggest *value* is a process not a substantive aim, and this process is called democracy. Therefore not sovereignty in the British sense, nor the state in the Leninist sense, but pluralism, therefore democracy, therefore devolution of government. These ideas are now extremely strong in the rank and file of the Labour Party. Centralised state planning has everywhere failed. But the social consequences of an uncontrolled world market are already, or once again, proving morally appalling. Political compromise is not the enemy of morality. Morality demands political compromise. We do not have to destroy the price mechanism to achieve social justice – we only have to modify its consequences. Perhaps Burke was right. Liberty always turns on questions of taxation; but not always right in the way he meant. A free market and liberty for all implies far higher taxation than our politicians care or dare to recognise.

The Influence of Liberal Ideas
in Post-War Britain

ANTHONY SELDON interviews
LORD DAHRENDORF

SELDON: In general terms, to what extent do you see ideas as influential in affecting the selection of government policies, as against individuals, or as against events and circumstances?

DAHRENDORF: In an odd way I agree with Keynes on the key point that in the end it is ideas which are formulated by people who thereby become influential, which ultimately determine policies. There are periods in which policy is essentially a reaction to events, but they are uninteresting periods of public policy, like the last five years. Basically I think it is ideas, which make their way by a peculiar route which is very hard to define, to those who are responsible for action. I think ideas are central.

SELDON: But how would you weigh them alongside events and individuals in affecting the outcome of history?

DAHRENDORF: The main point is that ideas have to find their proper moment, in which they become effective. I am quite sure that if one made the effort one could find important ideas which never were translated into policy, and one could also find important policy decisions which were accidental in the circumstances, which were not informed by any underlying ideas. But every now and again there are these meetings of ideas and political conditions which make a real difference. One book on that subject which seems to me very important is Keith Middlemas's *Politics in Industrial Society*,[1] which shows that at the end of both wars in this century there were both ideas and conditions which coalesced to bring about very major changes. I do not think it was the workings of the Labour movement which produced the great changes after 1945, it was as much the peculiar circumstance of the end of the war, in which Conservatives as well as Labour politicians felt that something had to be done to thank the people for

Lord Dahrendorf, St Antony's College, Oxford, interviewed by Anthony Seldon, ICBH, on 18 July 1995.

helping to win the war. The same was true after the First World War, for example universal suffrage.

SELDON: What is an idea?

DAHRENDORF: An idea, as I am discussing it now, is a notion of where we could go from where we are. In other words, an image, a vision of the future state of affairs, which may or may not be desirable.

SELDON: Has twentieth century British history been more idea-driven than say the history of Germany?

DAHRENDORF: That is a difficult comparison. British history has been driven by better ideas than the history of Germany, but there can be very little doubt that National Socialism, with all its disastrous implications and consequences, was to a significant extent idea-driven. So I am not suggesting that ideas of themselves are either good or bad.

SELDON: You mentioned the Attlee settlement, what other ideas do you see coming through and informing post-war political decisions?

DAHRENDORF: Starting today, it is perfectly clear that the Thatcher governments were highly ideological governments, and were more idea-driven than most of their predecessors. Perhaps the same can be said, and historians will have to write about that, for the Heath government, which in retrospect looks so very different because of the 'U-turn' two years into the government, but basically it was also a very ideas-driven government. It is a very interesting question to decide whether 1964 was an ideas-driven change to Labour or not. Many of those who at the time supported Labour felt that a new age would begin, and they had some notion of that new age being a combination of technological progress and social awareness. It sounds quite topical today. I think the 1964 Wilson government was ideas-driven, and certainly 1945 was. So, I think there has been a very important role for ideas at crucial points in British policy since the war, notably in 1945, 1964, 1970–79.

SELDON: To what extent do you think that Labour governments in the 1960s, with its emphasis also on individual freedoms, were ideologically coherent?

DAHRENDORF: It is often said that Roy Jenkins, the Home Secretary, who had a particular notion which I suppose in America would now be called libertine rather than liberal, had an enormous effect on giving legitimacy and practical legal expression to an underlying change in the public climate so far as the rights of individuals to be different, even to be outrageous, are concerned. So that was an important period. Incidentally, similar events occurred in several European countries, and also in the United States, so there was this general climate of ideas. Reform of the criminal law was another practical application of these ideas.

SELDON: What is a climate of ideas?

DAHRENDORF: A climate of ideas is one in which you do not get a policy studies institute drafting the manifesto for a political party, but in which you get a change in people's preferences which affects all sorts of possible paths into the future. I think in the 1990s there is a pretty clear climate of opinion which wishes to add social awareness to economic effectiveness. So you will sometimes get dozens of individuals, occasional speakers or party leaders, all expressing views which somehow add up to a change in vocabulary and in direction.

SELDON: I am interested in why it is that some ideas are adopted, and how climates of ideas are formed, and why others are dropped. What is the role of intellectuals in that adoption, and what might be the role of think tanks?

DAHRENDORF: That is a very important question. I think in recent decades, certainly in the last three decades, think tanks in the sense of institutes which attracted decision-makers, but were run by academics interested in practical affairs, have had a very important part to play. In America this tradition is much older. The Brookings Institution has been a resource for the Democratic Party for quite a long time, and more recently other institutions like the National Heritage Foundation have informed both parties, but perhaps more the Republicans. So think tanks, where they are set up to mediate, to straddle, the world of thought and the world of action, have come to be very important, and that is true to the present day. In fact I think London is probably the outstanding place in Europe for think tanks of this kind.

There are other ways of translating thought into action – and there again London is the outstanding place – and that is Op-Ed. pages. Op-Ed. pages in newspapers do not exist to the same extent in continental Europe, and they are extremely important and do make a difference. There are about two dozen commentators, the Hugo Youngs and Will Huttons and so on, who have a real influence, and they are after all peddlers of ideas.

SELDON: Do you see the influence of Op-Ed. pages in newspapers being relatively recent in British history?

DAHRENDORF: Yes, I see it as quite recent. In a sense Alan Watkins now seems old-fashioned, those who write columns in the old sense are almost all old-fashioned, it is more the William Rees-Moggs and Simon Jenkinses on the right and the Hugo Youngs and Will Huttons on the left who have an influence. It was not there in 1945, and not in 1955, and not in 1965.

SELDON: Why have think tanks grown up and why has there been this resort to newspaper being used, and television, as platforms for expounding ideas?

DAHRENDORF: I do not know. It must be something about politics and the way political decisions are taken. It must be something about a desire on the part of leading politicians to find a background for what they are doing which extends beyond idiosyncrasy and the old amateur politics.

SELDON: Why have universities themselves not been more influential on government policy?

DAHRENDORF: That is a very interesting question. I think it has more to do with the internal dynamics of universities than with doubts of governments or early interests of particular members of universities. Universities have just become huge institutions, highly bureaucratised, very strongly oriented to teaching, too big and too busy to establish a sensible relationship to the outside world. Sixty, seventy years ago I would have said it was universities, and it was.

SELDON: So is that the post-Robbins expansion?

DAHRENDORF: Partly.

SELDON: And the Thatcherite changes to universities?

DAHRENDORF: I do not know about the Thatcherite changes. They have led to bureaucratisation and an inward-looking approach, but essentially it is the great expansion.

SELDON: The two major areas of academic intellectual influence on government have been the medical/scientific and the economic departments. It is hard to see much influence from say pure philosophy departments, even sociology departments.

DAHRENDORF: I am not at all sure. The medical/scientific is classical, that is always there, and what kind of input it provides is highly debatable. The economic has not been highly organised in this country. It is much more organised in other countries in which you get for instance joint reports by private institutes of economic research, which have a major impact on the interpretation of the needs which determine interest rates and other economic decisions. It has been much more tenuous here. Who now speaks of the Chancellor of the Exchequer's economic advisers? There are these seven economic gurus, yet one does not hear an awful lot about any of them. But I think philosophy, political philosophy, has been astonishingly important over the last 15 years or so and continues to be that. After all, what was the Policy Studies Institute, what was the Institute of Economic Affairs, what is the Social Market Foundation? They are all in some sense philosophical.

SELDON: But if one looks say at the traditions of moral philosophy, general philosophy, philosophies of knowledge, there does not seem to be a tremendous amount of interactions between these areas of academic research and government?

DAHRENDORF: Well yes, naturally I think the government would have done better if it had listened more, but I think actually the influence of what I would call philosophy in the wider sense has been rather considerable.

SELDON: Why is it that at certain points in history ideas are taken on board; why should politicians in liberal democracies become receptive to new ideas at certain junctures?

DAHRENDORF: In an odd way, there is this dialectic of popular support and the generation of ideas, and politicians are mediators between these two. Just think of Beveridge and the Beveridge Report, and the notion that there should be a universal entitlement based on a universal contribution, this notion of citizenship, and then thousands of people queuing up to buy the Beveridge Report. Well, that is quite a visible combination of thoughts about needs and pressure for needs or interest in needs, and politicians were well advised to link the two and translate one into the other. I think it makes a lot of sense.

SELDON: If one looks at the ideas of Beveridge and Keynes, or Friedman and Hayek, they are grounded in empirical observations ... .

DAHRENDORF: Beveridge and Keynes are, Friedman and Hayek are more debatable.

SELDON: They would all claim to be based on observations, readings of real evidence, and yet it appeared in the 1950s and 1960s that the ideas of Hayek and Friedman were unacceptable to the British government. Why?

DAHRENDORF: Politics can never bring about ninety degree changes. We are always talking about a fairly limited range of possible policy changes and very often that is very limited on the 360 degree scale, very often it is no more than five degrees or so. And great politicians are able to extend that range and use ideas to extend the range. But a whole lot of ideas are way outside and they will not have a major effect at the time at which they are put on paper.

SELDON: Is this something to do with the strength of money to implement ideas, and with the perception of what the electorate would want to see implemented?

DAHRENDORF: I do not think it is money. I think they are just ideas which in given electoral circumstances are not likely to carry the support which is needed in order to make their implementation realistic. So it is much more the public mood or the dominant interests, whichever way you want to put it.

SELDON: Could you comment upon the role of interests in post-war history in actually forming the outcome of decisions?

DAHRENDORF: Every one of your questions requires a book to give a comprehensive answer to it! Clearly I believe the question of class is central. There was obviously a period in which a working class interest in the widest sense of the term had to find expression in policies, and any policies in conflict with that interest, like not having general education or not having housing the way it was done, would have failed, certainly in the electoral sense. And there followed a period in which a middle class interest was made dominant. I regard the whole period of Heath-Thatcherism as the protest of the lower middle class against a long tradition of British politics. And that creates an interest structure in which some things can be done and some things cannot be done. It has a lot to do with the factor of taxation, for example.

SELDON: What is it about certain individuals, such as Attlee, such as Mrs

Thatcher, which permitted them to change the agenda of politics. Are there particular attributes of leadership that you can see?

DAHRENDORF: They are a combination of a condition of some volatility in which a lot of people do not quite know where to go, and someone who knows exactly where to go, perhaps too much so, but someone who can therefore widen the range of acceptable options. That seems to me one of the secrets of politics. There are the bureaucratic politicians who go straight down the middle of a narrow range of possible options, and there are the non-bureaucratic, perhaps the charismatic, politicians who widen this range. And also, there are situations in which the constraints are enormous. Take 1973, the energy crisis, when we did not have much choice and whoever you were, however charismatic, there was not an awful lot of choice. And there are other conditions in which there is so much uncertainty, in 1979, the 'winter of discontent', that you can move some way beyond the central point of the existing range. That is how I see politics: as a permanent conflict really between available options, a range of available options, and the readiness and ability of individuals to take them as far as possible, or else just to do a John Major and try and remain somewhere in the middle without ever knowing where exactly the middle is, but nevertheless staying on for quite a while. Thatcher and Major in that sense are the two conflicting prototypes of policy making.

NOTE

1.   Keith Middlemas, *Politics in Industrial Society*.

The Influence of Sociology in Post-War Britain

ANTHONY SELDON interviews
ANTHONY GIDDENS

SELDON: What are the main ideas that have come out of work done by sociologists that have affected government thinking anywhere, in any country?

GIDDENS: If one starts at the 1945 period, I would say that sociologists filled in the institutional side of Keynesianism. In the UK in particular, they produced ideas which made sense of the Keynesian 'welfare-state compromise' and made it look feasible for the time that it did indeed look feasible. Some of the sociologists prominent in this country during the first twenty or so years after the war were influential in this respect more or less world-wide. T.H. Marshall's theory of citizenship and social class, for instance, justly became very widely-known and was deployed in a practical way as a guide to policy making. Marshall provided a rationale for arguing that you can have a competitive, capitalistic society which is economically effective but which does not produce the class polarisation anticipated by Marx. We can develop an acceptable compromise between social justice on the one hand and reasonable material prosperity on the other, without either relapsing into authoritarian rule or succumbing to deepening class division. That work was very important and indeed, whatever its limitations, remains so today. It influenced S.M. Lipset and also Reinhard Bendix in the US, and it was widely taken up on the Continent too. It was probably almost as influential as Keynes's theories, because Keynesianism could not have worked without this filling in of the social or institutional side.

Roughly speaking, one can say that sociology over the post-war period has gone through three stages of development, of which this was the first. Sociologists like Marshall were politically of the reformist Left; the interpretation and further development of the welfare state were central to their concerns. With Thatcherism, a certain model of economics took over and sociologists found themselves on the outside. And on the outside, many became predatory, like sharks circling around. Authors like Stuart Hall –

Professor Anthony Giddens, University of Cambridge, interviewed by Anthony Seldon, ICBH.

who might or might not have coined the term 'Thatcherism' – were greatly affected by the rise of the new outlook, while at the same time wanting to show it to be fundamentally inadequate. Today, in the post-Thatcher era, there is something of a reconciliation of political positions and sociologists have a different role again. Much more diverse, sociology has a key part to play in the attempts now being made to find a way beyond the collapsed categories of Left and Right.

There is a lot of ground to catch up upon. In my view modern society is deeply sociological; it can not work without constant reflection on its own institutions. Therefore if you look at debates about the family, about inequality, education and so forth, you would not find many areas where sociological research is not vital, and where policy based on some basic sociological ideas does not set the agenda. This was true through all three periods, although rather hidden away during the second.

SELDON: How far can one categorise three sociological traditions: of Marxist sociologists, social democrat Keynesian sociologists and the right wing anti-statists? If one can, would that have been the case throughout the whole fifty year period?

GIDDENS: Such a division does make some sense, in so far as the connections between sociology and politics are concerned. But different fashions became pre-eminent at different times. In the immediate post-war period, just as the dominant political consensus was a Keynesian compromise, in this country the leading perspective was Fabian-style sociology, linked quite closely to the investigation of social problems such as inequality, poverty and social exclusion. At that time there was a distinguishable Right, but for the most part it was regarded as eccentric. When I first started studying sociology Hayek, for example, was read, but his ideas were seen as distinctly on the fringe. This changed, of course, with the collapse of Keynesianism – which it has to be said few working within the Fabian-style framework actively foresaw. Marxists had long proclaimed that such a thing would happen, but were equally taken aback by what replaced it. The last thing they anticipated was the triumph of free market economics and neo-liberalism.

Since 1989 things have changed again. Not even the most hostile critics of the Soviet Union predicted the events of 1989 and after. Most neo-liberals held the system was doomed, but they believed this only as a longer-term prospect. The fact that a monolithic power system could suddenly fade away, almost without any violence – that is an extraordinary event in modern history. It sits uneasily alongside the writings of Robert Michels, Max Weber and other theorists of bureaucratic power. Bureaucracy, and the overweening power of the state, seemed to be the main enemies of freedom. Suddenly, states seem to have too little power rather than too much, and a great deal of rethinking of social and political theory is necessary.

SELDON: So in the 1940s and 1950s the ascendancy was held by the social democratic tradition?

GIDDENS: On the whole, yes. That was a period, though, when sociology was not very well developed in Britain. There were only a few universities where sociology was firmly established. The LSE was the main one and was the home of much Fabian-style sociological thought.

SELDON: Then in the 1960s and 1970s?

GIDDENS: The 1960s was a period marked by the internationalisation of sociology – and by the widespread introduction of the subject into British universities. American sociology became more influential in this country than it was before, but it became joined with a whole series of other influences and traditions, coming in particular from France and Germany. Marxism, or left wing radicalism of one kind or another, was prominent during this period, but was never as dominating as some Marxist authors liked to think, or as their rightist critics alleged either.

SELDON: What accounts for the internationalisation of the subject in the 1960s?

GIDDENS: Several things. One was the collapse of the social democratic consensus – something which no-one really at that time properly understood. Fabian-style sociology started to lapse when the institutional order to which it was geared began to falter. Another factor was the expansion of the new universities and the flourishing of sociology within them. The new generation of younger sociologists started to comb the world for new ideas. A third influence was the rise of the so-called 'new social movements' such as feminist, ecological, consumer and student movements, all of which operated mainly on an international level.
    The impact of American sociology by and large preceded traditions of thought taken over from the Continent. During the early 1960s, American sociology was fairly well dominant on a global level. Later on, Continental influences made themselves felt more strongly. Some such influences were Marxist in outlook. For example, the writings of Louis Althusser were for a while well regarded in some quarters. But a variety of non-Marxist traditions of thought for the first time became well known in this country.

Among these one would include structuralism and post-structuralism, hermeneutics and phenomenology – cumbersome names which hide some sophisticated yet accessible sociological ideas. Sociological theory in particular 'returned to Europe' at this time as the influence of the leading American theorists, such as Talcott Parsons and R.K. Merton, declined.

SELDON: Who were the main people who mediated this change to a greater Continental influence on British sociology?

GIDDENS: They were mostly the younger generation of up-and-coming thinkers. They were not all professional sociologists in the narrow sense, but were concerned to cope with social and economic issues of the time. Perry Anderson and his colleagues at the *New Left Review* played a major role in introducing Continental thought to an Anglo-Saxon audience. One should also note, however, the influence of feminism. Many British feminist authors took their points of departure from their counterparts in the United States, but some also looked for inspiration to Continental Europe.

SELDON: Publishing houses in this country have been very willing to mediate this change, Fontana Modern Masters and Penguin, for example.

GIDDENS: I think so. Smaller publishers also played a significant role. I have just referred to the impact of New Left Books. In the early 1980s, together with John Thompson and David Held, I helped establish Polity Press. One of our main objectives was to foster connections between Continental and Anglo-Saxon thought, not just in sociology but in a whole variety of academic and more popular areas. As an English-speaking country which is nonetheless part of Europe, we thought that the UK is particularly well situated to mediate American thinking and Continental traditions.

SELDON: And right wing sociologists in the 1960s and 1970s, like Julius Gould, were very much a minority?

GIDDENS: Yes, pretty much swimming against the tide and not popular within the main body of the sociological profession. On the whole there have not been too many sociologists of distinction in this country directly affiliated to the Right. Most tend to have been either liberals or leftists of the two kinds distinguished previously. This has not been so in other countries: the idea that most sociologists are leftists of one kind or another does not stand up to much scrutiny. Some of the main founders of sociology in Europe, such as Max Weber or Vilfredo Pareto, were quite rightist in their leanings. In the US there have been plenty of sociologists who write from a conservative standpoint, whether or not they have been affiliated to the Republican Party. Peter Berger or Nathan Glazer are examples. In the UK, with the exception of some Fabian-style sociologists mentioned previously, many sociologists have felt themselves to be outsiders. They came to the subject when it was expanding in the 1960s and hunting for a place within established university circles.

Sociology had a retarded development in this country partly because of the position enjoyed by anthropology. The hegemony of anthropology was marked by its strong presence at Oxford and Cambridge at a time when sociology hardly existed there at all. The flourishing of anthropology, to put things a bit crudely, was an artefact of Empire. It was okay, as it were, to write about exotic peoples, but not to subject our own society to sustained scrutiny. Or at least it was permissible only to study the 'exotic creatures' – the poor, the excluded – in our midst. Right up to the early 1980s the most prominent figures internationally in the social sciences – outside of economics – were social anthropologists. They included a brilliant galaxy of names: Meyer Fortes, E.E. Evans-Pritchard, Audrey Richards, Edmond Leach, Raymond Firth and many others. There are few comparable figures among younger anthropologists in this country today. Sociology, at least broadly defined, could by contrast nowadays boast a pantheon of authors well known on the international level – such as Steven Lukes, David Lockwood, Ann Oakley, Ray Pahl, John Goldthorpe and so forth.

The recent generation of sociologists, on the whole, however, has not been directly involved in politics. They have not sought out, or perhaps been offered, the sort of role played by Fabian-style sociologists, like Michael Young, Chelley Halsey or Peter Townsend in earlier years. Those who have been close to orthodox political circles, however, have mostly been involved with the Labour Party.

SELDON: Why is that?

GIDDENS: Oh, I think this is fairly clear. Fabian-style concerns have remained important in sociology even though the subject has become so much more variegated. And the 'outsider status' which many sociologists had was hardly conducive to them choosing to work alongside the Tories. Some sociologists who have come to fame in the UK were either émigrés from other countries or were fleeing from authoritarian regimes. They also mostly gravitated to the Centre or Left. As in other intellectual disciplines, sociological thought in this country has received an important injection from the work of authors who began their intellectual careers elsewhere. Ralf Dahrendorf is a prominent instance.

SELDON: Has Dahrendorf had a strong influence?

GIDDENS: Yes, I think so. One of his early books, *Class and Class Conflict in Industrial Society*, was very widely read. Together with other authors, including David Lockwood and John Rex, he forged a distinctive intellectual position. This looked to achieve something of a marriage between Anglo-American and Continental influences. Dahrendorf and the others were critical of the leading figure in world sociological theory at that time, Talcott Parsons – and they were critical on the basis of ideas adopted from Marx and Marxism. At the same time, none were Marxists. They sought to show that Marxism was valid neither as a version of social analysis nor as a political programme. Dahrendorf accepted much of the critique of Marxism offered by the philosopher Karl Popper and has remained steadfastly politically liberal. He has played a significant political role both in Germany and in Britain as well as producing a remarkable series of sociological works.

SELDON: The right-wing, anti-state, anti-welfare reaction among sociologists, when would you date that from? Was that a British phenomenon?

GIDDENS: It certainly was not primarily a British phenomenon. Some sociologists, like David Marsland, hold views of this sort. But such an outlook comes mainly from the United States and its roots lie quite deep in American Republicanism. 'Conservatism' in the US has traditionally been linked to a mistrust of central government. In her recent book on the welfare state, Theda Skocpol argues, convincingly I think, that debates about welfare in the US have consistently been shaped by this deeply ingrained mistrust of federal government on the part of the Right. Newt Gingrich in current times constantly stresses the need to utilise 'third wave' information technology, which he claims implies the decentralisation of political power. Yet such calls for decentralisation also reflect these long-standing anti-statist traditions.

A few sociologists in the UK have been drawn to the Hayek revival. Hayek's critique of collectivism, however, does not have much in common with the American political strands just referred to. Hayek was much more concerned to counter Continental forms of totalitarianism, such as he conceived of them.

SELDON: Moving on to more concrete policy influences, can one see the influence of sociology on the creation of the welfare state by the Attlee government?

GIDDENS: This goes back to our earlier discussion. Sociology helped to provide a coherent theoretical interpretation of the welfare state which linked it explicitly with reformist socialism. If one looks at its longer-term history, the welfare state did not originate primarily from socialist sources, either in this country or most others. It owes just as much to the Right as to the Left. Socialists had to do quite a lot of intellectual work to appropriate the welfare state as their own – and Fabian-style sociology played an important role in this.

SELDON: Then I can see an influence in the 1960s, with the move towards comprehensive education conspicuous.

GIDDENS: Yes, that influence was quite direct. Crosland drew upon a range of sociological authors in *The Future of Socialism*, and in his educational policies.

SELDON: So an influence in the 1960s, and informing perhaps some of the liberal Jenkins reforms in divorce, women's rights and so on?

GIDDENS: That influence was probably quite diffuse. While no doubt there were some sociological thinkers and researchers directly involved, there was not the same sort of overall theorisation which was developed in relation to the post-war welfare state.

SELDON: Then perhaps less influence in the 1970s, but more in the 1980s, particularly the late 1980s and 1990s, with the Right's reaction against solo state provision; again one can see sociological studies influencing government thinking, from a certain kind of academic?

GIDDENS: If, as I have said, sociological thinking and research are intrinsic to our society, there are few areas of policy making where the influence of sociology has not made itself felt. After all, what else can we depend upon if we are cogently to discuss issues such as the position of the family, gender and work, the changing role of cities or the nature of the educational system?

SELDON: Could British sociology be said to be more prescriptive, or descriptive, compared to say the trends of European sociology?

GIDDENS: Until the 1960s sociology in the UK was probably more descriptive and more empirical than was the case in Europe. Since then, however, things have changed in relation to the series of intellectual developments noted earlier. Sociologists in this country over the past quarter of a century or so have made important contributions to theoretical thinking; at the same time, they have also done a lot of valuable empirical research which has helped to provide substance for such theorising. Many of the differences which used to be found between sociology in Britain, as compared to that in France or Germany, have disappeared – or are in the process of so doing. Sociology is not now just becoming internationalised, it's becoming globalised: much the same ideas and issues are debated everywhere.

SELDON: Is that the media, computers?

GIDDENS: Instantaneous electronic communication, plus the ease of access which makes it so quick to shuttle to conferences around the world, tend to produce a globalising of intellectual culture. But globalisation also tends to mean that the practical problems and intellectual challenges are often very similar in otherwise quite disparate parts of the world. On the level of sociological theory, for instance, notions associated with post-modernism are being debated everywhere – in Western countries, in what was Soviet Eastern Europe and in many so-called Third World countries too. Sociologists have actually done a great deal of interesting work on the issue of globalisation as such: together with geographers, they were the first to bring the concept to the fore. Sociology has a new and urgent relevance to political thought and practice today, partly as a result of the very changes introduced by the globalisation of political, social and economic life. We are all now on untrodden ground. Sociological interpretation and mapping of this new terrain is going to be politically vital now that the pre-existing divisions between Left and Right have largely dissolved away.

The Influences on Economic Policy

ANTHONY SELDON interviews
ANDREW GRAHAM

SELDON: When you arrived at Number Ten in 1964, what were the prevailing economic ideas informing government?

GRAHAM: At that stage most economists still believed that Keynesian macro-economic policy could sustain full employment, and the key item on the agenda was how to raise the growth rate. It was thought that if the economy could be run at a slightly higher pressure of demand than it had been in the 1950s and early 1960s, then this extra pressure from demand would encourage firms to invest and improve their working practices. At the same time workers would be feeling relatively secure in their employment position and so be willing to raise productivity without fear of job loss. So the aim was to use fiscal and monetary policy to keep the pressure of demand up; this, in its turn, would induce responses which would increase supply and so raise the growth rate. Incidentally, the levels of unemployment we were talking about then seem utterly incredible now. The level of unemployment the Labour government wanted to aim at was about 1.5 per cent, instead of the level of about 1.8 per cent it had averaged in the 1950s and early 1960s.

In terms of ideas, I think many people at the time were being influenced by the Kennedy experience in America. The Kennedy tax cuts had taken some time to come through (they were introduced in 1961–62), but by 1963–64 the American economy looked as if it might be expanding more rapidly than it had during the Eisenhower period. People could therefore see this happening and had theoretical reasons why demand would pull supply upwards. This was one of the main ideas of the people in and around the government in 1964, 1965, 1966 – though it is quite hard, if you look back at the academic literature, to find much that says this. Indeed, one of the rather paradoxical situations is that the process which I have described, that is one in which demand pulls up supply by encouraging more investment, would almost count as what economists today describe as endogenous growth, and yet this idea disappeared in the late 1960s and 1970s. Certainly

Andrew Graham, Balliol College, Oxford, interviewed by Anthony Seldon, ICBH, on 29 August 1995.

the *converse* idea, namely that low demand would depress supply, was completely ignored, or seems to have been, by those who advised Mrs Thatcher. I wrote a paper[1] in 1977 warning that monetarism would reduce the capacity of the economy, but most economists ignored such thinking probably because they were operating with over-formal models in which they found it difficult to capture the thought of the supply side responding in this way.

SELDON: Who were the major intellectual influences on ministers in the formation of economic policy?

GRAHAM: Let me respond to that by talking about particular advisers and particular ministers. The two people who I think played an especially influential role were Thomas Balogh, who had been a long-term adviser of Harold Wilson, and Nicholas Kaldor, who came in to advise Callaghan at the Treasury. Both of them played an important part. Kaldor in particular thought that by pressure of demand and various other devices (he was the creator of the Selective Employment Tax), it would be possible to raise the growth rate. Thomas Balogh's two enormously important contributions, in contrast, were to insist (a) that the growth rate could only be raised if you had some other way of controlling inflation than unemployment, and (b) that there had also to be *direct* action on supply. Therefore a central aim of the first two Wilson administrations was the attempt to establish first of all a voluntary and then a more statutory-based incomes policy, because if incomes policy could hold down inflation, then you would be able to have a more rapid rate of growth and lower unemployment, with the inflationary pressures contained. Balogh had noticed as early as 1942–43 the need for an incomes policy and was the first to document that need.

In terms of ministers, Harold Wilson himself was important, he had trained as an economist and had had close contact with Balogh; Douglas Jay was at the Board of Trade; and he was followed by Anthony Crosland, who had in the 1950s written *The Future of Socialism*,[2] which gave very considerable prominence to the role of fiscal and monetary policy. It is quite important to note that I personally think, and I know Thomas Balogh also thought, that the ideas of Crosland, and indeed of the academic establishment at the time, were far too sanguine about how much could be done by fiscal and monetary policy on its own. This was why the Wilson administration of 1964 placed so much emphasis on planning and on industrial policy. However, there were three great problems with this. First, these 'supply-side' policies were a good deal more complex in practice than many people expected. Second, many civil servants, especially in the Board of Trade, were not sympathetic to them. Third, and most important, the government shot itself in the foot by refusing to devalue early enough. With an overvalued exchange rate, industrial policy was like pushing water uphill.

Looking at the situation more generally, I would say that the major mistake made by the economists and fostered by economists in the post-war period, was the belief that there were 'fixed points' in the economy, things like the Phillips curve, that you could rely on as a stable trade-off. Balogh never believed that.

SELDON: What do you mean by 'fixed points'?

GRAHAM: Economists are always looking for laws, for something stable, so when people lost faith in fiscal policy and Keynesianism, they shifted to monetary policy and monetarism, but this depended on a 'stable' velocity of money. But this did not work either. People who think like this view the economy as working like a mechanical system: all economists have to do is turn the knobs and predict reasonably reliably what would occur. Whereas in practice it is much more like an organism, a biological phenomenon, integrated, much more malleable, much more difficult to predict.

SELDON: Was this what Professor Paish thought?

GRAHAM: I am not sure what Paish thought on that point, but he certainly published articles which had been extremely influential in their impact on some Treasury economists. The force of these articles was to make it appear that the British economy could have got rid of its inflation, if it had only been willing to have unemployment at about 2 per cent. I remember going to a meeting held between the Treasury and the Department of Economic Affairs, it would have been late 1964 or early 1965, and at the centre of that discussion was whether it was sensible to do what the DEA wanted to do and try to run the economy at this rather low pressure of demand with 1.5 per cent unemployment, or whether, if only the economy could be run at about 1.8–1.9 per cent, you could avoid the stops and goes that had been occurring and obtain growth through a different route. Brian Hopkin, who later became Chief Economic Adviser at the Treasury, held very strongly to the view that 1.8–1.9 per cent was right and the DEA were arguing against it. So Paish's view at that stage appeared as highly mechanistic, as simply saying there was a different number to be aimed at and all would be well.

SELDON: Was this view of the economy as something predictable or mechanistic based on Keynes, or on experience, or on academic literature?

GRAHAM: It was certainly not based on the Keynes of the 'General Theory'. In terms of the history of ideas, I think one would have to say that theoretically the key move was the one made by Sir John Hicks, who literally only months after Keynes published *The General Theory*, brought out an article[3] which subsequently has been taught to every generation of economists, the so-called IS/LM curves. These made it look as if the economy could be manipulated by moving one or other of these curves. I think that anybody who reads *The General Theory* carefully will see that Keynes never believed that, and I know that Balogh always felt that Hicks, by publishing this article, had done great damage to the possibility that economics might be seen as an open-ended, evolving system rather than as a deterministic one.

On the empirical side the absolutely key article was the publication of the so-called Phillips curve in 1958,[4] and one has to say that this looked extraordinarily persuasive. Phillips plotted a relationship between unemployment and wages, going over the whole period from 1861 to 1912, and he then found not only that these points all seemed to lie along a curve, but, even more striking, the points after 1913 seemed to lie along the *same* curve. Now by the standards of modern day economics, to be able to have a relationship running over a forty or fifty year period and to find that it holds for a *subsequent* forty years, looks very persuasive indeed. The trouble with the Phillips curve, when you look at it more closely, is that it really combined three quite different data areas. One is the period before the First World War, when clearly the way economies functioned was rather different from how they functioned in the post-war period. The second is the inter-war period from 1919–20 to 1939 when, with the exception of a few years immediately after the First World War, unemployment was hardly ever below ten per cent, and not surprisingly you had very low inflation. Then there were a rather small number of points representing the period from 1945 onwards, and they were all clustered in a sort of blob, which didn't perhaps depict the strong, nice, stable curve that Phillips thought they did.

SELDON: How did Alec Cairncross fit in?

GRAHAM: I did not see a lot of Alec Cairncross. You have to remember that in 1964 he was the Head of the Government Economic Service, whereas I had only just joined it! However, I think that Alec Cairncross, like many of the actual advisers at the time, understood that the position was rather more complex than academics liked to believe. I think this would be true of many of the people who have been close to government. I don't think they necessarily thought that you could rely on these very stable relationships, and I think that Alec Cairncross, although I cannot be sure of this, was probably somewhat sceptical of the ability to run the economy at that lower level of unemployment without inflationary pressures. Partly because I think he would have been sceptical about being able to establish a viable incomes policy and, as I said, Balogh's position always was that you could only run the economy with lower unemployment if you did have an incomes policy, so one policy required the other. In that sense policy was quite vulnerable, and indeed that vulnerability is really a much bigger story and it is part of the reason, looking a long way further forward, why Thatcher eventually came to power. Wilson was trying to struggle with exactly the same dilemma in 1977–75: could you contain inflation without unemployment? For a period incomes policy was in operation, and the Labour government from 1974 to 1977 was very successful in getting inflation down, with unemployment at nothing like the levels of the 1980s. But the success depended on an incomes policy that eventually collapsed, and Thatcher came to power in many ways as a reaction.

SELDON: Was MacDougal a more abrasive, assertive, louder figure than Cairncross?

GRAHAM: No, I don't think he was. I think he was more inclined to want to see the economy expand, more inclined to push in that direction and more inclined to the view that the British economy had become uncompetitive and probably needed a devaluation. However, both Cairncross and he were well aware of the fact that the economy operates in a more complex way than some academics suppose.

SELDON: Who were the most influential amongst the officials of the DEA and the Treasury?

GRAHAM: Again, I did not see quite enough of that to give an informed view, because during the period of 1964–66 when I was at the DEA,' I was only seeing small parts of the system and from the DEA standpoint. In contrast, from 1966 onwards, when I was at Number Ten, I saw the ministerial side of things and not necessarily the officials all that much. But the people who I think were taken seriously would include the following. William Armstrong, Permanent Secretary at the Treasury, was regarded with awe by many people – too much so, I thought. Douglas Allen was extremely important, as was Eric Roll when he was at the DEA. He was trained as an economist, he was Permanent Secretary, but I do not think he was as tough as Douglas Allen. My impression of Eric Roll, even allowing for the fact that he was a civil servant and Permanent Secretary, was that he seemed as a person somehow interested in the debate in a slightly detached way, whereas some of the others were more intensely involved.

Another person, at a somewhat lower level, who I think played an important part in the work of the DEA, was John Grieve-Smith and, though he wasn't an academic economist, John Jewkes. But in that period of 1964–66 I did not see that much of either Balogh or Kaldor. I know that Kaldor in particular was very influential with Callaghan.

SELDON: At the Bank?

GRAHAM: One of the peculiarities of the British system at that time was that the work of the Bank was kept extraordinarily secret. The relationship was handled entirely by the Treasury, to such an extent that it was thought almost improper for any other department to have any contact with the Bank of England. Bank officials only came to forecasting meetings occasionally and did not seem to have any input into the regular advice giving. However, when the chips were down, the Governor would come to see the Prime Minister and then the Bank had *enormous* influence.

SELDON: All these people you have described as advisers subscribed by and large to the Keynesian interpretation of the economy?

GRAHAM: Probably speaking, yes, except that Balogh would have been sceptical.

SELDON: Sceptical because of its political values, rather than principally its vision?

GRAHAM: Enormously sceptical of the ability to control the economy *precisely* just through fiscal and monetary policy. However, he was convinced that you did need to try to control the economy. You could say that for quite a significant period of time he convinced Harold Wilson, because in the first Wilson government of 1964 there was a whole range of other controls on the economy. There was an import surcharge in operation, there was the tightening of exchange controls, the use of Industrial Development Certificates, the setting up of the Industrial Reorganisation Corporation, the establishment of the National Board of Prices and Incomes, not to mention the National Plan. All of these were alternative ways of intervening in the economy to try and get it to do what you wished it to do, rather than standing back and assuming it would happen automatically.

Of course where Balogh was most successful was when he was pushing for things which others supported. For example, Sir Donald MacDougal had been in the National Economic Development Office from its inception in 1961, and they had produced a publication called *Conditions Favourable to Faster Growth*, and this advocated establishing an incomes policy, trying to reorganise industry and so on. So in that area Balogh would have been getting support.

SELDON: Were there any bodies, think tanks, that were influential?

GRAHAM: At that time there were only two bodies that one might have thought of in that sort of way. One would have been the National Institute of Economic and Social Research, because it had been the place which the Treasury had used to carry out research on macro-economic policy when it wanted it to be in the public domain. The second, the opposite extreme, would have been the Institute of Economic Affairs, which was still trying to maintain the view that you could run the economy in a more market-oriented manner. They weren't being listened to very much – certainly not by Labour – but they were there, and indeed Frank Paish had written pieces for them. I would add to that, that although the National Economic Development Office was a quasi-governmental office and therefore not a think tank, some people quipped that NEDC stood for the Nuffield Extended Discussion Centre as it was a place in which academics and civil servants mixed rather easily and where new ideas could come.

SELDON: Did they?

GRAHAM: Quite a lot of the people who were in the DEA in the early days had been in Neddy before that. MacDougal had been there, Francis Stewart had been there, Roger Opie had been there. John Grieve-Smith had been at the Steel Board, also a body believing in planning.

SELDON: And the National Institute?

GRAHAM: The National Institute, as I would have seen it, was mainly doing the research that derived from and supported the view that the economy was rather mechanistic. Trying to find out what the numbers were; trying to find out, if you cut taxes by x, how much the economy would expand by. Not at all challenging the conventional wisdom, but operating within the conventional wisdom.

SELDON: So the only challengers were the IEA?

GRAHAM: Yes, with one important qualification. Neither Kaldor nor

Balogh fit into any of these camps very easily. In that sense they were both challengers of the conventional wisdom. However, for that very same reason they may have been less influential, because they didn't easily find other allies.

SELDON: Did any journalists make a distinctive impression on government thinking?

GRAHAM: The amusing thing, I suppose, is that in 1964-65 Sam Brittan was in the DEA and Peter Jay was in the Treasury, and at that stage, as I recall it, Sam Brittan was quite taken with all of these ideas. The idea that you could improve the economy by better manipulation of it.

SELDON: How do you mean?

GRAHAM: Well, the title of the book he wrote, *Steering the economy*,[6] is itself indicative.

SELDON: Any others?

GRAHAM: One of the things I would say that has changed dramatically over the last 25 or 30 years is that at the time, in the late 1960s, although politicians would have been reading the press, the economic com-mentators were not taken anything like as seriously. Of course, politicians were watching the press for headlines that could cause trouble in the House of Commons or wherever, but I did not have the impression of the press and television running the agenda of debate in the way that they do now.

SELDON: Would there be copies of the economic journals floating around the DEA or the Treasury or Number Ten?

GRAHAM: Yes, they would have been looked at – if there was time. However, my main impression was that most academic economists seemed very distant. I remember Max Corden coming to give a seminar at the DEA and he seemed to be from a different planet. There was almost no connection between what he was worrying about and what we were worrying about.

SELDON: Why did the Keynesian model eventually fail?

GRAHAM: Let me try and give an answer to that very difficult question, but to do so I shall have to make some rather broad generalisations. I think that the Keynesian model failed in the eyes of the public because it had been over-sold. People thought that Keynes had produced a way of combining relatively low unemployment and relatively low inflation, and yet, in truth, there is nothing whatsoever in the 'General Theory' that should really lead you to that conclusion. The result was that once we hit the periods of stagflation, with unemployment and inflation combined – particularly in the years 1974, 1975 and 1976 – people felt that if you can have both unemployment and inflation *together*, this must deny the proof of Keynes's theory.

In my view the reality was exactly the opposite. What had actually happened, most obviously in 1974 when the oil price had gone up dramatically, was that this acted exactly like a very large indirect tax increase. So, exactly as if you were doubling or trebling VAT, prices rose, which was inflation, but exactly like doubling or trebling VAT you were reducing people's spending power, which created unemployment. Therefore the oil price rise had the effect of creating both unemployment *and* inflation. Moreover, in many ways the unemployment occurred because Keynesian remedies were *not* applied, rather than because they were applied. If the whole world economy at that moment could have said: this has been an enormous tax exerted on the industrialised economies, we have got to offset this by an injection of extra demand, then the world slump of 1974–75 need not have occurred. Of course, some disruption would have been inevitable because of the large shift in *relative* prices that had taken place, but the macro-economic disturbance need not have been on anything like the scale that emerged. Paradoxically, people thought that unemployment and inflation were the proof of the failure of Keynes, but it was actually a failure to use Keynesian policies that brought about this transformation.

SELDON: So are you saying this was the fault of the IMF or whatever?

GRAHAM: I said before these are broad generalisations. The question you are putting presupposes that the IMF and the major industrialised countries could at that stage have reached agreement on a different set of policies. I do not think they were capable of doing that. If there had been a particular country that had been very powerful and a kind of godlike economic adviser, then I think that it would have been possible to devise policies which would have meant much less recession, much less inflation. For example, if all the industrialised countries had cut their indirect taxes on goods other than petrol which had genuinely gone up in price, but if all other prices had been cut, inflation would have been lower, purchasing power would not have been reduced and unemployment could have been lower.

SELDON: When you went back to Number Ten in March 1974, how had things changed?

GRAHAM: The most important thing is that the 1974 government was dominated by a sense of crisis from the beginning. The time to think about academic ideas was pretty small. You must remember that Wilson had never been expected to be elected in 1974 – nor did he expect it – he had come to power as a result of the miners' strike; inflation was high and accelerating; the balance of payments was in huge deficit; there were enormous quantities of sterling held in London by the Arab countries, the OPEC countries, which could have been removed at the drop of a hat; the whole situation had an immense feeling of fragility. At the very outset, in the March 1974 budget, a set of Cambridge economists, in particular Wynne Godley and possibly Nicholas Kaldor, tried with some success to persuade Denis Healey that the policy of sustaining demand in the economy was the right thing to do. However, at least the following things went wrong: first of all, and most dramatically, other countries didn't do the same, so that, given that all other countries were slowing down and Britain was not, or slowing down less, Britain picked up more than its fair share in terms of the balance of payments deficit and that made us exceptionally vulnerable. The second thing that went wrong was that people hadn't fully appreciated how a rather technical matter to do with the taxation of stocks, combined with rapid inflation, would put an incredible squeeze on company finances. So through the spring and summer of 1974 the company sector in the UK found itself in large financial deficit. It was being taxed on nominal gains on stocks and the prices and incomes policy at the time meant they were unable to pass this on in price increases. By the autumn of 1974 Healey found himself firstly with other countries having gone in the opposite direction from him, and secondly with the company sector in crisis, so he had to introduce another budget.

Although there were intense analytical discussions going on, which would have been coloured by prior Keynesian thinking or prior monetarist thinking or prior market thinking, the situation was so fresh that people were really having to work things out from first principles.

SELDON: The two issues we still need to look at are, first, the process by which monetarism came to be accepted, talked about, and then adopted, and the reality of the extent to which monetarism was adopted – was there really a change in thinking at the core of Treasury economic policy making? And secondly, your caveats about the 1980s.

GRAHAM: The major transition to monetarism, I think, came about from the following factors. First of all it would be true to say that in the original 'General Theory' Keynes had stressed that monetary factors could play an important part, but throughout the 1950s and 1960s fiscal policy had really dominated policy. This was not the result of the General Theory, but of a fixed exchange rate system. Whenever there was a sterling crisis the government had to use the interest rate to defend the exchange rate, so it could not also use it to control the domestic economy. What began to dawn on people from the mid-1970s onwards when sterling was floated, was that monetary policy became free to operate in its own right. Also people were very struck by the enormous expansion of money in the boom of 1972–73 and believed that this had contributed to inflation. So there was both a serious change in the structure of policy, from fixed to floating exchange rates, that pulled money back in importance, and secondly in the more practical sense a realisation that it did seem to have been very powerful.

Of course, these developments coincided with the long campaign of Milton Friedman, who maintained that money played a very particular role in generating inflation. As a result, there is no doubt that some people in the Treasury – I do not know how much they had been studying the underlying theory – became persuaded that monetary policy had been greatly underrated in its importance. In a sense I think they were right about this. However, there is a crucial distinction to be made here. You can agree that monetary policy had been underrated without thereby moving to monetarism. You might think that interest rates were playing a more important role in determining people's spending decisions than perhaps some Keynesians had done, and yet not be in any way committed to monetarism. Monetarism is the belief (a) that money affects inflation and *only* inflation, and (b) that, as a result, you should hold the quantity of money constant. The view that you can use monetary policy and, in particular, interest rates to influence the economy does not commit you to either of these propositions.

What I think pushed forwards the transition to monetarism was a combination of the IMF crisis of 1976 and a very strong belief within the IMF that countries should have targets for monetary aggregates. Then, in part as a direct result of that, but in part occurring separately, there was the growing belief in the City of London in the financial markets that government needed to worry much more about these things than they had previously done. This also coincided with the opening up and expansion of financial markets, so their role in policy making was growing in importance, at the same time that monetarism was becoming the idea that seemed to be more crucial. All of these things led a set of people in the Treasury to begin writing papers about the need for monetary targets. The IMF in 1976 insisted on what is called domestic credit expansion, which is a form of monetary aggregate, and Denis Healey agreed, as part of the IMF rescue package, to go along with this. At that stage I think it would be fair to say that Denis Healey and the upper echelons of the Treasury saw this as a buttress, as supporting fiscal policy, rather than a full-scale conversion to monetarism.

Then in 1977 there was an extremely important change of policy, one that has been greatly underrated in my view in terms of the subsequent development of British policy. From late 1976 to approximately September 1977 the exchange rate began to rise, and there was an extremely important discussion in the Treasury about whether the exchange rate should be allowed to continue to float upwards or whether it should be held down. This came to a head in the autumn of 1977, when eventually the exchange rate was allowed to float freely upwards. This was because the *act* of holding down sterling meant that the Bank of England would have been supplying sterling to the market and so increasing the domestic sterling supply. In other words, any decision about the exchange rate was also a decision about monetary aggregates. I think that this unpegging of the exchange rate in an upwards direction in late 1977 was an event of great importance, and one that hasn't been sufficiently discussed. From then on the exchange rate continued to rise, and it was rising at a time when British inflation was *above* that of the rest of the world. On competitiveness grounds, if British inflation was above that of the rest of the world, the exchange rate ought to have gone down, but it was going up. So British competitiveness was deteriorating both because of higher inflation than other countries and because of a rising exchange rate. From the trough of 1976 (of 1.70 to the dollar or even lower) to the peak, then under Mrs Thatcher, when sterling reached 2.45 to the dollar, British goods lost in excess of 50 per cent of competitiveness. This played an enormously important part in the destruction of manufacturing industry in the early 1980s.

By 1977 there was a sense in which the original move of the Labour Government to use monetary targets as a buttress to fiscal policy had moved towards a much greater implicit commitment to try to meet monetary targets, and in that sense it had become more monetarist. However, it had not – this is very fundamental – become fully monetarist in the sense of thinking that control of the money supply would thereby be a relatively painless form of controlling inflation. The really significant claim of monetarism is that inflation is caused *only* by an excessive growth in the money supply, and that if you stop that you would stop inflation; and linked is a further claim that in the relatively medium run you can do so fairly painlessly – unemployment might rise for a short period, but will then revert to its former level. So if you could stop inflation by controlling the money supply without having any higher unemployment, why not do so?

It was that second view, that you should adopt monetary targets for the purpose of controlling inflation, and that it would be relatively painless, which was the full-scale version of monetarism adopted by the first Thatcher government in 1970. This was a major transformation in macro-economic policy. Suddenly the government believed that *its* responsibility was inflation. Unemployment, in contrast, was the responsibility of the market. So policies to tackle unemployment were micro-economic, not macro.

Of course, there have been a lot of very important subsequent developments because, early on, monetarism was found wanting. It was found wanting firstly because the people who had advocated it hadn't anticipated the extent to which sterling would rise and cause this contraction of manufacturing. In a famous article published in the *Oxford Review of Economic Policy* in 1985,[7] David Laidler confessed that the monetarists hadn't thought these things through properly in an open economy. So monetarism was found wanting early on because the exchange rate proved to move much more dramatically upwards than had been anticipated.

It was also found to be wanting in two other important senses. The first of these was that controlling monetary aggregates proved to be far more difficult than monetarists had expected. The fundamental point there is that in a modern capitalist economy, most of the money supply is private money, created by the banking system, so it is not directly under the control of the central bank. As a result the critics said it was not possible to control the quantity of money directly – at best you do it indirectly, through interest rates. If so, you are halfway back to a Keynesian interpretation. The second and even more fundamental problem was the recession of the early 1980s. This was the result of monetary policy and, it had to be said, tight fiscal policy as well – in many ways it was a very old-fashioned deflationary policy. This recession did reduce inflation, but it did so at enormous cost in terms of unemployment and, most important of all, this unemployment *persisted*. All the earlier monetary theory had claimed that, at worst, there would be a short period of transition. Unemployment would rise, then it would go back to its earlier level. But it did *not* go back to its earlier level.

It is that last point which has caused fundamental re-thinking of how the economy operates and whether monetarism is really fatally flawed – or, if you like, monetarism is just an old-style deflation, not a new theory at all.

After this we move on to attempts to put something in place of money. First, we had fixed exchange rates, the ERM and the failure of that, and now in the 1990s, with the ERM having been abandoned, it is proposed that in its place we should have an independent central bank. All of these approaches are, to my mind, looking for too simple a cure for a very complex problem. All the time there is the attempt to try and find a sort of magic fixed point in economics. In the 1950s and 1960s it was the Phillips curve, in the 1980s it was controlling the money supply, followed by fixing the exchange rate, and now it is an independent central bank. But so far the results have been much less promising.

SELDON: Across the whole range of government policy in the 50-year period, what have been the significant shifts in policy thinking and policy delivery, and to what extent have the shifts in policies been determined by the change in ideas, or the change in personnel, which could be change in government, or the change in circumstances?

GRAHAM: Trying to summarise that, I would say that the two really big shifts in macro-economic policy have been firstly away from Keynesian in the years after 1976, followed by, in 1979, the belief that you could control money and that, thereafter, the economy would be on autopilot. The Keynesian need to control the level of demand disappeared completely. This was an absolutely fundamental shift, and it is impossible, I think, to say that any one individual brought it about. Certainly the monetarist set of ideas would have to be given enormous weight. They maintained a theoretical campaign over a very long period, even when Keynesianism was at its height and monetarism arrived virtually unnoticed. But these ideas only came to fruition because they had the right moment. The right moment was the combination of the growth of power of the financial markets in the 1970s and 1980s and the rise to power of a completely different kind of Conservative government – it wanted to have a revolution in thinking. Moreover, people wanted inflation stopped – they were no longer worrying about unemployment (or at least viewed it as less important) – and people were all too ready to believe the monetarist claims that this could be done at small cost. Whether monetarist ideas would have made it on their own is nothing like as clear. They were also influential in the States, but not to the same extent. It really came most dramatically into play in the UK, because of the higher inflation here, because of the Thatcher government and because of the ever increasing integration of the world's financial markets with London as a key player.

SELDON: So it was ideas intertwining with circumstance and with people?

GRAHAM: Absolutely. The two big shifts, staying within macro-economic policy, are, first, the rediscovery in the late 1980s that the economy cannot be left on autopilot and, second, the realisation that macro-economic policy in Britain in the 1990s *has* to be done in a more co-ordinated fashion, at a minimum as part of the European Union. That takes us on to a whole new agenda: how do you fit monetary and fiscal policy into the European Union, what structures do you need, who decides what and so on and so forth. But that is a debate that is still going on. I think it is a very important debate, the shift to Europe, and, alongside this, the recognition that monetarism and leaving the economy on autopilot are insufficient. It is driven, I think, partly by ideas, but more in this case by circumstances and evidence. Monetarism has produced very high levels of unemployment, the UK has become an increasingly open economy, financial markets have become more and more inter-related – and the UK is part of the European Union. Countries have been forced to think far more about macro-economic policy as part of international economic policy, and that has been a long process, going on since 1945.

SELDON: Personnel was not particularly significant in this second shift?

GRAHAM: Not in the same way.

SELDON: You mention two shifts, you are not mentioning the original shift to Keynesianism because you are predating this to 1945?

GRAHAM: Yes. Keynes published *How to Pay for the War* in 1940 and the running of the wartime economy in the Second World War was done on a far more Keynesian basis than in the First World War. We had already made the transition at that stage. Taxes were increased so as not to have excessive demand, whereas the 1914-18 war was financed far more by borrowing and was more inflationary.

I have been talking throughout about macro-economic policy, I would like to say something briefly about micro-economic policy. I have emphasised within macro-economic policy the extent to which I believe that for quite a long period economists have thought of the economy far too much as a machine, and the search – in my view, the mistaken search – for fixed points or constants in much the same way as physicists do. There is a mirror image or an analogy with these fixed points in micro economics, where economists by and large had an image of people as individuals acting in accordance with rational behaviour. At the micro-economic level this assumption of rationality had acted much like the fixed points in macro economics – it was the 'given' – whereas I would say that people are, and always have been, more complex than that. There always is a social element to people's behaviour as well as an economic element. The extent to which individuals are partly motivated by economic incentives, and partly by social commitments, social obligations, loyalty to institutions and commitment to others, is extremely important and is a factor that was greatly underestimated in the whole shift towards the market-oriented economy in the 1980s. You can see this mistake most dramatically in areas of the public sector – nursing, education, the police – where people go into these professions partly out of commitment to these activities themselves. Yet in the 1980s people in these jobs have almost been attacked for having such commitment. Indeed they have been regarded as stupid if they didn't quite respond as economists wanted them to, for example to performance-related pay or to greater inequality in the distribution of incomes. What we have seen is people acting in ways that many economists find surprising – though of course they ought not to have been surprised. As a result, the market-oriented reforms haven't worked anything like as well as people who advocated them expected. Again, what we are seeing here is the failure to understand the extent to which individuals, whether we are seeing them at the micro-economic level or at the macro-economic level, have to be seen within particular institutional structures.

SELDON: One way of summarising rather glibly what you are saying is that the erroneous belief through much of the economics has been to assume at the macro-economic level that economic agents and economic indicators are going to behave in a mechanical way, whereas in fact they behave in an organic way; and the mistake in micro-economics has been to try to make individuals, who are in fact organic, behave in a mechanistic way.

GRAHAM: Absolutely.

NOTES

1. A. Graham, 'Demand Management Policy in Changing Historical Circumstances', in *Contemporary Economic Analysis, Vol.2, Papers presented at the AUT Conference 1978* (London: Croom Helm, 1978).
2. C.A.R. Crosland, *The Future of Socialism* (London: Jonathan Cape, 1956).
3. J.R. Hick, 'Mr Keynes and the "Classics": A Suggested Interpretation', *Econometrica*, Vol.5 (April 1937).
4. A.W. Phillips, 'The Relation Between Unemployment and the Rate of Change of Money Wage Rates in the United Kingdom, 1861–1957', *Economica*, Vol.25, new series (Nov. 1958).
5. The Department of Economic Affairs was a new ministry established by the Labour Government in 1964 to focus on the longer-term development of the economy.
6. S. Brittan, *Steering the Economy: The Role of the Treasury*, new edn. (London: Penguin, 1971).
7. D. Laidler, 'Monetary Policy in Britain – Successes and Shortcomings', *Oxford Review of Economic Policy*, Vol.1, No.1 (1985).

The Influence of Ideas on the Modern Conservative Party

ANTHONY SELDON interviews JOHN RAMSDEN

SELDON: Which of the nineteenth-century figures most influenced the development of the twentieth-century party?[1]

RAMSDEN: I think that nineteenth century thinkers were not as important as Conservative politicians – some of whom thought, some of whom did not think. Disraeli is the one that most practising twentieth century politicians, until relatively recently, would have automatically cited as the most important influence on them; still, into the 1960s, Rab Butler would hark back to Disraeli and 'One Nation'. The very phrase 'One Nation' as a pressure group for progressive Toryism in the post-war years is a Disraelian concept, and of course the phrase is taken from a Disraeli novel. These Conservatives would certainly have traced Disraeli as an intellectual antecedent in that sense, though they had a very peculiar idea of what Disraeli actually stood for.

SELDON: To what extent then has each generation interpreted Disraeli to their own ends?

RAMSDEN: Enormously so. With a political life as varied as Disraeli's you can find justification for almost anything at some point of his career, which made him a particularly handy antecedent. The one theme that has probably been most useful to the Conservative Party which was derived from Disraeli was the one Paul Smith talked about when he concluded that Disraeli had not got much of a record of social reform, but that he persuaded the Conservative Party that it had.[2] So the liberal Tories of the twentieth century have been able to quote nineteenth century antecedents for that. Quintin Hogg, in *The Case of Conservatism* and in his CPC lectures of the 1950s, regularly harked back to that social reform and condition of the people tradition, the idea that somehow the Conservatives were the party of social reform when the Liberals were the party of *laissez-faire*, which is a way of viewing nineteenth-century history, but a pretty skewed one.[3] We

John Ramsden, Professor of History, Queen Mary and Westfield College, University of London, and Visiting Professor of British History, Westminster College, Fulton, Missouri, interviewed by Anthony Seldon, ICBH, on 12 and 15 July 1995.

have even had aspects of that drawn into Margaret Thatcher's idea of Victorian values.

SELDON: Did Smith go rather too far in belittling Disraeli's achievements in social reform?

RAMSDEN: I think you could make a more positive case for Disraeli, although I do not think I would personally wish to argue with Smith's conclusions. I think that the positive case is a tenable one.

SELDON: Why was Lord Randolph Churchill's influence so slight?

RAMSDEN: It is difficult to know what Randolph Churchill ever really stood for as a person. But clearly he stood for a brand of politics as opposed to a philosophy or a programme. And as a brand of politics it was of a kind that orthodox Conservatives at the time did not approve of, barnstorming at a time before it was very common in the country, visibly manoeuvring for power when it was still very much not the done thing in the Conservative Party. A bounder and cad if you like; there were plenty of bounders and cads who concealed their bounderism and caddishness, but Randolph never tried. One of the major influences was that people tended to judge Winston Churchill by his father, not least because Winston was so proud of his father, and wanted to be identified with him.

SELDON: Is not that interpretation of Randolph Churchill a little over-traditional?

RAMSDEN: Well, I was careful to say that that was about his politics rather than his policies. I am not suggesting that there was nothing in the ideas that he put across, but a major reason why the ideas he put across did not have a lasting impact was the popular view of his politics.

SELDON: Salisbury has been rediscovered by right wing Conservatives in the 1980s and 1990s. What has been the legacy of Salisbury on the Conservative Party this century?

RAMSDEN: The Salisbury they rediscovered was the young Salisbury who was an ultra-Conservative, always the reactionary figure, and completely contrary to the alternative tradition of cautious progress and timely concession. They have tended to understate quite a bit of what Salisbury actually did in the office, which was much more Disraelian, or even Peelite, than the Tory ideologue they discovered when founding the Salisbury

Review et al. Again, as with Disraeli, a long political career in a period of rapid political change is susceptible to all sorts of interpretations. Clearly Salisbury was crucially important for someone like Baldwin, as representing a cautious and ultra-respectable form of Conservatism as Prime Minister. Baldwin, in contrast to admirers today, derived his Salisbury entirely from the latter part of the career. But in terms of Britain's position in the world, the primacy of foreign policy and national prestige, it has been a really important lasting tradition, through say to Anthony Eden.

SELDON: So Salisbury was important for redefining the Conservative Party with a commitment to an external role, which was not so central for Disraeli?

RAMSDEN: Disraeli has been called 'the impresario of Empire'. There was a certain amount of marching the circus down the road and making a big fuss and noise about Empire in Disraeli, but Salisbury clearly was the person who made Empire central to Conservative Party thinking and policy. To an extent of course we are simply saying that they were Prime Ministers during two different periods, when all British politicians of all parties tended to be imperialist by nature. Gladstone after all added the largest tracts of territory to the Empire, not Salisbury or Disraeli, largely because he happened to be in office at the moment when those decisions were inescapable. There is no reason to believe that Disraeli would not have been a genuine imperialist, had he been alive and kicking in the 1890s. But there still was for Salisbury a way of consolidating Empire in a hard and fast manner that Disraeli never achieved, never intended, even though the glitter and the show was very much Disraeli's.

SELDON: Vernon Bogdanor has recently written about the 'ghost of Peel' having an enduring influence on the party. To what extent would you subscribe to that?

RAMSDEN: Until the most recent generation of politicians maybe, there was the constant belief that the great false dawn of Conservatism in the 1840s, followed by the long period in the wilderness and the desperate attempt to keep the party alive and come back from the dead, was blamed overwhelmingly on Peel. He was seen as providing the perfect example of bad leadership, a leader who provided no positive legacy; this is the myth, not necessarily the reality. So you have in 1903 Balfour wandering around saying 'I will not be another Sir Robert Peel' over the tariff reform issue. In that case, Balfour's determination to avoid a split at all costs kept the issue rumbling on for years, with no decisive action taken, which did create a split and, I would argue, was the worst way of dealing with the problem. Way into the post-war years you have Macmillan imagining in 1961 that Rab Butler is going to be the Disraeli to his own Peel over the Common Market, which had taken over as the divisive issue rather than the Corn Laws. Only two years later, in the late spring of 1963, Butler said just before the leadership crisis that if he did not win, 'whatever happens in the coming crisis, I could not act like Peel'.

Enormous significance is thus put on keeping the party together at all costs. This was not always honoured in practice, for example in the First World War period to the Carlton Club meeting of 1922, which was a period of deep division. But the belief affected most of the party's leaders, most of the time, (though not the Chamberlains who came from a different stable) but it is very true of the traditional Tories right through to Butler. Probably it does not hold after Butler. I am not aware of anybody saying quite that after the early 1960s, until of course recently again, when the European issue has been frequently compared to the Corn Laws or tariff reform and people ask 'Is Major a Peel figure?'. But I would argue the analogies are almost impossible to make work at this point. I am not at all clear that Major is in any way influenced by Peel in what he is doing anyway. Up to Butler it was clearly very important.

SELDON: Why exactly did the tariff reform issue tear so deep?

RAMSDEN: Because it actually raised, as very few political issues do, all the key elements of international and domestic policy at once. After all, it was meant to deal with the serious problems of British agriculture, the problems in part of British industry; it washed over in to social policy, in the views of some of its supporters anyway, with the question of whether social reform could be funded out of non-re-distribute taxation; and of course it influenced, or was meant to influence, the future direction of the British Empire. It is extremely rare for any political issue to unite that range and combination of interests, in a way that everybody on either side of the argument saw as being a high-salience, once-for-all political battle. You could not fudge it, you went one way or the other. People saw the scale of what was at stake, Britain's role in the world, and the landed interest's last fight to protect its special position at the same time, against the different demands of industry and the urban working class voter. It was not an issue on which people were going to accept compromise.

Most governments, when they face the really big political battles, usually have large policy areas they can fall back on to unite the party, because they are not part of the divisive framework. But the three issues of the Corn Laws in the 1840s; tariff reform from the Edwardian period right into the 1920s, but especially in the Edwardian period; and Britain's role in Europe from the 1980s onwards (not so true of the period of Britain actually joining in the 1970s, but only after Britain joined), all have that tendency to unite all the major strands of policy in a way that people care about so deeply that they are not prepared to settle for the usual political give and take.

SELDON: Might the party split over Europe?

RAMSDEN: Well, the party is split over Europe. But it would not be as in the 1840s, in the sense of a group seceding and joining another party, unless there was a much more fundamental realignment of British politics. I do not think it would be initiated from the Conservative side in the first place. A Labour government that also split over Europe, and failed miserably, say in the second half of the 1990s, would open up all sorts of possibilities for British political realignment. But I do not think it would actually happen from the Tory side first.

SELDON: What are the consistent ideas that have informed Conservative government thinking in the twentieth century?

RAMSDEN: They are I would say twofold. One is the protection of property and with it the extension of property-owning. The first has been rather more actively pursued than the second. It is well known that the phrase the 'property-owning democracy' was coined in 1925, but it was not actually until 1946 that anybody on the front-benchers used it. Even then, middle-class private housing was all that the property-owning democracy actually meant in the 1950s, for all practical purposes. There was not any concerted attempt to widen ownership any further than in housing until the Thatcher period and certainly not in relation to land. It always seems one of the great paradoxes that the Heath Conservative Party had in Edward du Cann and Peter Walker two of the inventors of unit trusts and yet no one seemed interested in widening share ownership as a political principle. As we know, the Party hit on it in the Thatcher period only as a device for raising money to cut taxes, and only subsequently found that it had considerable political benefits too. So the protection of property has always been a greater priority for Conservatives than actually diffusing its ownership.

SELDON: Are those the only two common factors in Conservative outlook this century? What about the preservation of the constitution?

RAMSDEN: I find it difficult to detect much evidence of that in the Conservative Party. It clearly is the third leg of the Disraeli stool. Preserving the constitution when attacked has been important, and Unionism involves both the preservation of the constitution and the prestige of England at the same time. But defending the House of Lords when attacked, defending the monarchy when it was attacked very briefly in the mid-nineteenth century, it is hard to see that that is more than a tactical gambit as opposed to a matter of ideological approbation.

SELDON: What about 'the condition of the people'?

RAMSDEN: Well the condition of the people was for many humanitarian Tories from Shaftesbury onwards clearly a matter of conviction, all the way through to Iain Macleod, Edward Boyle and Peter Walker. It was also very strongly tied up for more than a century now with the need to hold on to the working class vote.

SELDON: But you would not place it as one of your two ideological consistent principles?

RAMSDEN: No, I think it has much more to do, as the preservation of the constitution has, with tactical necessities. The preservation of the constitution has more to do with actually preserving the Conservatives' position as a powerful political party. Both defending the House of Lords, or whatever, and the elevation of the condition of the people, to quote Disraeli, has much more to do with holding on to working class votes.

SELDON: The enduring influence of Balfour and Bonar Law on the development of the Conservative Party?

RAMSDEN: I am not clear that there was much of an enduring influence of Bonar Law, except maybe through Richard Law, Lord Coleraine, his son. His book, *For Conservatives Only*, is one that leading Tories constantly refer back to as an influential post-war book, but which was not much noticed outside the party.[4] Robert Blake gave it a very strong review and referred back to it regularly in his own writings, but outside the Conservative Party is was hardly noticed. With the title *For Conservatives Only*, that perhaps is not surprising. But it was clearly an important book in starting to steer the Conservative Party back in a rightish Bonar Law-like direction after the long interlude of Baldwinism. So I do not think that Bonar Law personally had all that much of an impact. He is as much an unknown Prime Minister to the Conservative Party as he is to the rest of the world, I should think.

SELDON: And Balfour?

RAMSDEN: Balfour I think is simply, in as far as he is regarded at all, regarded as a reinforcement of the Peel story.

SELDON: And Joe Chamberlain?

RAMSDEN: He is inseparable, is not he, as a political legacy, from the sons? Joe Chamberlain as wrecker, and the ultra-conformism of the sons Austen and Neville in order to live down the reputation of their father was clearly a permanent factor right through to the Second World War. What it does bring into the Conservative Party on the other hand, and reinforces those genuine Tory humanitarians, is the idea that the Conservatives are really a workmanlike Fabian type of social reformers. Neville Chamberlain clearly being the prime example of that. They were people who actually understand the nuts and bolts of practical social reform. It was all a long way from Disraeli talking about sewage as a grand gesture, when clearly he had not the foggiest understanding of the details of the municipal ethics and codes of the 1870s. The Chamberlains filled that gap.

SELDON: So, contrasting the influence of Baldwin and Neville Chamberlain, you would put who as having the more enduring influence on the direction taken by the party post-war?

RAMSDEN: They are difficult to separate, are not they, because they were such an inseparable partnership when they were working together in the 1930s? We still do not know which was putting some of the input into their activities, particularly in the 1930s, which are much less well covered by the literature than the 1920s. And neither was a figure that people wanted to associate themselves with by name after 1945, Chamberlain even less than Baldwin. So one has to detect their influence where people were not claiming that they had been influenced, and only much later did people start harking back to them, as Major has done very firmly in the 1990s in talking about Baldwin as his great political influence. Of course, given his age, it can only be based on reading secondary literature; he was not in any sense directly influenced by Baldwin but may have absorbed that influence through people like Butler. Rab Butler was a man who was never ashamed to admit his association with Baldwin, and harked back to it at regular intervals. Through Butler it passed to Macleod, and Macleod, almost unique among that generation, was also prepared to associate himself with Neville Chamberlain, writing his biography in order to try and clear Chamberlain's name as a social reformer.[5] That low-profile, cautious, incremental reform that was associated with Chamberlain, plus the social harmony that was associated with Baldwin's name, was what influenced in practice a lot of moderate Tories of the 1940s and 1950s, but very few of them apart from Macleod wanted actually to put Chamberlain's and Baldwin's names on it. In the age of Winston Churchill that is not surprising; after what Churchill did to the reputation of his predecessors, nobody wanted to associate themselves by name. Macleod is the good and typically honourable exception to that rule.

SELDON: We have had an excellent book from Paul Addison on Churchill on the domestic front.[*] He was party leader for fifteen years; to what extent did he remould the Conservative Party?

RAMSDEN: Addison of course does not have room to say much about Churchill on the home front after 1945, which was two-thirds of his time as party leader. Clearly he provided an umbrella under which the Conservative Party could regroup on the home front, because much like his father he had a colourful career in which you could find all sorts of things. In the late 1940s, when opposing some aspects of the Labour government's domestic policy, he was adept at using bits of his own past career. For example on welfare reforms he was regularly pointing out that he had been a part of Asquith's government (1908–15) that had passed the biggest dose of welfare. Now this was a curious thing for the Conservative leader to say, given that his party had opposed those reforms at the time, and it is a wonderful bit of selective pulling out of his own past in order to give his party credibility in the present. Given that the Conservative Party was in such a desperate state in the late 1940s, nobody challenged it. In view of those, as surveys and election results show, who thought of the Conservative Party as hard-faced men of the slump, the party found it quite convenient to refer back to Churchill's role as a social reformer before the First World War.

Now that was all cover, because Churchill's actual interest in the consideration of Conservative policy after 1945 was minimal. He tried to stop the review of policy under Butler actually happening at all; he did not read the documents when they were actually produced, until the end of the Parliament when he insisted on reading everything and redrafting much of it in his own prose. But when the real decisions were being taken in 1947 and 1948, Churchill was not listening. The most you can say is that he did not stop it happening, or that he could not stop it happening, though he tried.[*]

SELDON: Which has been the most Conservative premier since the war and which the least Conservative?

RAMSDEN: I think which has been the least conservative with a small 'c' is the easier question. Clearly Churchill was a very conservative old man when he was party leader, Macmillan was in all sorts of ways conservative but with a radical undercurrent too, Home was certainly a natural conservative, and we have not had a natural conservative since. Heath certainly was not conservative, Thatcher very certainly was not; Major has more conservative instincts, but we have not yet seen enough to judge. But the trouble about asking the same question with a large 'c' is precisely the range of beliefs that have passed for Conservatism over the past hundred years, and therefore you can call somebody who pursues a Peelite policy a natural Conservative. But a Disraelian would be doing something very different and also be a natural Conservative. Now the dominant strand, clearly, from Salisbury onwards, Salisbury through Baldwin through Macmillan and maybe through Major, is respectable, cautious, inch-by-inch incremental and establishment-minded, which perhaps Major is much more so than his immediate predecessors. That has been the dominant strand of Conservatism, but it has been punctuated by such eruptions in a radical and populist reforming direction from the Randolph Churchill–Joseph Chamberlain–Ted Heath–Margaret Thatcher school that that is just as valid a tradition, and it is just as 'Conservative'.

SELDON: The non-premier thinkers or politicians who most influenced the direction of the post-war party?

RAMSDEN: Rab Butler has to be the most important single figure, because he was always there for twenty years: chairman of the Conservative Research Department, chairman of the Advisory Committee on Policy. In a sense, even beyond those institutional posts he was always the person at the leader's right hand whenever it came to any issue of domestic policy, right through till Heath's arrival.

SELDON: And he was at the height of his influence between 1945 and 1951?

RAMSDEN: I do not think so. I think he was actually at the height of his influence in government after 1951. I do not think it declined after 1951, because in party terms the political input was even more marked; Rab went on paying attention to the party mechanisms when the rest of them got involved in their departments. So right through his work on the Steering Committee in the late 1950s, his time as Party Chairman in the early 1960s, he was always there. He had influence directly, and indirectly through the acolytes, the Maudlings and the Macleods, not Powell clearly, and through many others of a very different political stamp like say John Biggs Davidson, whom one would not think of as a Butlerite at all, but who had clearly imbued from his time at the Butlerite Research Department, through Michael Fraser, a lot of Butler's thinking in all sorts of ways.

SELDON: The ideas that inform the party from the 1950s–1970s, to what extent were they based on actual new thinking?

RAMSDEN: The property-owning democracy idea was the property of the left of the party and the radical wing in the 1920s, which was picked up by Eden, who did not really know what it meant, and turned by the Butler team at the Conservative Research Department and then by Macmillan at the Housing Ministry from 1951 and 1954 into an actual policy afterwards. And in a way you could say the same thing about Macmillan's 'middle way' ideas, that they became the focus of party policy in the *Industrial Charter* whereas they had been one extreme wing of the party in the 1920s and 1930s. What the official party now said is what Macmillan had said as a lone voice, almost a lone voice anyway, before the war. The period through to 1965 was heavily influenced by inheritance from the inter-war years and the Wartime Coalition Government. It was only really from the mid-sixties onwards that a new thinking began to come through. You can find people demanding a new attitude to trade union policy for example before 1965, but they were very easily marginalised by the front-bencher who wanted to have nothing to do with it, right through to after the 1964 election defeat. The same is true of a number of other areas. But then the tilt began to happen very quickly. It really happened around the new front-bencher that Ted Heath constructed in 1965/6. To some extent again they were people who argued the same lines before. Rob Shepherd in his biography of Macleod shows that his early 1950s statements had quite a lot in common with what he was saying in the Heath Opposition period in the late sixties, but that he had then become a rather more powerful figure, who was able to say it on behalf of the party rather than on behalf of a pressure group like One Nation. It was the same type of generational shift that you saw earlier with Macmillan, in the centre of power in the 1950s, having been an oppositional figure earlier on. Macleod was able to move the One Nation group into the driving seat by the mid-1960s and into the 1970s. They were not the only advances of that sort. Quite a lot of what Geoffrey Howe was saying way back when he was Bow Group chairman is very consistent with what he did as Chancellor of the Exchequer in the 1980s. But the advance of that generation of what I would call sound money men came later; they only discovered monetarism late, but they dreamed of and argued for sound money right from the beginning of their political careers. They came of age as inflation re-started after the war, of course.

SELDON: So one has three distinct generational waves?

RAMSDEN: There is the Butler-Macmillan wave, Butler inside the hierarchy but quite junior in the 1920s and 1930s, and Macmillan more senior but outside, both coming into their inheritance after 1945. There is the One Nation group, which got into Parliament in 1950 and became by and large Cabinet ministers in the early 1960s. And then there is the first generation of Bow Groupers, those very young men in the 1950s, who came into their inheritance pretty well when Thatcher became leader.

SELDON: But to what extent were the Bow Group ideas new and where were those ideas coming from, from outside the party, from inside the party?

RAMSDEN: They were influenced from outside the party, yes, as well as inside. For instance Geoffrey Howe was aware of the Institute of Economic Affairs. Not all that many were, but ideas did permeate through people like Howe. It is one of the great misconceptions, that the Bow Group was sort of left wing and therefore somehow must be consensus orientated; it is not correct at all, it never was. They had a curious combination of policies, which Howe after all pursued at various times of his career and still is doing, which is moderate on social policy and hard-line on economics. That applies to Keith Joseph as well.

SELDON: How does that differ from the One Nation approach?

RAMSDEN: I do not think it necessarily differs from some of them. Powell and Macleod after all were both One Nation people, but it certainly differs from the way that the majority of the One Nation people (like, say Robert Carr) became committed to substantial public spending as their career developed and this conflicted with the objectives of lower taxation and keeping down inflation.

SELDON: So why did the ideas of Enoch Powell not actually win through earlier? To what extent do you see the Heath government as an early day Thatcher government, which failed only because of high unemployment and the U-turn that followed upon it?

RAMSDEN: I do think that many in the party in 1970 thought of themselves as making the same sort of tilt that they actually made after 1979. What they did not have of course was a viable economic theory to back them up, because it is fair to remember that hardly any British economists had discovered monetarism in the 1960s either, and those few who had were regarded as rather wild men, not to be taken too seriously. It was only in the mid 1970s, that monetarist economists won real acceptance; Hayek and Friedman did not get their Nobel prizes till the mid 1970s. Even with the same sort of programme in 1970 as in 1979, the philosophical and theoretical underpinning was much more secure by 1979. Robert Blake argued this a long time ago, that after 1979 we had the theory attached to the detail, and he is dead right.[7] When the going got rough after 1972 the Heath government did not quite know *why* they were doing what they were doing, whereas the Thatcher government knew exactly why they were doing it, but probably were less good at knowing the details of what they were doing. So the Thatcher Government actually worked better than the other in the end. There is also a big question about how far Heath himself was committed to a totally fresh approach, and I go along with John Campbell in thinking that Heath was never as deeply committed as his words suggested to some Tories in 1970.[8]

SELDON: So the belief that 'Selsdon man' was articulating a fresh new phase of Conservative thinking is exaggerated?

RAMSDEN: It is exaggerated if you are referring to Heath, but it is certainly not exaggerated if you are looking at people like Joseph, who despite his tameness during the Heath government, was a pretty rabid free marketeer during the Opposition period up to 1970. As soon as Powell left the front-bencher, Joseph was the flag-waver of the free marketeers. A lot of what he said then looks remarkably close to what he came back to in 1974.

SELDON: What speeches or writing would you refer to in the period up to 1970 on Keith Joseph's part?

RAMSDEN: There was a series of speeches he made just about the time of the Selsdon conference in the first few months of 1970. Tony Benn wrote in his Diary about 'an important new initiative' and started making speeches to refute them. There is an absolutely fascinating piece which Michael Harrington wrote just before the 1970 election which discusses Joseph speeches. Joseph is characterised as the exponent of abandoning the 'lame ducks' of industry; the actual phrase lame ducks does not appear, but he talks about more carrots and more sticks for industry.[9] Exactly the same sort of approach – less feather-bedding, more rewards for success, more bankruptcies for failures – that we see after 1974.

SELDON: So looking at the Heath government overall from 1970 to 1974, how much intellectual coherence is there and to what extent was the U-turn symbolising a Heath I and Heath II?

RAMSDEN: It was so overwhelmingly a Heath government, was it not, and we know so little about the Prime Minister's own thought processes. It still remains a mystery to most people who worked with him, quite what made him make decisions at particular moments in time. He had an enormous power to persuade his colleagues, and he had relatively compliant colleagues, in all of the key economic departments anyway. So quite what made the government tick becomes a question of what made Heath tick, it is a big question and the answer is that we do not really know. We do know that Heath was a man who was not all that excited by big philosophical ideas: he tended rather to react to problems. Heath was a problem solver, and to that extent the government became a problem-solving government, and that is one of the reasons it is difficult to place it precisely. It is not easy looking back at it to see where exactly the Heath Conservatives were going.

SELDON: The impact of the Salisbury Group and the Conservative Philosophy Group has been what actually, has it been felt on the direction of party policy?

RAMSDEN: It has been felt in the sense that they gave detailed support to Mrs Thatcher, but whether they really made much difference to policy, I'm not so sure. David Howell is a good example, he was very much an ideas man. He did not survive long in the Cabinet, but was after that an important figure on the back-benches, one of those sacked ministers who kept up morale on the back-benches even when things were going badly. It did not make him a rebel, ever. But clearly, if the Heath government was very much a Heath government, then the Thatcher government was very much more a Thatcher one. The influence of ideas on Thatcher was profound and diffuse: the influence of people from outside coming in, very often people who had switched over from the left, like Paul Johnson, who then became more right than the right very quickly afterwards. They had quite an impact strengthening the morale of the leader, of the leadership.

SELDON: To what extent do you see Europe as a straight left-right issue? How do you place Europe ideologically in the Conservative Party in the 1970s to 1990s?

RAMSDEN: I think you have to be careful about two quite separate phases. The 1960 to 1974-ish period was to a certain extent left against right, but the old-fashioned right rather than the Monday Clubbers and Thatcherites of the more modern right, because it was the traditional right who were the more suspicious of the EEC in that first phase. Even in that phase one should mention that there were left wingers like Peter Walker who were inveterately opposed to the EEC because they thought of the Commonwealth as the great experiment in multi-racial co-operation, which would be wrecked by Britain opting out of it to go into Europe. But predominantly it was the old colonial hands who were the opposition to Europe in the 1960s and early 1970s. But clearly, things changed after Britain got in with the overwhelming support at that stage of the Conservative Party, and especially of the leading figures in the party; in the big vote in 1972 there was virtually nobody of any importance who voted against it. Apart from Powell, virtually no Cabinet minister past or future voted against it. It was only the disappointment with what happened afterwards, and the slow seeping into the Tory consciousness of the sovereignty argument that failed to get across to them at the time. Just as Heath failed in a way to get the economic argument across until he had gone as leader, Powell failed to get the sovereignty argument across until he had left the Party altogether. But the opponents gradually started to matter and then of course is did become much more a conventional left versus right issue.

SELDON: Why do they start to matter more?

RAMSDEN: They start to matter more because they become practical rather than theoretical, and they become, particularly from 1979 onwards, more of a restraint on what a Tory government can actually do, and potentially a permanent defeat of what any Tory government can do. If a Labour government in Britain nationalises something, you can denationalise it by winning an election and passing a bill. If the EC introduces the Social Chapter and we end up getting compelled to join it, or we end up getting back into some form of monetary union, you cannot ever opt out of that again at some future date. It becomes absolutely impractical. Even those who say otherwise clearly know it is not true. So the growing sense of a permanent form of interventionist state from outside the UK, which a British general election cannot reverse or impede, becomes steadily more worrying as the anti-statist nature of Conservatism in the 1980s starts to clash with the interventionism of the European Commission. That does become very clearly a left versus right sort of issue. The Commonwealth has nothing to do with it by that point.

SELDON: Do you see Heath essentially as an old-style Tory harking back to Macmillan and Home, or do you see him as an early day Thatcherite, or both?

RAMSDEN: I see him as actually a transitional figure. I think it was Andrew Roth who made the point even in 1972, because of the U-turn that happened at the beginning of the year, that Heath was clearly a non-establishment figure who had worked his way up within the establishment to become very much an establishment type of Prime Minister.[10] So you have a grammar school Tory, but you also have the Anglican, Balliol and army man who in that sense infiltrated the establishment, whereas the whole Thatcher approach is all about subverting the establishment from the outside.

SELDON: Heath was initially the master but ultimately the servant of events?

RAMSDEN: Yes, I think that is absolutely right, and it is my own view that there are bound to be such consequences if somebody who is inherently a problem solver and not an ideas man holds office at a time of enormous pressure on government. There are going to be so many problems to be solved, you are never actually going to find the time to allow ideas to shape your agenda.

SELDON: What was the influence on the shape of government policy of Enoch Powell, Keith Joseph and Chris Patten?

RAMSDEN: Interesting trio, and not one I would put together! Joseph is the chief figure in getting the new economics through to the front-bencher, actually more than the front-bencher, getting it onto the major pages of the newspapers in 1974–75. It is interesting that Thatcher, in the earlier volume of her memoirs, goes public in the sense of accepting Powell as her intellectual ancestor. Joseph had already done so at an ICBH seminar; he had gone on the record saying that, but he would, would not he, because he was always so intellectually honest?[11] In a way it is slightly more surprising that Thatcher should have done it in her memoirs quite so fulsomely, since Powell has been so scathing about her. But it is entirely deserved, and there is no doubt at all that Powell is the intellectual ancestor of Selsdon Man – and indeed Finchley Woman – and all that follows from it.

SELDON: You give Selsdon Man there an importance that some would not attach to it.

RAMSDEN: I certainly am giving Selsdon Man an importance that John Campbell (in his biography of Heath) would not attach to it, and Ted Heath would not attach to it now either. I do not know how far Ted Heath really meant what he said in 1970, and he has now rethought his own view of what he thought about it, so I am not sure that even he could ever get back into his frame of mind of 1970. But if you look at the documents at the time, there is no reason to believe that Ted Heath was the sort of politician that said things he did not mean in order to get elected. That is just not what we think Ted Heath is like, is it? What he did though was to say things that meant different things to different wings of the Party.

SELDON: And Lawson maintaining the intellectual thrust?

RAMSDEN: Yes I think that is right. Clearly he was very important from early in the Thatcher government, but there was a whole range of other people early on who were arguing in the same direction.

SELDON: And Chris Patten's role?

RAMSDEN: Chris Patten is very consciously in the Butlerite tradition and he was clearly seriously disadvantaged by that for most of the time Thatcher was Prime Minister. Talent will out in the end, but the Thatcher memoirs are very dismissive of Patten as Director of the Research Department when she was first leader. She kept him on, but at the price of in the end axing the Research Department as a separate organisation, and never treating its leader as a real confidant in that period. The best years of Patten's life were wasted really, one might say, in the early 1980s, until he finally fought his way into the Cabinet only later on, and was then of course one of those with the brightest smile on his face when he had to tell her she had to go in 1990.

SELDON: Does Majorism mean anything, other than a return to an incremental type of conservatism?

RAMSDEN: It is easier to define in the negative form as what it is not, but clearly the excesses of Thatcherism have been pruned. What can you say of a leader who was elected in 1990 predominantly with the votes of the centre and right, and re-elected in 1995 predominantly with the votes of the centre and left? What is Majorism in those circumstances?

SELDON: It means he is a consummate politician, what else!

RAMSDEN: It is a view!

SELDON: How do you view John Gray's argument that the Conservative Party has allowed itself to become alienated from its various core interest groups and supporters in the 1980s and 1990s, thus spelling in some sense the end of Conservatism?

RAMSDEN: I do not think the Conservative Party in the 1980s as a whole can be said to have alienated itself from the core group of supporters. You can argue quite the opposite, that it was actually doing more for its real middle-class battalions of voting support, though it did not manage actually to hold the whole middle-class vote in that process. What it did manage to do was to do rather well among its core middle-class private sector support, at the cost of creating the impression of 'rolling back the state' and thereby upsetting the very large proportion of the middle-class salariat in the public sector who had also been loyal supporters in the past. Among the socially-aspiring working class voters the Conservative government did better in the 1980s than ever before. So there are the three different components, and it did well by two of them and not really well at all by the third.

SELDON: And in the 1990s?

RAMSDEN: I do not like drawing conclusions from short-term evidence, because what we may have seen so far is no different from what we saw in the middle of every Parliament in the 1980s. Until we see the second half of this Parliament I shall find it very difficult to grasp where we have actually got to. There may well have been a really significant draining of core support that is not going to come back. I think that is now a quite likely situation. But I thought that in 1986 as well, you probably did as well, I thought it in 1981, and we were both wrong. Everybody was wrong basically about that. I think the trouble is that the Government's recovery was so steep and so rapid before all of the last three general elections, that none of us are going to know much about the next general election until it happens.

SELDON: But the party is no longer seen to be supporting the Church, the monarchy, the House of Lords, the professions, it is no longer seen to be supporting the Union, in Northern Ireland at least.

RAMSDEN: It is not an establishment party any more. It is striking if you read the pre-Number Ten volume of Margaret Thatcher's autobiography, albeit of course with all the benefits of hindsight, how much hostility there is in her view to the Conservative Party she joined, how antagonistic (she now says anyway) that she felt then, right up to 1975, about the grandees who did not want to select women candidates, who did not like people from her social background, who did not like the sort of food she served at her table, and so on.[12] Clearly that anti-establishmentarianism is now a chip-on-the-shoulder sort of feeling that predominates. Julian Critchley wrote a wonderfully prophetic piece in the summer of 1973, when he did not know which way things would go. He thought that the moderates might hold on, in which case the Conservative Party would largely continue as it had since he joined it. But he also said that 'if things go wrong and the right seize control, we could become the party of the aggrieved motorist'.[13] There is some sense in which that anti-establishmentarianist populist line became dominant, clearly, up to the end of Thatcher. We are now in another time of transition, of not knowing where it is going now.

NOTES

1. John Ramsden is the author of three twentieth century volumes in the Longman History of the Conservative Party: *Age of Balfour and Baldwin, 1902–1940* (1978), *The Age of Churchill and Eden, 1940–1957* (1995) and *The Winds of Change, Macmillan to Heath, 1957–1975* (1996). He also published the Longman *The Making of Conservative Party Policy, the Conservative Research Department since 1929* (London: Longman, 1980), and *Real Old Tory Politics, the Political Diaries of Sir Robert Sanders, Lord Bayford, 1910–935* (London: The Historians' Press, 1984).
2. Paul Smith, *Disraelian Conservativism and Social Reform* (London: Routledge, 1967).
3. Quintin Hogg, *The Case for Conservatisim* (London: Penguin, 1947).
4. Lord Coleraine, *For Conservatives Only* (London: Tom Stacey, 1970).
5. Iain Macleod, *Neville Chamberlain* (London: Muller, 1961).
6. Paul Addison, *Churchill on the Home Front, 1900–1955* (London: Cape, 1992).
7. Robert Blake, *The Conservative Party from Peel to Thatcher* (London: Fontana, 1985), p.310.
8. John Campbell, *Edward Heath* (Cape, 1993), pp.264–6.
9. Michael Harrington, 'Sir Keith Joseph', in *Here Come the Tories* (eds.) T. Stacey and R. St. Oswald (London: Tom Stacey, 1970).
10. Andrew Roth, *Heath and the Heathmen* (London: Routledge, 1972), pp.224–5.
11. Witness Seminar: 'Conservative Party Policy-Making, 1964-70', *Contemporary Record*, Vol.3, No.4, (1990), p.34.
12. Margaret Thatcher, *The Path to Power* (London: HarperCollins, 1995).
13. Julian Critchley, 'Strains and Stresses in the Conservative Party', *Political Quarterly*, 445 (1973), p.403.

The Influence of Ideas on
Economic Policy (I)

ANTHONY SELDON interviews
LORD ROLL OF IPSDEN, KCMG, CB

SELDON: Let me ask you a broad question to begin with. What do you see as the main economic ideas and economic thinkers to have influenced the direction of government policy since 1945?

ROLL: Let me begin with a general observation on that question. I do not in the least want to minimise the effect of ideas and the effect of people who had these ideas during this period of fifty years. Having been myself brought up as an economist in Britain, the last thing in the world I would want is in any way to denigrate the place of that science. Nevertheless, I have to say that at my age, with those experiences that I have had, in the academy, in government service, and later in private sector finance, I have become increasingly doubtful about the precise weight and place to assign to ideas in formulating or fashioning economic policy, as distinct from the continuing influence of what is called by Pareto the residue of social and economic ideas,[1] of the history of actual economic policies, and so on, and of personalities, and of the influence of the political seesaw, especially in our country with our type of party politics. So my general observation to you is that now I feel it is hazardous to correlate, too closely at any rate, what has been happening between the so-called real world of politics and the world of economic ideas. You can point to the influence of Keynes and Hayek, of Arthur Seldon and Ralph Harris, or to the planners, the Gaitskells, Evan Durbin, the deviant New Jerusalem authors of the post-war period. But to correlate all that too closely with what has actually been happening can be hazardous, for example with the chances of Mr Major leading his party to victory again next time round and on what basis he can do that, or even with the extent to which the Thatcher era was really so much of a revolution against dirigisme as it appeared to be at first sight. So that is my general observation on that whole complex of things.

SELDON: That said, and I accept your caution, whom would you then pick

Lord Roll of Ipsden was interviewed by Dr Anthony Seldon, ICBH, on 8 August 1995.

out, what ideas would you pick out, that have actually changed the shape of post-war history?

ROLL: Obviously this is a matter very much of personal choice and predilection and the extent to which one's own experience is expressed in one's views, but I would say despite everything else, and despite the number of people who obviously appear to qualify for this, I still would regard Keynes as most important. Not only because I think he was in fact the most seminal of thinkers, and not because he was universally successful, far from it but simply because friend and foe even today operate with the kind of apparatus of ideas that he did. The whole concept of influencing the course of economic progress and influencing growth in an upward or in a downward direction by certain defined instruments: fiscal policy, deficit financing, monetary policy etc., in one way or another goes back to Keynes. So whatever may be the ultimate outcome of Keynesianism, or the effect of the *General Theory* and all the tremendous body of theory and analysis and implications for practical policy that has been built up on the basis of the *General Theory* by a large number of economists on both sides of the Atlantic. Whatever may be the ultimate fate of that, I do not think one can in any way ignore the fact that it is still to a large extent Keynesian.

SELDON: When do you see his ideas beginning to affect the government, and how were his ideas mediated?

ROLL: Apart from the immediate period of very vigorous debate between Keynes and Denis Robertson, between Keynes and Hayek, and all that kind of thing in the years just before 1936 when the *General Theory* came out and immediately after to the outbreak of war, I would say that the real influence on British policy came during the war. A number of people were responsible, including some originally hostile to Keynes, through the Cabinet Office, through the Economic Section, through James Meade, through Lionel Robbins and Robert Hall, both of whom were not to start with pro-Keynes by any means. It started with the Economic Advisory Council before the war, but continued through the Economic Section during the war and into the immediate post-war planning period initiated through the Economic Survey and the white papers on full employment and social policy.

SELDON: So what were the circumstances that made for his economic ideas to be translated into policy outcomes?

ROLL: The key was the upsurge of broad, if you like popular, discontent with the operation of the economy and the attitude of governments during the 1930s. That period was marked by heavy unemployment in the industrialised countries, by the absurdities of agricultural and raw material surpluses, which affected mainly the primary producing countries leaving them in tremendous misery, while at the same time helping the industrialised countries to recover more quickly by getting their raw materials and food more cheaply. If it was not exactly an intellectual revolt, nevertheless there was a broad feeling of 'that's not the way it ought to be'. This was vividly demonstrated by the hunger marches from Jarrow, the marches onto Washington from the Midwest. There was a general and widespread turbulence of popular opinion.

That was the substratum. Then you put on top of that Keynesian ideas, I say Keynesian broadly speaking, coupled with the difficulties faced by governments. If you look at the history of the British Labour government at the time of Philip Snowden (which I dealt with in my recent book, *Where Did We Go Wrong*)[2] the difficulties of the 'New Deal', first successful and then gradually, as always happens in these cases, running into great difficulties, what you see is an eagerness of the active politicians to find something that will help them. After all, they are to find solutions to such problems. Then you can understand why this was very much a formative period.

SELDON: So a revulsion against the operation of the free market, and the inequities and maldistributions that resulted, provided the seedbed into which these ideas could be accepted?

ROLL: Yes, but the discontent was very widespread and sometimes it even led to a strengthening of the 'left' and admiration of the Soviet Union, which involved shutting one's eyes to the horrors that were going on there because they were thought to be so successful economically. All these developments provided a climate in which something new was required.

SELDON: To what extent do you see Keynes creating these ideas, to what extent were they more autonomously generated, as similar ideas were being articulated elsewhere as a reaction against the free market and against *laissez-faire*?

ROLL: It was undoubtedly very important to him, and to the acceptance of his ideas more generally, that he was not alone, not only in reacting to the general background that I have just described, but in regard to his own ideas themselves, in academic circles, particularly in the United States. Galbraith wrote an interesting pamphlet about Keynes in America,[3] and the effect he had on Harvard, MIT and various other schools in the United States – apart from Chicago and California, where his ideas were not quite so welcomed. So it helped that there was a general feeling of acceptance. But the other point I would make is this. Up to 1936 Keynes was very much a man of the world, who knew what was going on in the City and knew the politicians. He was nevertheless working within the academic field, in Cambridge, writing books which were somewhat esoteric and obviously would not be read by everybody. But he kept in touch with the world of affairs, with business, and knew a lot about business. He was chairman of the National Mutual Insurance Company and he did extremely good work in speculating in commodities, providing as is well known a lot of money for King's College, Cambridge, as a result. When the war came he was associated with active policy formation. He is sometimes unfairly accused of being simply a depression and deficit financing guru, but he was well aware of the need to suppress inflationary pressures during the war, and how the free market could be used. As in points rationing⁴ for example. I know about that because Ted Lloyd, the adviser to the Ministry of Food, where I was for a while, was one of the originators of the technique of points rationing together with some of the Board of Trade people, but Keynes was very much in the background being consulted about this. He saw there an extremely useful instrument to preserve some of the virtues of the free market and choice within a limited range of possibilities.

SELDON: What do you see as his distinctive theoretical contributions?

ROLL: That is very difficult to answer, because on that, as we say nowadays, the jury is still out. Quite apart from any tremendous cleavage between Keynes and the 'free market school' as represented by Hayek and Mises and some of their latter day followers, quite apart from that difficulty, even within the Keynesian canon itself, there are considerable differences: the post-Keynesians, the reconstructed post-Keynesians, the mainstream Keynesians and so on. If you look at people like Bob Solow, Nobel prize winner at MIT, Paul Samuelson, Nobel prize winner at MIT, Franco Modigliani, Nobel prize winner at MIT, James Meade in this country, and so on, you will find shades of opinion. There is something that unites them of course, as compared, say, with the total anti-Keynesians, on broad philosophical grounds, but there are still considerable differences. I would hesitate to say here and now what is lasting and will prove to be continually seminal, and what is not. It is too early. I think some of the categories that he has left behind are still very much alive. They include liquidity preference, consumption function, production function, and so on, although not exclusively his, and the whole nexus between monetary policy (credit volume; interest rates, short and long), fiscal policy (deficits; how long you can keep them; what is the threshold of tolerance in regard to the percentage of GDP made up by the public sector borrowing requirement and so on.) All these things are still somewhat imprecise – there are lots of different interpretations – but they all owe much to him.

SELDON: When did the critical mass inside the Treasury change from being sceptical to embracing Keynesianism?

ROLL: During the war you still had the old school at the head of the Treasury, and I mention names not in any derogatory manner but simply to illustrate signposts. You first of all had Edward Bridges as Permanent Secretary, who then became Secretary of the Cabinet as well, and he was Head of the Civil Service. He once said to me he spent much more time on administering the Civil Service than he spent on Treasury policy. There was Bernard Gilbert, Wilfred Eady, and then there were a lot of newcomers like Rowe-Dutton and others at a lower level. Gilbert and Eady were the outstanding Treasury officials. They were very much the old school, but one could argue that the tremendous influence and pressure of the war made them open to new ideas. I am sure they did not altogether understand them. Even Bridges, who was a very clever man, did not really quite understand the Keynesian canon, but he knew enough of what was going on to appreciate its relevance. Then there were the outside advisers. There were people like Edwin Plowden and the planners; there was Robert Hall, who was very close to Plowden and influenced him to some extent. And Robert Hall, though not an out-and-out Keynesian, was nevertheless open to his ideas, being essentially an academic. Alec Cairncross' is another who would fit into that category. Though the Gilberts and Eadys, and even Bridges, did not quite understand the significance of Keynes's ideas; they realised that these were something new, and the war was something which did not allow for fixed positions and for ignoring new ways of doing things.

So I would say it was in this period, and particularly when Keynes and Harry White (under-secretary of the Treasury) and others in America started preparing for post-war reconstruction, when the International Monetary Fund and the International Bank for Reconstruction and Development were born. All that was an avenue for introducing these ideas into very important practical international post-war arrangements. That again had an influence on the traditionalists, like Gilbert and Eady. Thus, there was not that degree of opposition to new ideas that one might have expected. Then gradually the personnel changed too. For example, there was Frank Lee. He started in the Colonial Office, then went to the Ministry of Food, then Permanent Secretary at the Board of Trade, then finally ended up as Head of the

Treasury. Frank Lee was a very open person, very pragmatic, not a theorist but very clever in understanding what was going on in the theoretical field. I mention him as an example, though there were others who were gradually replacing the old guard. I would say from 1941, especially when the weight of carrying the war started moving to the other side of the Atlantic in 1943, and when the Anglo-American negotiations for lend-lease, the post-war settlement, the British loan, and for IMF/IBRD started, that was the period when the whole complex of new ideas got more or less firmly established and formed the climate in which the post-war policy was going to be fashioned.

SELDON: How significant, as a reaction, do you see the 'Robot' plan of 1952 with Clark and Rowan and Bolton?

ROLL: Owing to my last book I am regarded as a defender of Robot.[6] Looking back over developments in economic policy since 1945, I singled out Robot as a rather remarkable opportunity for doing something new which *might* have made a very significant difference, not so much immediately in our economic affairs, but rather in redirecting our whole thinking and our planning into different channels. Up to that point the fixity and the strength of the exchange rate were practically untouchable. This can be seen in the return to the Gold Standard in 1925, in regard to the American loan and our obligation to convertibility and so on. Robot would have meant a departure from that clinging to certain principles, whether or not the practical proposals were either feasible or immediately useful. I am quite prepared to accept it was not politically possible, because neither the Americans nor the Europeans, nor the Commonwealth, would have been pleased by what was involved in it: different settlement of the sterling balances, making sterling convertible and so on. So it may not have been feasible. But the decisive thing was the line-up in Whitehall, as it often is, a sort of gladiatorial contest between ministers or between ministers and advisers. On Robot there were Plowden, MacDougall and Cherwell, lined up one way, and on the other side you had that slightly wayward genius Otto Clarke, Leslie Rowan, who was not an economist but was an important official (he had been Churchill's Private Secretary and then a high official in the Treasury), and George Bolton from the Bank of England. This was a somewhat unorthodox little group, compared with the very powerful orthodox phalanx that stood against them. And in this gladiatorial contest, in the end ministers did say 'well if we cannot do it, if we are going to get into trouble with the Commonwealth, and the Americans and the Europeans, let's forget about it, whether it is a good scheme in theory or not'. I am sure that is what happened, and that's really what I tried to bring out in my book. Had it not been so, it is quite conceivable that Robot would have worked. Some of my colleagues at the time with whom I have talked about this say 'well, even then it would not have worked, because our underlying economic situation, in terms of availability of resources for exports and so on, was such that freeing the exchanges would not really have had a very beneficial influence because we did not have the possibility of taking advantage of a decline in the exchange rate to boost exports'. That may be true. But looking back there is a certain nostalgia in this not having been tried, because after all we implemented a lot of other policies which turned out not to be all that good.

SELDON: But to what extent did the defeat of the plan actually mark a victory for a consensus view in economic thinking amongst the influential policy-makers?

ROLL: It was not so much that the Keynes-anti-Keynes argument, whatever that may be worth, operated on this occasion. I do not think the MacDougall–Robert Hall–'Prof' (Lord Cherwell) axis was so to speak just anti-Keynesian, while the Bolton-Rowan-Clarke axis was pro. It was not on that plane that the battle took place. It was more in terms of whether in sheer practical terms it was better to let the ups and downs of our balance of payments position be reflected in the reserves, or in the exchange rate.

SELDON: So it did not constitute new thinking?

ROLL: I do not think so. I believe that, although it was novel, it did not represent fundamentally new thinking.

SELDON: When do you think Keynesian ideas were at the high point in their influence on government policy?

ROLL: I suppose it was at its height just before Keynes died in 1946, although that might imply that it came to an end then. But I think that first burgeoning of the 1945 Labour government – with Cripps as Chancellor; and the planners, the Central Economic Planning Staff, which was put into the Treasury shortly after its formation and was headed by Plowden, who although not a politician was very close to Cripps through his work at the Ministry of Aircraft and Production, and in the Cabinet Office – seems to have been the peak. Keynes was still there. He had come back having negotiated the American Loan, which had relatively little to do with Keynesian ideas in the narrow sense of the word. But it shows how realistic Keynes was and had to be, before he actually died. This was probably the high point. Once that passed, then you had the difficulties of convertibility, which led to an almost immediate return to a regulated regime with exchange control and you had the gradual decline in the power of the Labour government, which finally led to Attlee calling an election in 1951 and the Tories coming back for thirteen years. Not that they instituted a totally anti-dirigiste programme or a totally anti-Keynesian programme, far from it; Butler and Maudling were not of that ilk at all. But there was a certain shade of difference. So I would regard 1946 or 1947, probably right up to 1949 and the devaluation of 1949, as being the period when Keynesian ideas still ruled strongly.

SELDON: To what extent do you see Keynesian ideas informing British government economic policy all the way through to the 1970s?

ROLL: With variations the Keynesian ideas continued up to the Thatcher government, although I would maintain, though many people would disagree, that even after 1979, despite the *rhetoric* of the post-1979 policies, even beyond that period, the residue of economic management, via the main instruments of fiscal policy and monetary policy, remained very largely in place. The rhetoric was different. Direct intervention came under a cloud, not always effectively, and you had issues as over Westland in 1980 which showed that there was still an argument as to which way government should influence industrial policy. But in terms of budgetary policy on the one hand and monetary policy on the other, you could even argue that the rule of monetary policy, particularly on short-term interest rates, was if anything increased, even though the rhetoric changed after 1979.

SELDON: An influential Treasury figure from the 1980s said that he thought that the influence of ideas and indeed economics on the Treasury had been greatly exaggerated; that there was next to no influence on Treasury thinking of economic ideas or even economics.

ROLL: I would not dissent from that. What I said at the beginning of our conversation tended rather in that direction. When you are sitting in the Treasury, whether you are the Chancellor or a junior minister, or whether you are the Permanent Secretary or the adviser, the problems do not present themselves day in day out as a choice between, let us say, Hayek or Keynes. They present themselves in quite specific decisions that have to be taken fairly quickly, that are influenced by what is going on in Brussels, by the fact that the Chancellor might have to attend a summit meeting next week, by the fact that the Americans at the moment may be devoting themselves to benign neglect of the dollar, or the other way round and so on. You have to deal with these realities, which cannot be dealt with or resolved just on the basis of broad principles. Economic thinking in my view, whether Keynesian or not, has not progressed to such an extent that you could have a handbook and look up in the index 'what do I do today on this particular problem that I have to advise the Chancellor on today'. I would have to agree once again that one should not seek either justification or condemnation for what is being done in the Treasury day in day out on the basis of a choice between fundamental ideologies, or ideas.

SELDON: More generally, in the post-war period, we see a great mushrooming of the study of economics at schools and universities, a tremendous expansion in the number of economic books and articles, economic branches and economic journals. To what extent has all of this intellectual activity helped inform better policy making by government? To what extent does government command better understanding of the operation of the domestic and international economy as a result of all this work?

ROLL: You bring me back again to what we said right at the beginning. First of all I agree with you. Economics has been a growth industry in the last few decades. The job opportunities for those studying economics have grown immeasurably in international organisations and national trade associations, in businesses, in private companies, to say nothing of the governmental machine itself, although this trend has come to an end. All of this activity, including the springing up of new journals, has helped. I would be very reluctant to adopt an obscurantist attitude, to say that going on rummaging in these ideas and seeing whether, say, the Phillips curve could be presented in a more effective way, or exploring the whole relationship between unemployment, investment decisions and short-term interest rates, is not worth pursuing. No, not at all, I think it is very important.

Nevertheless, I would be forced to the conclusion that if you compare the growth of the economics industry with the actual practical results of what used to be called 'keeping the economy on an even keel', that relationship is very, very hard to demonstrate. There have been short periods in which the economy has gone moderately well and you could say 'it's been working quite well, the ups and downs of interest rates and the influence on the exchange rate, the decision as to what you do in response to what the Fed has done and so on, it's worked out quite well'. But these are almost accidental if you look at the whole chain of factors. Therefore I put it this way: on the one hand the correlation is very difficult to establish, on the other hand it would be very wrong because of that just to reject all the economics that has been done, and continues to be done (some of it extremely esoteric and very difficult to follow, particularly when it involves of very sophisticated mathematical procedures). At the Lionel Robbins Memorial Lecture in Bologna in 1995, I argued that the mainstream economists deserve a great deal of credit that they continue to work and continue to try to refine their ideas, despite the fact that they must obviously be disappointed and frustrated that they have not always succeeded, and despite the fact that whatever they do, ideological battles continue and they do not get the recognition they deserve. Continued work of the mainstream should go on, but practical politicians and businessmen should not be tempted to expect too precise results that could be used straightaway. However, I should add that in business economics in particular there is a whole range of work and that is relatively successful in a narrow sense of the word.

SELDON: In the sense of being prescriptive, having some scientifically predictable value; if various policies and levers are followed one can to an extent predict outcomes?

ROLL: Yes, I would say that but it has been most precise in certain highly specialised fields. The financial ideas, such as those which have emerged from Modigliani for example and the recent recipients of the Nobel prize, are very much practised, particularly in banks like ours. The whole science of derivatives and what you do about them is very much influenced by quite specific theoretical ideas, which do not have much to do with the broader ideological conflicts that we have been talking about. They simply accept certain market phenomena and certain market conditions and try to evolve series of consequences that follow from certain actions.

SELDON: What problems fundamentally do you see Keynes trying to solve?

ROLL: I think they are probably best described by the title of his most renowned book, namely *The General Theory of Employment, Interest and Money*. He was trying to bring together, as economists always do and have to do, certain relatively simplified concepts or categories of the economy, of the economic universe (employment, interest and money), and trying to see what their relationship is under certain influences. Now this involves a series of subsidiary categories like liquidity preference. You could argue that this has always been the procedure of the greatest economists, from Adam Smith onwards. It has not always been the same categories that have interested them, obviously, but this idea of trying to isolate from the actions that go on every day by what are nowadays called economic agents, whether the agents are enterprises like Lord Hanson's or ICI or whether the agents are just individual operators in the financial markets, to try and distil from their actions certain specific categories of a very broad character, which describe and at the same time influence the state of the economy as a whole, growth, employment and so on. Now that has always been the programme of economists I think, and Keynes has done it in a certain way. Whether that has been the most successful way or not is of course a matter of argument. For those economists of a general character in their thinking and their analysis, they cannot really get away from this process of abstracting a series of broad categories from the economy and then seeing what is the relationship between them and what alters said relationship as a result of action by 'the authorities', that is to say the state, the central bank, of whatever it may be that can influence it.

SELDON: So much is talked, about the era from the 1940s to the 1970s being the great era of Keynesian social democracy. Could I ask you to clarify what you see as the ideas informing government policy which were specifically derived from Keynes?

ROLL: I would not want to extol this as a sort of golden age, a paradise of economic thinking, but I do believe that it represents thinking that is not going to go away.

SELDON: What specifically would you pick out from Keynes as the core ideas?

ROLL: The core idea I think, and what I believe the General Theory tried to establish, is that the economy does not spontaneously and automatically tend towards equilibrium at a high, full, or at any rate adequate level of employment and growth. Now underlying the whole nineteenth-century 'liberal economics' was the belief that, left relatively alone, or entirely alone, the economy will tend to establish an equilibrium. Whether that takes a long time, and in the meantime all sorts of things happen to people, is another matter. But that school holds that the natural tendency of the economy, left alone, is for markets to establish an equilibrium at an adequate level of growth and employment.

The real hard core of Keynesian thinking is to start off by saying analysis, as well as historical evidence, shows that this is not the case, that you cannot rely, at any rate in a period that matters for human action and human reaction, on the economy tending to equilibrium. Starting from that, he says that you cannot be sure that you will have adequate growth, that you have full employment or relatively full employment. Once you start from that point you say what can I do about it? how can I ensure that this natural tendency not to produce an equilibrium can be countered? That leads you to what is by the enemies described as dirigisme, excessive deficit financing in times of depression, a lax monetary policy and so on. And that may be true. I am not necessarily denying that there have been such consequences. What I am saying is that it is a fundamental difference of approach to say 'don't accept just like that the theory that the economy automatically and spontaneously tends towards equilibrium of a satisfactory kind'.

SELDON: Why then was it not until the 1970s that the attack on that approach began to make itself felt?

ROLL: Because it was not until the late-1970s that the excesses of policy were politically manipulated. You may accept Keynesian principles, but you may not accept the way people went about trying to act accordingly in their attempts to influence the economy. Indeed there have been gross mistakes right through the period made by both political parties when in power, as I try to prove in my recent book. For instance I argue that it would be absurd to regard Rab Butler and Reggie Maudling as skinflints, and Cripps and Callaghan as spendthrifts. It was almost exactly the opposite, but we try to think in these stereotypes. Nevertheless, there were very considerable errors, and these errors, rightly or wrongly, were then related to the principle that you can intervene to do something about the economy, when in fact you could demonstrate that you had simply taken the wrong action. Whether that means that you cannot do the right thing ever is another matter. But there was that tendency in the 1970s, largely in rhetorical terms I must say rather than in actual policy terms, to say 'yes, you can be quite sure that intervention will always produce a worse result than non-intervention'. Nevertheless there was a lot of intervention even in that period.

SELDON: To conclude, in looking at this matter of the swing back and forth of ideas, the belief at one time in the free market, at another the belief in the need for intervention, has it actually been circumstances and the discrediting of a belief in one system that has led to a search for a new solution, rather than a change of individuals or individuals' new ideas?

ROLL: I think this really comes back to the point of what is the role of this clash of ideas in terms of practical politics. And that comes back to the question of whether the important politicians who really make opinion and win or lose elections etc., regard help from this ideological stockpot or the other ideological stockpot as being real from their own point of view. Lady Thatcher obviously did think so and made of that a prominent feature of her policy formation. As I say, I think one ought to make a distinction between apparent and real. Nevertheless she did, others did not. I do not think Mr Major as of now seems to have regarded ideas as quite so important a factor in creating a favourable climate of political opinion. Labour has varied from time to time, presently the party is virtually exclusively pragmatic and not doctrinaire.

I am very dubious whether in the end politicians derive much comfort and help at crucial periods, such as the run-up to an election, from being sort of Hayekian in the extreme or from being old-fashioned Keynesian in the extreme. I doubt it. I do not think the general British public reacts all that much to that. Maybe it helps a little bit here and there. But the general British public is more inclined from time to time to say 'well, we've had enough of these, let's give the others a chance. It is time for a change', that sort of thing, rather than to say 'I now believe Mises and Hayek had the right ideas, and this wretched man Keynes thought that we would always be living in a depression'.

NOTES

1. Vifredo Pareto, *Traité de Sociologie Generale*, 1917–19.
2. Eric Roll, *Where Did We Go Wrong?: From the Gold Standard to Europe* (London: Faber & Faber, 1995).
3. 'How Keynes Came to America', reproduced in J.K. Galbraith, *Economics, Peace and Laughter* (Boston, MA: Houghton Mifflin, 1971).
4. In addition to the basic ration, there was a distribution of points, which could be used to acquire a certain number of other commodities, each carrying a different 'price' in terms of points.
5. Alec Cairncross succeeded Robert Hall as Chief Economic Adviser to the government.
6. Robot was essentially a project for making sterling largely convertible, thus 'taking the strain of the balance of payments fluctuation on the exchange rates rather than on the reserves'. The name was derived from its three protagonists.

The Influence of Classical Liberalism and Monetarist Economics

CHRISTOPHER MULLER interviews
ARTHUR SELDON

MULLER: How did you come to your economic and political convictions?

SELDON: The roots of my beliefs lie in my early childhood. I grew up amongst the working classes in the East End of London between the wars and learned something of their efforts at self-help: the sacrifices parents made for their families. My experience illustrates the times. My parents had died in their 30s from the Spanish 'flu; I was the youngest of five: two were taken to live with uncles, two were sent to an orphanage; after several attempts to find carers for payment I was adopted by a childless couple. My foster-parents treated me as their own.

That experience of family cohesion may be where I derived my later philosophic resentment of the welfare state for usurping the role of parents and weakening the bonds of family. On earnings of three pounds a week, of which ten shillings went on rent, my foster-father paid two shillings for private violin lessons so that I might learn better than in the sixpenny class lessons.

Like other local husbands, he had joined a friendly society to ensure help in sickness and unemployment and on the death of a bread-winner. When he died at 47 the friendly society secretary promptly arrived with £100, then an enormous sum in our world. And when it ran out after a year or so, and our slightly better-off neighbour wanted to help my foster-mother, she was too proud to accept 'charity' and insisted on scrubbing her friend's front step for half-a-crown.

Perhaps that childhood recollection inspired my present interest in the early self-help of the working classes in the nineteenth century that was almost destroyed by the welfare state. This forgotten history was examined in the counter-factual in the IEA journal by ten economists, sociologists and historians to be expanded into book form.[1]

Our neighbours were manual workers in nearby furniture or clothing

Arthur Seldon, founder-president of the Institute of Economic Affairs, interviewed by Christopher Muller, St Dunstan's College, 4 August 1995.

work-shops, some self-employed, some tradesmen – bakers, shopkeepers in groceries, butchers, barber shops. So in my early years it was natural for me to think that Labour was the party for people like us, though our parents did not know much about socialism – except what they were told about the new Jerusalem in Russia.

It was not surprising for a child born in that kind of environment and listening to the conversation of adults to think that if only the right sort of politicians were in government they would save the common people from hardship. So at age eight I cheered the Labour candidate when he drew up in a car at a polling booth in a General Election. We children had no idea what he stood for; neither did our parents. But anybody labelled 'Labour' must want, and be able to do good for the labouring classes.

MULLER: By whom were you influenced?

SELDON: My earliest mentors were two teachers at the nearby grammar 'secondary' school at which I had won a free place (fees £2 50 a term). The sixth form economics teacher's sympathies were Fabia, although he did not bias his lessons. (He told us of the new economist at the London School of Economics, our sixth form goal: name-Hayek). If there was any Fabian flavour it was neutralised by the economic history teacher, the first to leave me with a sense of the classical liberalism I later embraced.[2] He was what Hayek later called an Old Whig (of the early 18th century to whom Burke sent his celebrated Appeal). Although I had thought of myself as vaguely left-wing in my 'teens, he taught us of the invasion of liberty by mercantilism. And when he recognised a budding kindred spirit he lent me his student notes on the medieval guilds.

A State Scholarship, the only state subsidy I recall with approval, opened the universities to me. But I could not leave my foster-mother for Oxford or Cambridge. So I turned to the LSE. It was the best intellectual powerhouse I could have chosen. It was then – the mid-1930s-at its intellectual height in resisting the Cambridge Keynesians and the prevailing spirit of collectivism. The middle-aged American economist, Professor James Tobin once applied to Keynes Wordworth's evocative welcome to the French Revolution:

> Bliss was it in that dawn to be alive,
> But to be young was very heaven.

But in the light of the record of what Callaghan called 'spending yourself out of depression' Wordworth's lines could more justifiably have been used by a young undergraduate arriving at the holy of holies of academic liberalism in the 1930s

By then I had abandoned my early Labour sentiments and veered toward the economic liberalism that would let the people do what they wanted for themselves. In that mood I came under the influence of the three senior economics professors: Arnold Plant, a specialist in the economics of industry, Lionel Robbins, who taught mostly economic theory and F.A. Hayek. And I should add that through them I learned much from economists overseas – F.H. Knight of Chicago, Knut Wicksell of Sweden, the Austrian School of which Hayek with his teacher Mises of Vienna was the leading light, and other liberal economists around the world – all dissatisfied with the fashionable reliance on government to correct the 'market failures' of unemployment , inflation, poverty, insecurity, and all the ills of mankind attributed to 'capitalism'.

Plant was my Tutor for the Commerce degree I had decided to take because it would teach subjects like statistics and accounting that I could sell to employers in the aftermath of the Great Depression. He taught the classical truths of economics, not least the power of markets in trade and industry and the role of private property seen by Locke and Hume, then very much out of favour in the midst of the promise of 'public' ownership in 'nationalisation'. Plant did not publish much[3] but passed his teaching mainly in lectures and seminars to his colleagues and students, including two future Nobel Laureates – (Sir) Arthur Lewis and R.H. Coase, still a close friend of the IEA. On graduation Plant offered me a Cassell Travelling Scholarship, which would have taken me overseas for a year of research but which I could not accept because of the usual family reason, or a year's stint as his Research Assistant, which I accepted to complete a Master's degree. Owing to Hitler's indecisive intentions about war and peace the appointment was renewed for a second and third year. I was awed to find myself working next door to Plant, Lionel Robbins, Hayek and later D.H. Robertson who had left Cambridge because of the discord with the Keynesians.

Robbins was the leading liberal influence in my early undergraduate years. His lectures and writings were the bugle blast of classical liberalism in counter-attack on the left-inclined socialism of his more politically-minded colleagues – the political scientist Laski, the public finance economist Dalton, Attlee's Chancellor of the Exchequer, the 'public' administrators Robson and Finer, the historian Eileen Power.

Although a socialist in his early days as an assistant to Arthur Greenwood, Robbins became disillusioned by socialism and the failure of academic socialists to see its dangers. He was on good personal terms with them but did not disguise his uncompromising rejection of their fallacies. He offended Laski with lines he quoted at the end of a chapter in a book

> Lilies that fester
> Smell far worse than weeds.

I then wondered at their simplistic faith in government and the state to solve economic and social problems, but did not see the underlying naiveté of their thinking until the emergence of the new school of 'public choice' which elucidated the ramshackle economics of politics. Its two founders, Professors J.M. Buchanan and Gordon Tullock, Americans with appropriately Scottish names, established the underlying weaknesses of the political process[4] that explained Adam Smith's (and at one stage John Stuart Mill's) scepticism of politicians.

As my interest turned from economic theory to applications in policy the strongest influence became Hayek through his writings on capitalism and the market near the end of my undergraduate years.[5] He and I went our separate ways to Cambridge when Dalton took over the LSE building as the Ministry of Economic Warfare. As he moved to the University of Chicago after the war my next contact with Hayek had to wait for the early years of the Institute of Economic Affairs in the late 1950s. They led to an intellectual relationship that became closer as he saw the IEA become the most influential vehicle for the application of the market thinking I had learned from him and others at the LSE. I edited his shorter writings on inflation, unemployment and the trade unions in his last 15 years and the longer study of 'The Denationalisation of Money'[6] of which he sent me a draft for polishing and editing for publication. The revisions were extensive since after a spell in Germany or Austria his prose used strings of subordinate clauses and language that required clarification for the English reader. When he thought that ill-health might prevent him from completing Volume III of his 'Law, Legislation and Liberty'[7] he indicated that he hoped I would complete the script with similar attention.

Three incidents illustrate my sympathetic relationship with Hayek. When I felt I knew him sufficiently to venture a gentle admonition I wrote to remonstrate against a causal reference to the Institute as 'a publisher' of market studies. The Institute published the works it sponsored but they often went through considerable editing in conjunction with the authors to amplify the conclusions implied in their analyses. I said he may have overlooked the many original studies we had sponsored. He wrote promptly to regret his lapse and added that he well knew the source of the academic repute of the Institute. After a Liberty Fund seminar in Freiburg, where I had put it to a gathering of eminente from Chicago, the home of 'empirical testing' and several later Nobel Laureates, that Hayek had rarely used statistical evidence to support his penetrating deductive insights, I wrote to ask why he had remained silent. (Homer may have nodded off; he was near his 80s.) He replied that he did not wish to stir differences between the world's leading liberal scholars. And a few years later he hustled from another part of England to an IEA lunch to celebrate my modest honour.

MULLER: When did you begin teaching classical liberalism?

SELDON: Oddly the Army gave me my first opportunity. During the war spells in North Africa and Italy I wrote occasionally to Plant. My LSE research had studied the economics of large in retail distribution. A letter described the diseconomies of scale in large-scale armies: they were 'planned economies', much praised in peace, without markets or consumer reaction. I detected much waste, bureaucratic abuse, and inefficiency. Plant used my letter in a talk to businessmen on the deficiencies of wartime planning without prices. (He had devised a system of points rationing to simulate pricing at the Ministry of Trade.)

As the end of the war approached, the Army Bureau of Current Affairs taught the coming demobbed men of the new free welfare services they could expect following the Report of the economist called Beveridge. So I began ABCA talks, in a headquarters near Naples, on the economics of 'free' services and their long-term effects that would be overlooked by politicians anxious for short-term votes (a General Election was expected after the outbreak of peace).

When, after the war, as Chairman of a Liberal Party Committee on the Aged, I went to see my political crony, Beveridge, the former Liberal MP, for his view on technical aspects of state pensions, he began gruffly: 'You seem to know more about all this than I do'. The advice, in his famous report on the social services for deferring the full payment of the new state pension for 20 years until the National Insurance Fund was built up, was being ignored for political reasons by a weak excuse – even by Gaitskell, one of the more responsible post-war scholar-politicians. Beveridge was beginning to doubt the effects of spreading social insurance on the private insurance of the voluntary Friendly Societies. But his book came too late.[8]

Later I taught LSE students the liberal market aspects of economics overlooked by textbook writers caught up in the fashion of the times. I spent ten years as Tutor to evening students at the University of London and ten more years with the honorific title of 'Staff Examiner' at the LSE – partly to supplement the modest salaries the new IEA could pay in its early years.

My doubts about the beneficence of government even if led by well-meaning politicians were mounting. The remark of a respected academic economist with Fabian leanings in Whitehall, James Meade, to whom Plant sent me for a possible job on the return from the army, alerted me further. He regretted, he said with a confidential smile, he did not have the vacancy I wanted, as his job was 'to inaugurate the millennium' which he did not think was my purpose.

MULLER: How was your LSE thinking built into the IEA?

SELDON: The IEA was established to inform – 'teach'-the general public the economics long neglected in the universities. I asked IEA authors to raise question on the operation of market systems: how far they were a neglected way to deal with problems not solved by government. And here I suggested they should not dismiss effective economic solutions on the grounds of so-called 'political impossibility'.

In a sense I was 'teaching' the economics of politics to the authors commissioned at the IEA who had been doing good work on unusual subjects not normally thought to be within the competence of economists – from water (droughts) to fire-fighting (outdated) and from human blood (shortages) to animal semen (shortages). The purpose throughout was to show the confusions unnecessarily encountered in the absence of market pricing in 'public' services usually misunderstood by the sociological mind.

That was also the 'teaching' I did in 'Charge'.⁹ It was written during the water shortage of 1976 but I extended the use of pricing to a wide range of other 'public' services. The book offended critics who thought 'public' services should be 'free' but overlooked the rising government costs, the mounting taxes and the swelling government debt then plaguing the welfare states of Europe and later risking social conflict if not civil war, as recently in France.

This was the original task of re-examining the neglected principles of classical economics. The more topical subjects that formed the substance of conventional economics and contemporary history like unemployment and inflation, and their cures in counter-cyclical government financing or monetarism, also formed a large part of the IEA output analysed by economists dissatisfied with the established solutions of Keynes and the Fabians.

Two aspects are of interest in the teaching of economics at the IEA in the last four decades. First, these newer approaches and solutions were generally under-taught in the universities. Often our younger authors spoke of the distaste they encountered from the faculty colleagues in their departments. And the student at Cambridge who told us he had never heard of the Hobart Papers, the flagship of the IEA becoming known and respected by leading journalists like (now Sir) Samuel Brittan, William (now Lord) Rees-Mogg and Peter Jay, was not exceptional. It is a subject for study by historians of contemporary Britain that the teaching by the IEA of the unfamiliar but fundamental truths left to us by the classical economists did not inspire the newer 'market think-tanks' until they began to appear after 20 years in 1975. Either academics were otherwise engaged or politicians were slow to realise the relevance or urgency of the new/old study of classical liberalism. It is significant that these truths, rediscovered belatedly by academics in the former communist countries and even some politicians like Vaclav Klaus, now Prime Minister of the Czech Republic, are still neglected by British academics and by politicians in all three parties.

MULLER: At what stage did Hayek become more influential with the establishment?

SELDON: As I saw it interest in his writings was highest for a time after his 'populist' *The Road to Serfdom*. When I visited him in Salzburg in 1972 with proofs of *A Tiger by the Tail*, an anthology of his writings collected by a clever young Indian economist, Sudha Shenoy,[10] he was in a period of intellectual doldrums. He felt the world was not listening to his anxieties and warnings. The publication of the anthology seemed to remind the world of his prescience. Samuel Brittan wrote that it had caused his critical views of the post-war orthodoxy to 'have suddenly come back into prominence'.

Hayek followed with five shorter IEA Papers in the next few years on aspects of unemployment and the unions and on the 'tiger' of inflation, then rampant.[11] These were the pressing problems that drew the attention of politicians, as suggested by Callaghan's confession on the futility of government spending and Sir Keith Joseph's reading of Hayek's *The Constitution of Liberty*[12] on a Scottish holiday and his tutoring of Mrs Thatcher.

The Nobel Prize in 1974, even though shared with a Swedish economist, no doubt revived his spirits. And the award of Companion of Honour, marked by a private word with the Queen, made him feel, even at the age of 85, that his naturalisation as British in 1938 and his eminence as a British economist had been recognised at last after 46 years.

But his long-term thinking on the role of money in the causation of inflation is taking longer to be acknowledged or heeded by both academics and politicians, or by bankers of the world. The message of 'Denationalisation of Money' is revolutionary. It is no less that inflation will remain a risk as long as it is controlled by the monopoly of the state. Here Hayek agreed with Milton Friedman that inflation is a monetary phenomenon. But where Friedman looks for constitutional disciplines on government to control the money supply, Hayek finds salvation only in the competition of the market. He looks to the painful penalty of heavy financial loss to induce limitation of the supply of money. The solution is intellectually obvious and simple. Money is to be supplied by firms that will lose heavily if it is issued to excess because its value will then fall. Loss and bankruptcy are the ultimate guarantors of the value of money and the mastery of inflation.

That solution is hardly likely to commend itself to governments, or to central bankers under close political control. When I tentatively put the solution to a Governor of the Bank of England, the response was an indulgent smile and a diplomatic rejoinder: 'That may be for the day after tomorrow'. But tomorrow may come sooner than the politicised bankers suppose. The Austrian economist Eugen von Bohm-Bawerk wrote in 1914 a short classic in the 'Austrian' school of economics: it argued that in the end the market would prevail over political power. If government does not learn to master inflation, the people will use the moneys of other countries or, for some purposes, evolve private moneys.

The argument is relevant for the current debates over the best currency for Europe. It suggests that the solution is not a single currency. Nor is it competing national currencies. the reason is the same: that both systems would be controlled by the political power that has failed to prevent inflation.

MULLER: What was the purpose of your book *Capitalism*?

SELDON: This book was written as the communist socialist system was collapsing. They had failed to produce the living standards of the capitalists economies, which were typically four times higher. Blackwell had asked me to write the book after my first retirement in 1981, but I had continued working at the IEA until I finally retired in 1988. The collapse of the anti-capitalist world seemed the right time to refine the achievements and the powerful intellectual case for the capitalist market systems.

There was a more personal reason. *Capitalism*[13] had several themes running through the argument and the evidence. The important theme as seen by reviewers was that capitalism as it was practised, rather than it had been promised by Lincoln, had degenerated into government of the politically active, by the political managers, for the politically influential – of the busy, by the bossy, for the bully.

The more personal theme of the book was that the common people would fare better under capitalism than under socialism. The more the market and the less the state decided economic life, the better for the working classes. There were inequalities under both systems: in the market the inequalities were financial – differences in income and wealth; in the state the inequalities were cultural – differences in social, occupational or other influences that explain why the better-connected middle income groups derive more from the state than the less influential lower-income groups. But it is easier to reduce differences in financial power, by supplementing the lower incomes, than to reduce differences in cultural power, which derive from accent, social background or other faculties in making a case with a headmaster, a hospital official, a local government housing manager. The evidence is now amply documented, not least by the Fabian-inclined Professor Julian Le Grand, and not only for Britain but also for Australia and the USA.[14]

Moreover, *Capitalism* argued, the market was itself the most powerful equalising force in economic life under any system. The poor of England among the farm workers of the Home Counties were recruited for the new higher-paying textile mills of the North in the early nineteenth century. The poor of Europe moved to the higher-paid opportunities of America in the early twentieth century. The power of the market is that it gives the common people the power to escape from poverty and from the state. And there is now increasing scope to increase their power by replacing 'free' state services, not least in welfare, by purchasing power.

MULLER: The IEA spent much time publishing the monetarists. Was it the most important part of its activities in the 1960s and 1970s?

SELDON: In the anxieties of these years the most urgent on which we considered we could shed light still ignored by other economists was that of the monetarists. Inflation was a monetary phenomenon: it was futile to suppose that it could be mastered or suppressed by government decree. The fallacy was to think that because government had seemed to master inflation during the short years of the war, they could do the same in the longer years of peace. Not only did they overlook the underground economies that developed during wars and disguised the true price of many commodities, so that official statistics were falsified. They also confused the impulses that moved people to observe government decrees in the imperatives of war with the new personal impulses that moved them to put their closer family interests first in peace. So 'incomes policies' of varying economic breeds and political colours were resisted or trampled by the unions and other organised employees in the anxiety to raise wages and salaries. Wilson thought he could tame his allies in the unions. Heath thought he could sober them by constitutional confrontation. Yet the economists in the universities and in Whitehall continued to offer government specifics of precisely the kind that had been failing.

This was the economic impasse that caused us to emphasise the arguments for the control of the supply of money. And here the authors were the influential and the famous – and the Nobel Laureates-whose world was often overseas more than in Britain.[15] And 'monetarism' is now the established anti-inflation cure in all continents.

Yet the more fundamental long-term purpose of the IEA founders was to discover how far, if at all, was the market as the most effective mechanism for deciding the efficient use of resources to satisfy the preferences of the people. That is why we searched for and found and published the work of economists, many of them young and unknown, who had been working on the less topical but more enduring solutions for the long-ignored economic problems – not only in the socialist countries but nearer home in Britain. And now few economists anywhere scoff at the use of markets to solve tensions between supply and demand.

In the end the problem, the solution for which is still being refined by the IEA researches, seminars and publications, remains that of refining the use of markets where they are still being under used. But now there is a new urgency.

When government confined itself to supplying the 'public goods' that could not be produced in the market its authority could be respected. Now that it is persisting in supplying them when the conditions of supply and demand – rising incomes, technological advance – have made market supply more possible and efficient, the state is driving economic activity to the private market, as most evidently in education and medical care, and moreover into 'unofficial' markets. Government is still needlessly raising too much in taxes and other imposts to finance services and functions that are outdated by economic forces larger than itself.

The IEA founders saw this trend in the 1970s with a study of the reactions between tax avoidance and evasion.[16] Economists overseas are now talking about 'parallel' markets. Government in Britain and elsewhere is endangering respect for the rule of law and therefore democracy itself. And here again the solution may be to allow markets to develop where people are using them. That is what Lincoln meant on the battlefield of Gettysburg in 1863 by declaiming that democracy was government of the people, by the people, for the people. That could be the next phase of intellectual leadership into the twenty-first century.

NOTES

1. Articles in *Economic Affairs* (Oct. 1994); to be enlarged into book form, (Spring 1996). The continuing distortion by historians and the 'condition of England' novelists of the evidence on poverty and its causes in the nineteenth century was rebutted by economists and historians in *The Long Debate on Poverty* (London: IEA, 1972).
2. The best recent study of classical liberalism and its superiority over egalitarian, communitarian and conservative societies is David Conway, *Classical Liberalism: The Unvanquished Ideal* (London: Macmillan 1995).
3. I assembled his main original writings on patents, copyrights and other aspects of property rights in 'Selected Economic Essays and Addresses' (London: Routledge for the IEA, 1974). The Economist spoke of 'his Marshallian sweep of theory allied to observation ... this scholar and pragmatist (has had) influence out of all proportion to his published work'.
4. The *locus classicus* is J.M. Buchanan and Gordon Tullock, 'The Calculus of Consent' (Ann Arbor, MI: University of Michigan Press, 1962). The application of economics to the political process has produced a stream of new writing, spreading to Europe, and attracted the attention of political scientists who accept that it reveals facets of politics not discussed by conventional political science.
5. F.A. Hayek, *Collectivist Economic Planning* (London: Routledge, 1936).
6. F.A. Hayek, *The Denationalisation of Money* (London, IEA, 1976), 2nd Edition 1978,

reprinted 1990.
7. F.A Hayek, *Law, Legislation and Liberty*; Vol.1, *Rules and Order*, (Chicago, IL: Chicago University Press, 1973); Vol.2 *The Mirage of Social Justice* (Chicago, IL: Chicago University Press, 1976); Vol.3 *Political Order of a Free People* (Chicago, IL: Chicago University Press, 1979).
8. W. Beveridge, *Voluntary Action* (London: Allen & Unwin, 1948).
9. A. Seldon, *Charge* (London: Temple Smith, 1977).
10. S. Shenoy, *A Tiger by the Tail* (London: IEA 1972).
11. F.A. Hayek, *Full Employment at any Price?* (London: IEA, 1972), *Choice in Currency* (London: IEA, 1976), *1980s Unemployment and the Unions* (London: IEA, 1980).
12. F.A. Hayek, *The Constitution of Liberty* (London: Routledge, 1960). The IEA published an assessment by economists and philosophers in A. Seldon (ed.) *Agenda for a Free Society* (London, IEA, 1960).
13. A. Seldon, *Capitalism* (Oxford: Blackwell, 1990).
14. J. Le Grand and B. Goodin, *Not Only The Poor: The Middle Classes in the Welfare State* (London: Allen & Unwin, 1987).
15. The monetarists published by the IEA: Milton Friedman, *The Counter-Revolution in Monetary Theory* (London: IEA, 1970); *Monetary Correction* (London: IEA, 1974) *Unemployment versus Inflation* (London: IEA, 1975); *Inflation and Unemployment: The New Dimension* (London: IEA, 1976); Axel Leijonhufvud, *Keynes and the Classics* (London: IEA, 1969); A. Walters, *Money in Boom and Slump* (London: IEA, 1969); *Crisis '75?* (London: IEA 1975); *Economists and the British Economy*' (London: IEA, 1978).
16. A. Seldon (ed.) *Tax Avoision* (London: IEA, 1979).

Lightning Source UK Ltd.
Milton Keynes UK
UKOW03f0004120914

238446UK00001B/87/P